THE NEW TESTAMENT DOCUMENTS

THEIR ORIGIN AND EARLY HISTORY

THE CROALL LECTURES FOR 1911-12

THE NEW TESTAMENT DOCUMENTS

THEIR ORIGIN AND EARLY HISTORY

BY

GEORGE MILLIGAN, D.D.

PROFESSOR OF DIVINITY AND BIBLICAL CRITICISM IN THE UNIVERSITY OF GLASGOW

ἔχομεν δὲ τον θησαυρὸν τοῦτον ἐν ὀστρακίνοις σκεύεσιν

WITH TWELVE FACSIMILES

Wipf & Stock
PUBLISHERS
Eugene, Oregon

Wipf and Stock Publishers
199 W 8th Ave, Suite 3
Eugene, OR 97401

The New Testament Documents
Their Origin and Early History
By Milligan, George
ISBN: 1-59752-641-X
Publication date 4/14/2006
Previously published by Macmillan and Co., 1913

ALMAE MATRI
ABERDONENSI
SACRUM

PREFACE

THE following Lectures were delivered in Edinburgh on the Croall Foundation in the end of the year 1911. And the time that has since elapsed has given me the opportunity of revising them carefully, and of adding a number of notes, which may prove useful to those who desire to carry the study further.

In attempting to cover so wide a field in the course of six lectures, I have naturally been obliged to indicate, rather than to discuss, many of the problems that emerge, while not a few points to which I would gladly have drawn attention have been omitted altogether. I trust, however, that enough has been said to show how fascinating are the questions suggested by the making of our New Testament, and, above all, how impossible it is fully to understand the varied documents of which it is composed, unless they are studied in connexion with their origin and early history. The very outward form of the autographs, on which recent discoveries have thrown so much welcome light, has its value from this point of view. And the story of the gradual process, by which writings in themselves so occasional and fragmentary were at length brought together in one sacred volume, so far from obscuring, tends rather to emphasize the Divine power that has been operative in them all along.

It remains only to record my grateful thanks to the Croall Trustees for the honour they did me in appointing me to the Lectureship, and to the many friends who have assisted me with valuable suggestions in the discharge of its duties. Nor can I forget the officials and readers of the Glasgow University Press, whose constant courtesy and care have materially lightened the work of revision.

G. M.

THE UNIVERSITY,
GLASGOW, *January* 17, 1913.

CONTENTS

LECTURE I
THE ORIGINAL MANUSCRIPTS OF THE NEW TESTAMENT

	PAGE
Introductory	3
I. *The rise of Christian writings*	4
Disappearance of the New Testament autographs	6
II. *Outward form of the original manuscripts*	7
1. The material on which they were written	8
2. History and manufacture of papyrus	9
3. Other writing materials	16
4. Sealing and addressing of rolls	17
5. Preservation of rolls	20
III. *The manner in which the books of the New Testament were written*	
1. Dictation	21
Autographic conclusions	24
Character of the handwriting	25
The amount of liberty left to the scribes	26
2. General results from the use of dictation	
(1) Vividness of language	27
(2) Quotations embodied from correspondents' letters	27
(3) Differences of style	30
IV. *Delivery of the New Testament writings*	30
Use of private messengers	31
The permanent value of the New Testament writings	32

CONTENTS

LECTURE II

THE LANGUAGE OF THE NEW TESTAMENT WRITINGS

                                                             PAGE

I. *The linguistic conditions of Palestine* - - - - 35
    Wide-spread use of Aramaic - - - - - 36
    Use of Greek by the New Testament writers - - 37
    Reasons for their preference for Greek - - - 39

II. *The character of New Testament Greek*
    1. Use of the common Greek of the day - - - 43
        New light on this Greek - - - - 44
        General uniformity of the Κοινή - - - - 48
    2. *Influences affecting the Greek of the New Testament*
        (1) Hebraisms - - - - - - - 50
        (2) Certain literary tendencies - - - - 55
        (3) The transforming power of Christianity - - 58

III. *Recent Gains to our knowledge of the Greek New Testament*
    1. Direct additions to our New Testament texts - - 60
    2. Indirect gains as affecting
        (1) Orthography and Accidence - - - - 62
            Morphology - - - - - - 63
        (2) Syntax
            Examples of laxer usage in the case of prepositions - - - - - - 65
            and in the construction of ἵνα - - - 67
            Grammatical niceties in the New Testament
                Tense construction - - - - - 68
                Case construction - - - - - 68
        (3) Vocabulary
            (*a*) Reduction in the number of 'Biblical' words - - - - - - - 70
            (*b*) Confirmation of traditional meanings - 72
            (*c*) Choice of meanings - - - - - 74
            (*d*) Suggestion of new meanings - - - 75
            (*e*) Fresh life and reality imparted to familiar phraseology - - - - - 77
    The ultimate aim of New Testament study - - - 80

CONTENTS

LECTURE III

THE LITERARY CHARACTER OF THE NEW TESTAMENT WRITINGS—THE EPISTLES AND THE APOCALYPSE

	PAGE
The earliest books of the New Testament were epistles	83

I. *The Pauline Epistles*

	PAGE
Their authenticity	84
1. The epistolary form	
Antiquity of letters	85
Classical collections of letters	86
Letters in the Old Testament and the Apocrypha	86
2. The adoption of the epistolary form by St. Paul	87
(1) The personal side of the Pauline Epistles illustrated from contemporary papyrus letters	88
(2) The literary side of the Pauline Epistles	94
3. The style of the Pauline Epistles	95
4. Some general points regarding the Pauline Epistles	
(1) Their speech-character	103
(2) Their artistic and rhetorical structure	104
(3) Their relation to Jewish literature	104

II. *The other Epistles of the New Testament*

	PAGE
The other Epistles of the New Testament	107
Their general and yet personal character	108
The Epistle to the Hebrews	109
The Epistle of St. James	111
The First Epistle of St. Peter	112
The pseudonymous character of 2 Peter	113
The Johannine Epistles	115

III. *The Apocalypse*

	PAGE
The Apocalypse	117
Its Hebraic and its Hellenic sides	118
Its barbarous Greek	119
Its structure	121
Bearing of language and date on the question of authorship	123
The religious significance of the Apocalypse	126

CONTENTS

LECTURE IV

THE LITERARY CHARACTER OF THE NEW TESTAMENT WRITINGS—THE GOSPELS AND ACTS

	PAGE
Oral teaching	129
The earliest Christian records	130
The 'Gospel' name and form	130

I. *The Synoptic Gospels*
    (1) The character and complexity of the Synoptic Problem — 132
        The Two-Document Hypothesis — 133
        The Original Mark — 134
        Reconstruction of Q — 136
        Special Lucan Source — 138
    (2) The literary evolution of the Synoptic Gospels — 139
    (3) The conditions under which the Evangelists wrote — 141
        General aim of the Evangelists — 142
    (4) Characteristics of the individual Gospels
        (*a*) St. Mark — 143
        (*b*) St. Matthew — 146
        (*c*) St. Luke — 149
    General unity of the Synoptists — 152

II. *The Fourth Gospel* — 153
    Language and style — 154
    (1) Its relation to the Synoptic Gospels — 155
    (2) Its unity — 157
    (3) Its authorship — 158

III. *The Acts of the Apostles*
    Relation to the Third Gospel — 161
    The sources of Acts — 162
    The writer's literary skill and historical accuracy — 165
    The double-texts of Acts — 166
    General conclusion — 167

CONTENTS

LECTURE V

THE CIRCULATION OF THE NEW TESTAMENT WRITINGS

	PAGE
Summary of previous lectures	171
The dates of the New Testament autographs	172

I. *The circulation of the New Testament writings in roll-form*
 1. The multiplication of copies due to practical needs and the facilities for intercourse amongst the first Christian communities — 173, 175
 2. The danger of textual corruption arising from
  (1) the material on which the autographs were written — 176
  (2) the employment of non-professional scribes — 177
  (3) the literary ideas of the time — 178
 3. Bearing of the roll-form on questions of structure connected with
  (1) the Epistle to the Hebrews — 181
  (2) the end of St. Mark's Gospel — 182
  (3) the closing chapters of Romans — 182
  (4) the composition of 2 Corinthians — 184
  (5) the arrangement of the Fourth Gospel — 186
 4. Marginal additions — 187

II. *Change from the papyrus roll to the papyrus codex* — 188
 1. Early use of papyrus codices — 189
  (1) Fragmentary New Testament texts — 189
  (2) The 'Sayings of Jesus' — 190
 2. Handwriting of the papyrus codices — 190
  'Poor Men's Bibles' — 191

III. *Parchment Codices*
 1. Manufacture of parchment — 191
 2. Use of parchment in connexion with Christian literature — 192

CONTENTS

	PAGE
3. Construction of a parchment codex	194
Character of the handwriting	195
4. Suitability of the codex-form for collection of writings	195
Pocket Bibles	196
General trustworthiness of the New Testament text	197

LECTURE VI

THE COLLECTION OF THE NEW TESTAMENT WRITINGS

The circulation of the New Testament writings	203
Light in which these writings were at first regarded	204
Supremacy of the Old Testament	205

I. *Influences leading to the collection of the New Testament writings*

1. The existence of the Old Testament Canon	206
The Greek Old Testament	206
Collections of *Testimonia*	207
2. The contents and character of the New Testament writings	
The words of Jesus	208
The Apostolic teaching	209
3. The use of the new documents in public worship	210
The Epistles	211
The Gospels	212
Apocryphal books	213
4. The part they played in controversy	214

II. *History of the Collection and Authorization of the New Testament writings*

1. From the time of writing to A.D. 200

(1) The *Corpus Paulinum*	215
Traces of the knowledge of Pauline Epistles in Christian literature	216
Canon of Marcion	217

CONTENTS

	PAGE
(2) The *Corpus Evangelicum*	
Witness of the *Didache* of Clement of Rome, and of others	217
The *Diatessaron*	218
Irenaeus—Clement of Alexandria—Tertullian	219
The Muratorian Canon	222
2. From A.D. 200–400	
Determination of the limits of the New Testament collection	222
Origen—Eusebius	223
General attitude of the Church illustrated in the case of	
the Apocalypse	223
and the Epistle to the Hebrews	225
Other Christian writings	226

III. *General remarks*

1. The collection of the New Testament writings was a gradual process - 226
2. It was largely informal and unofficial - 227
3. It included, on the whole, all that was best worth preserving in early Christian literature - 228
4. The unique character of the completed New Testament 229

APPENDIX OF ADDITIONAL NOTES

A Some Books for the Study of the Greek Papyri - 233
B The Titles and Subscriptions of the New Testament writings - 237
C Dictation and Shorthand - 241
D New Testament Texts on Papyrus - 248
E Greek Papyrus Letters - 255
F Dionysius of Alexandria on the Authorship of the Apocalypse - 262

CONTENTS

		PAGE
G	The Oxyrhynchus 'Sayings of Jesus'	266
H	Papias and Irenaeus on the Origin of the Gospels	269
I	Alternative Endings of St. Mark's Gospel	274
J	The Gospel according to Peter	281
K	The Muratorian Fragment on the Canon	286
L	The Order of the New Testament Writings	292
M	Extracts from Festal Letter XXXIX. of Athanasius, A.D. 367	297
N	Recent Literature on the Canon of the New Testament	301

INDEXES

I.	Subjects	307
II.	Authors	310
III.	References	
	1. Biblical	314
	2. Ancient Texts and Writings	318
IV.	Greek Words	321

PLATES

		PAGE
I.	Papyrus Roll of the First Century, showing part of Thucydides iv. 36-41 in non-literary hand - - -	11
II.	Papyrus leaf containing part of St. Matthew i., Third Century - - - - - - -	61
III.	Papyrus letter, Second Century A.D. - - - -	92
IV.	New 'Sayings of Jesus,' Third Century - - - -	131
V.	St. John dictating to Prochorus, Fourteenth Century -	161
VI.	Alternative ending of St. Mark from the Freer (Washington) manuscript, Fourth to Fifth Century -	182
VII.	Codex Sinaiticus, Fourth Century - - - - -	195
VIII.	Apocalypse iii. 19-iv. 1 from a pocket edition, Fourth Century - - - - - - - -	196
IX. X.	} The Gospel according to Peter, Second Century - -	213
XI.	Canon of Muratori, end of Second Century - - -	222
XII.	Waxen Tablet with Tachygraphic Symbols, probably Third Century A.D. - - - - - -	245

LECTURE I.

THE ORIGINAL MANUSCRIPTS OF THE
NEW TESTAMENT.

Οἱ θεσπέσιοι καὶ ὡς ἀληθῶς θεοπρεπεῖς, φημὶ δὲ τοῦ Χριστοῦ τοὺς ἀποστόλους, τὸν βίον ἄκρως κεκαθαρμένοι καὶ ἀρετῇ πάσῃ τὰς ψυχὰς κεκοσμημένοι, τὴν δὲ γλῶτταν ἰδιωτεύοντες ... τῆς τῶν οὐρανῶν βασιλείας τὴν γνῶσιν ἐπὶ πᾶσαν κατήγγελλον τὴν οἰκουμένην, σπουδῆς τῆς περὶ τὸ λογογραφεῖν μικρὰν ποιούμενοι φροντίδα. EUSEBIUS, *Hist. Eccles.* iii. 24. 3.

I.

THE ORIGINAL MANUSCRIPTS OF THE NEW TESTAMENT.

Ἔχομεν δὲ τὸν θησαυρὸν τοῦτον ἐν ὀστρακίνοις σκεύεσιν, ἵνα ἡ ὑπερβολὴ τῆς δυνάμεως ᾖ τοῦ θεοῦ καὶ μὴ ἐξ ἡμῶν.
2 Cor. iv. 7.

Τὸν φελόνην, ὃν ἀπέλειπον ἐν Τρῳάδι παρὰ Κάρπῳ, ἐρχόμενος φέρε, καὶ τὰ βιβλία, μάλιστα τὰς μεμβράνας.
2 Tim. iv. 13.

THE New Testament consists of twenty-seven writings, generally ascribed to ten different authors, and in themselves of very varying characters and dates. There are four Gospel narratives, a History, twenty-one Epistles, and an Apocalypse, while their composition must have extended over a period of not less than two generations.

So unique and authoritative is the place which these writings now occupy in the Christian Church, that it is not easy to realize that the Church had already been in existence for a considerable number of years before the earliest of them in their present form appeared. Our Lord Himself wrote nothing, nor did He lay any charge on His disciples to write. It was as living witnesses to Him and to

His truth that He sent them forth.[1] And they in their turn recognized that their primary duty was to produce not epistles written with pen and ink, but living epistles[2]—men and women who by their lives and conversation should bear witness to an unseen but ever-present Lord, until He Himself should return and set up His Kingdom in their midst.

Apart indeed from everything else, this anxiously expected Parousia of the Lord could not fail to tell in the disciples' minds against any thought of providing for future wants that might never arise. What need to write regarding Jesus when any day might see His appearance in glory, or to lay down rules for the guidance of His Church on earth, when in the new 'fulness of the times' all things, both in heaven and on earth, were about to be gathered up 'in the Christ'?[3]

1. The rise of Christian writings.

I. While, however, considerations such as these would inevitably tell against the production of a definite Christian literature, there is a strong presumption that from the very beginning of Christian history its principal events would be recorded in some form. Evidence is multiplying from many quarters as to the widespread habit of writing amongst all classes of the population at the time. And it is impossible to doubt that the leading facts of Christ's life and ministry, which had so profoundly stirred the hearts of many, were written down and circulated almost as soon as they took

---

[1] Matt. xxviii. 19 f.   [2] Cf. 2 Cor. iii. 2.   [3] Eph. i. 10.

place, even though at first it might be in a very fragmentary and rude form. Sir William M. Ramsay goes the length of saying that 'so far as antecedent probability goes, founded on the general character of preceding and contemporary Greek or Graeco-Asiatic society, the first Christian account of the circumstances connected with the death of Jesus must be presumed to have been written in the year when Jesus died.'[1] And as time passed and Christian communities arose and spread in different parts of the Empire, the necessity of supplying the scattered converts with authentic records of their new faith could not fail to assert itself in a very pressing and practical way.

St. Paul, for example, on whom was laid as a daily burden, 'anxiety for all the Churches,'[2] would quickly find that he could only keep in touch with the communities he had founded by means of letters or epistles. And there can be little doubt that those writings of his which have come down to us are only part of a large correspondence which he carried on in order to confirm and develop the work that had been begun in the course of his missionary journeys.[3] The same would be true in varying degrees of the other Apostles.

---

[1] *The Letters to the Seven Churches of Asia* (London, 1904), p. 5 f.

[2] 2 Cor. xi. 28.

[3] Cf. 2 Thess. iii. 17, 1 Cor. v. 9, 2 Cor. x. 10, Col. iv. 16, and 'On the probability that many of St. Paul's Epistles have been lost,' see Jowett, *The Epistles of St. Paul to the Thessalonians,*

In some such way as this, then, on practical rather than on literary grounds, a number of Christian writings gradually came into existence, out of which, in time, by a process of selection there came to be formed what we are accustomed to describe as the New Testament Canon, or, more briefly, the New Testament.

Upon the manner in which this was brought about, and the scattered writings, so occasional in origin and purpose, were transformed into a single and authoritative book, I shall have something to say later.[1] Meanwhile we are concerned with these writings only in their earliest form, long before either their writers or recipients had any idea of the future in store for them.

Disappearance of the New Testament autographs. Of the original autographs themselves there is indeed no longer any trace. They must all have perished at a very early date, if not in the persecutions that befell the early Church, then simply through ordinary tear and wear, and the comparative neglect which would befall writings, not at first supposed to be invested with any specially sacred character.[2] But while we are thus no longer in the

---

Galatians, Romans[2] (London, 1859), i. p. 195 ff. That a different view existed in the early Church seems to be implied in Eusebius, *Hist. Eccles.* iii. 24. 4, vi. 25. 7.

[1] See Lecture VI.

[2] By the 'ipsae authenticae literae' of the Apostles to which Tertullian (*c.* A.D. 200) refers as read in certain Churches (*de Praescriptione Haereticorum*, c. 36), we must understand, from the general usage of 'authenticae' at the time, the autographs,

THE ORIGINAL MANUSCRIPTS

possession of the original of a single New Testament book, we are able, thanks to the marvellous discoveries of contemporary documents in Egypt during recent years, to form a wonderfully clear idea of what its outward form and appearance must have been.[1]

II. It may seem, perhaps, in view of the absorbing importance of the contents, that such external features are of comparatively little moment. We do not, as a rule, linger over the casket in which the precious jewel is enclosed. And the 'earthen vessels' in which the treasure of God's revelation is contained are in themselves, as one of their artificers

II. Outward form of the original manuscripts.

---

and not simply genuine copies of the originals, but the rhetorical character of the whole passage prevents our attaching much importance to the statement. On the supposed autograph copies of St. Matthew's Gospel found in the grave of Barnabas in Cyprus, and of St. Mark's Gospel in Venice, see Nestle, *Textual Criticism of the New Testament* (London, 1901), p. 30. In the present connexion, the daring attempt of Constantine Simonides to palm off certain falsifications as original parts of the New Testament may also be recalled: see his *Facsimiles of certain portions of the Gospel of St. Matthew, and of the Epistles of St. James and of St. Jude, written on papyrus of the first century,* London, 1862.

[1] For a brief account of these discoveries I may be allowed to refer to the Introduction to my *Selections from the Greek Papyri*[2], Cambridge University Press, 1912. Fuller details with many valuable bibliographical references will be found in Deissmann, *Light from the Ancient East*, London, 1910, being the English translation of the second edition of *Licht vom Osten*, Tübingen, 1909. See also Additional Note A, 'Some Books for the Study of the Greek Papyri.'

has pointed out, a constant reminder of the weakness of human effort as compared with 'the exceeding greatness' of the Divine power.[1] At the same time, everything that bears on the history of writings that have now the supreme place in the world's literature cannot fail to be of interest. And, as a matter of fact, we shall have frequent occasion to notice that even the outward aspects of our New Testament writings have a closer bearing on many vexed questions of text and interpretation than may at first sight appear likely.

1. The material on which they were written.

1. Turning to these outward aspects, we begin naturally with the material on which they were written. There can be little doubt that that was papyrus, the ordinary writing material or paper of the day. The Old Testament Scriptures were apparently as a rule preserved on specially prepared skins, for which afterwards vellum was substituted.[2] But any such material would be beyond the scanty means of the New Testament writers, as well as inconsistent with the occasional character which they themselves ascribed to their writings. And we may take it that not only was

---

[1] Cf. 2 Cor. iv. 7.

[2] In the Old Testament itself skins are not directly mentioned as a writing material, but in the letter of the Pseudo-Aristeas it is expressly stated that the copy of the Law sent from Jerusalem to Egypt was written on διφθέραις (*Aristeae ad Philocratem Epistula*, ed. Wendland, Leipzig, 1900, § 176). See further Kenyon, art. 'Writing' in Hastings' *Dictionary of the Bible*, iv. p. 945, and the full discussion in Blau, *Studien zum althebräischen Buchwesen* (Strassburg i. E., 1902), i. p. 12 ff.

THE ORIGINAL MANUSCRIPTS

papyrus the material used for the original autographs, but that for a period of more than two hundred years, copies would be made and circulated on papyrus.[1]

2. In itself, papyrus as a writing material was originally an Egyptian manufacture, and at the beginning of the Christian era had already a long history behind it. The earliest extant papyrus is one found at Sakkara in 1893, containing accounts dated in the reign of Assa B.C. 3580-36. And from this period down to the ninth century after Christ, countless papyrus documents have been recovered in Egypt, where they owe their preservation to the singularly dry character of the climate.

2. History and manufacture of papyrus.

The origin of the word papyrus is somewhat uncertain, but it is probably derived from the Egyptian pa-p-yôr, 'the (product) of the river,' 'the river-plant,' a name given to a tall reed-plant which at one time grew in great abundance in the Nile, though it is now confined to the upper part of its course.[2]

From this plant (*Cyperus papyrus*, L.) the papyrus

---

[1] Cf. 2 John 12, πολλὰ ἔχων ὑμῖν γράφειν οὐκ ἐβουλήθην διὰ χάρτου καὶ μέλανος, and 3 John 13, οὐ θέλω διὰ μέλανος καὶ καλάμου σοι γράφειν, where by χάρτου we must understand a sheet of papyrus, and by καλάμου the reed-pen used for writing on it (cf. p. 17). For the meaning of 2 Tim. iv. 13, see p. 19 f.

[2] Lagarde (*Mittheilungen*, ii. p. 260) suggests that the word may be derived from Bura on Lake Menzaleh, where it was first manufactured, the opening syllable being the Egyptian article. If so, there is the more reason for pronouncing the 'y' long as ancient writers did (Juv. iv. 24, Mart. iii. 2, Catull. xxxv. 2): see Nestle, *Text. Crit. of the Greek Testament*, p. 42.

material was derived by a process of which the elder Pliny has left a classical account.¹

The pith (βύβλος) of the stem was first cut into long strips (σχίδες), which were laid down vertically to form an outward or lower layer. Over this a corresponding number of strips were placed horizontally, and the two layers were then pressed together to form a single sheet (κόλλημα), the process being assisted by a preparation of glue moistened, when possible, with the turbid water of the Nile, which was supposed to add strength to it. After being dried in the sun, and rubbed down with ivory or a smooth shell to remove any roughness, the sheet was ready for use.²

---

[1] *Nat. Hist.* xiii. 11-13. Cf. Birt, *Das antike Buchwesen* (Berlin, 1882), p. 223 ff.; Dziatzko, *Untersuchungen über ausgewählte Kapitel des antiken Buchwesens* (Leipzig, 1900), p. 49 ff.; Gardthausen, *Das Buchwesen im Altertum und im Byzantinischen Mittelalter*, being *Griechische Palaeographie*² (Leipzig, 1911), i. p. 45 ff., and most recently Wilcken in *Grundzüge und Chrestomathie der Papyruskunde*, edd. Mitteis and Wilcken (Leipzig, 1912), I. i. p. xxviii ff.

[2] An unused sheet was known as χάρτης (*charta*), but after it had been written upon, it was generally described by βύβλος or βίβλος (*liber*) from the material out of which it was made. From this came the diminutive βιβλίον, at first applied to any short writing such as a letter, but later used practically synonymously with βίβλος. Hence its plural τὰ βιβλία, meaning originally a collection of books or rolls, as in the Prologue of Ecclesiasticus (*c.* B.C. 130), when transliterated into Latin was adopted as a convenient designation for the Holy Scriptures, and eventually came to be regarded no longer as a neuter plural, but a feminine singular, *biblia*, 'the Bible.'

PLATE I.

FROM OXYRHYNCHUS, SHOWING PART OF THUCYDIDES IV. 36-41 IN NON-LITERARY HAND
CONTEMPORARY WITH THE AUTOGRAPHS OF THE NEW TESTAMENT.

Now in the Museum of Science and Art, University of Pennsylvania, U.S.A.
By permission of the Egypt Exploration Fund.

THE ORIGINAL MANUSCRIPTS 11

The size of the sheets thus formed would obviously vary according to the quality of the papyrus and the uses to which they were to be put, but Sir F. G. Kenyon has shown that for non-literary documents a very common size was from 5 to 5½ inches in width, and 9 to 11 inches in height, the height being always greater than the breadth, when the sheet was held in the way in which it was meant to be used.[1] *Size of the sheets.*

For a brief note, like the Second Epistle of St. John, a single sheet would therefore suffice; but, when more space was required, it was easily procurable by fastening a number of sheets together into a roll. For selling purposes, a roll seems frequently to have consisted of twenty sheets,[2] but this could easily be cut up into smaller dimensions to suit the purchaser's convenience, or, if desired, extended almost indefinitely by the addition of extra sheets. *Papyrus rolls.*

The beginning ($\pi\rho\omega\tau\acute{o}\kappa o\lambda\lambda o\nu$) and the end ($\dot{\epsilon}\sigma\chi\alpha\tau o\kappa\acute{o}\lambda\lambda\iota o\nu$) of the roll, as the parts most handled, were sometimes strengthened by attaching additional strips of papyrus at the back, while, in the case of more literary documents, the inner edge of the $\pi\rho\omega\tau\acute{o}\kappa o\lambda\lambda o\nu$ was often glued to a wooden roller ($\dot{o}\mu\phi\alpha\lambda\acute{o}s$), to the ends of which knobs or horns ($\kappa\acute{\epsilon}\rho\alpha\tau\alpha$) were attached. Hence, according to a common interpretation, the $\kappa\epsilon\phi\alpha\lambda\grave{\iota}s$ $\beta\iota\beta\lambda\acute{\iota}ov$ referred to by the author of the Epistle to the Hebrews in c. x. 7 (from Psalm xl. 7) may perhaps denote originally 'the little head of the book,' or the end of

[1] *The Palaeography of Greek Papyri* (Oxford, 1899), p. 16 f.
[2] Wilcken, *Grundzüge*, I. i. p. xxix.

the stick round which the roll was wound, and thence by a natural synecdoche the roll itself.¹

Price. The price would naturally vary with the size and quality of the papyrus sheet, as when in Roman times we find one sheet valued at 1 drachma 3 obols, or a little over a shilling of our money, another at 2 obols, or about 3d., and yet another at 3 obols, or about 4½d.² But in no case does papyrus seem to have been a very cheap material, the result being that the poorer classes of the population had often difficulty in procuring it, or made use of the backs of old documents, from which the original contents had been either washed or crossed out.³ For the same reason the despatch of a letter was often the opportunity for sending greetings from a large number of different friends—a practice which finds an interesting Christian parallel in the extended greetings at the close of several of the Pauline Epistles.⁴

---

[1] Cf. Ezek. ii. 9, ἰδοὺ χεὶρ ἐκτεταμένη πρὸς μέ, καὶ ἐν αὐτῇ κεφαλὶς βιβλίου, and κεφαλίς standing alone in Ezek. iii. 1-3.

[2] Cf. Schubart, *Das Buch bei den Griechen und Römern* (Berlin, 1907), p. 12, and for other figures, see Gardthausen, *Buchwesen*, p. 67.

[3] Amongst the Genevan papyri (*Les Papyrus de Genève*, ed. J. Nicole, Geneva, 1896, i. p. 76, No. 52) is a letter written on the back of a business document, where the writer explains— χάρτην (χάρτιον, Wilcken, *Archiv der Papyrusforschung*, iii. p. 399) καθαρὸν μὴ εὑρὼν πρὸς τὴν ὥραν εἰς τοῦ[τ]ον ἔγραψα.

[4] In a second century Berlin papyrus (*Berliner Griechische Urkunden*, Berlin, 1898, ii. p. 245, No. 601) the closing greetings occupy thirteen out of thirty-one lines.

THE ORIGINAL MANUSCRIPTS

As a rule, the original writing was confined to the side of the papyrus on which the shorter fibres lay horizontally, not only because it offered a smoother surface to the pen, and the clearly marked lines did away with the necessity of ruling, but also because the horizontal side was better adapted for being rolled inwards. The side thus used is technically known as the *Recto* in contradistinction to the *Verso* or back.[1] *Recto and verso.*

That the *Verso* was also occasionally made use of when space failed is shown by the long magical papyrus in the British Museum, in which nineteen columns are written on the *Recto*, and thirteen carried over to the *Verso*.[2] And when, accordingly, in Rev. v. 1 we read of 'a book written within and on the back' (βιβλίον γεγραμμένον ἔσωθεν καὶ ὄπισθεν) it is sometimes thought that the seer wishes us to understand that so great was the number of woes to be recorded that no ordinary roll could contain them, and both sides of the paper had to be employed.[3]

---

[1] Wilcken first drew attention to the distinction between *Recto* and *Verso* in *Hermes*, xxii. (1887), p. 487 ff.: see also his *Grundzüge*, I. i. p. xxx f., and for the disappearance of the preference for the *Recto* in Byzantine times owing to the deterioration of papyrus manufacture and the introduction of a new style of writing, cf. Schubart, *Das Buch*, p. 9 f.

[2] British Museum Papyrus, cxxi. in *Catalogue of Greek Papyri in the British Museum*, ed. Kenyon, i. p. 83 ff.

[3] It should be noted, however, that both Zahn (*Introduction to the New Testament*, iii. p. 405) and Nestle (*Textual Criticism of the Greek Testament*, p. 43, n²) follow Grotius in connecting

Arrangement in columns.

These columns (σελίδες) into which in the case of writings of any length the matter was arranged were from two to three inches wide, and, as a rule, were placed close together, leaving little space for the marginal additions, with which St. Paul and other New Testament writers are sometimes thought to have annotated the original documents.[1] When such additions were made, it must have been between the lines, or at the top or bottom of the papyrus sheet, and not until parchment took the place of papyrus can marginal comments on the text be said to have become common.[2]

Length of rolls.

The length of the rolls containing the New Testament books would obviously vary, not only with the length of their respective contents, but with the size and character of the writing made use of. But, anticipating for a moment what will be explained more fully directly, that the original scribes made use of the ordinary non-literary hand of the day, we may notice that Sir F. G. Kenyon has calculated that a short Epistle such as 2 Thessalonians would form a roll of about fifteen inches in length, arranged in some five columns, while the

καὶ ὄπισθεν not with what precedes, but with the following κατεσφραγισμένον. In this case βιβλίον is not a papyrus roll, but a papyrus codex (cf. p. 188), of which St. John saw only the outside: the contents were not known, until the seals were loosed.

[1] Cf. especially Laurent, *Neutestamentliche Studien* (Gotha, 1866), p. 17 ff., where a number of passages such as Rom. ii. 14, 15, xvi. 19, etc., are cited as examples of Pauline *marginalia*.

[2] Dziatzko, art. 'Buch' in Pauly-Wissowa, *Real-Encyclopädie der classischen Altertumswissenschaft* (Stuttgart, 1899), iii. p. 963.

longer Epistle to the Romans would run to about eleven feet six inches. In the same way, the Gospel of St. Mark would occupy about nineteen feet of an average-sized roll, that of St. John twenty-three feet six inches, St. Matthew thirty feet, the Acts and St. Luke's Gospel about thirty-one or thirty-two feet.[1]

The general sameness of these last figures has led to the conjecture that St. Luke wrote 'to scale,' making use of a certain stereotyped length of roll, and compressing or economizing his materials so as not to exceed it.[2] But, however this consideration may have influenced certain of the purely literary writers of the time,[3] it is difficult to think of it as extending to writings of such a spontaneous and informal character as the Gospels, especially in view of the ease with which, as we have seen, a papyrus roll could be cut or added to at pleasure.[4]

In the case of a long roll, the reader would require to use both hands, unrolling it with his right, and with his left rolling up again what he had finished

[1] *Handbook to the Textual Criticism of the New Testament*[2] (London, 1912), p. 34.

[2] Cf. Zahn, *Geschichte des Neutestamentlichen Kanons* (Erlangen, 1888), I. i. p. 76 f., and most recently Sanday in *Studies in the Synoptic Problem* (Oxford, 1911), p. 25 f.

[3] 'Für verschiedene Litteraturgattungen waren verschiedene Buchmaxima oder Formate üblich oder obligat' (Birt, *Das antike Buchwesen*, p. 288).

[4] The word $\tau\acute{o}\mu o\varsigma$, whence our 'tome,' had originally nothing to do with size, but meant simply a 'cut' of a papyrus roll, forming a volume by itself: see Birt, *op. cit.* p. 25, where $\tau\acute{o}\mu o\varsigma$ is defined as 'das Buch als Werktheil.'

reading,¹ a practice that enables us to understand the imagery of Rev. vi. 14, ὁ οὐρανὸς ἀπεχωρίσθη ὡς βιβλίον ἑλισσόμενον, where the expanse of heaven is represented as parting asunder, 'the divided portions curling up and forming a roll on either hand.'²

3. Other writing materials.

3. To complete our survey of writing materials, it is enough to notice that the ink (τὸ μέλαν: cf. 3 John 13) in ordinary use for papyrus was made of soot, mixed with gum, and diluted with water. A colour, which had a wonderful lasting power, was thus produced, as may be seen by examining any of the recently recovered texts. At the same time, the ink, through not sinking into the fibres of the papyrus, was easily washed out, when still fresh, a point which lends emphasis to the language of Col. ii. 14: by His atoning work Christ not merely 'blotted out,' but 'washed out the bond written in ordinances that was against us' (ἐξαλείψας τὸ καθ' ἡμῶν χειρόγραφον τοῖς δόγμασιν ὃ ἦν ὑπεναντίον ἡμῖν), so that it was as if it had never been.³

---

¹ Cf. Lucian, *imag.* c. 8, βιβλίον ἐν ταῖν χεροῖν εἶχεν, ἐς δύο συνειλημμένον· καὶ ἐῴκει τὸ μέν τι ἀναγνώσεσθαι αὐτοῦ, τὸ δὲ ἤδη ἀνεγνωκέναι, and the instructive illustrations in Birt, *Die Buchrolle in der Kunst* (Leipzig, 1907), p. 130 ff.

² Swete, *The Apocalypse of S. John* (London, 1906), *ad l.*

³ Cf. also Rev. iii. 5, οὐ μὴ ἐξαλείψω τὸ ὄνομα αὐτοῦ ἐκ τῆς βίβλου τῆς ζωῆς, to which interesting parallels are afforded by such passages from the inscriptions as Dittenberger, *Sylloge Inscriptionum Graecarum*², No. 439²⁰ (iv./B.C.), ὃς δ' ἂν δόξῃ μὴ ὢν φράτηρ ἐσαχθῆναι, ἐξαλειψάτω τὸ ὄνομα αὐτὸ ὁ ἱερεύς, and *Orientis Graeci Inscriptiones Selectae*, No. 218¹²⁹ (iii./B.C.), ἐξαλείψαντας τ[ὸ ὄνομ]α τὸ ἐκείνου.

THE ORIGINAL MANUSCRIPTS

The pen in ordinary use for papyrus was a 'calamus,' or reed, as we find in 3 John 13 (οὐ θέλω διὰ μέλανος καὶ καλάμου σοι γράφειν). According to Wilcken the point was at first prepared for use simply by being softened in the mouth, and not until Graeco-Roman times was it split after the same fashion as our quills or steel pens.¹

4. When finished, the roll was rolled round upon itself, fastened with a thread, and in the case of formal and official documents, sealed, as when in a second century papyrus a certain Ptolema acknowledges the receipt of a will 'with the seals intact' (ἐπὶ τῶν αὐτῶν σφραγείδων) which she had deposited 'under seals' (ἐπὶ σφραγίδων) in the archives, and now wished to revoke.² It is tempting to imagine that we have a reference to a similar practice in the 'book sealed with seven seals' (βιβλίον ... κατεσφραγισμένον σφραγῖσιν ἑπτά) of Rev. v. 1, where the symbolism has been explained on the ground that in Roman law a will had to be sealed *seven* times in order to authenticate it;³ but the seven is more probably simply the Jewish sacred number. And apart altogether from any such special references, we may, I think, take it that the original writers of

4. Sealing and addressing of rolls.

---

¹ *Grundzüge*, I. i. p. xxxii f.
For other references to writing materials, see *Selections from the Greek Papyri*², p. xxiii, note 2.

² *The Oxyrhynchus Papyri*, edd. Grenfell-Hunt, i. p. 173 f., No. 106.

³ Cf. Hicks' *Greek Philosophy and Roman Law in the New Testament*, p. 157 f.

B

the New Testament would be content, as in the case of ordinary letters, to secure their writings with a thread without going through the formal process of sealing.

In the same way, in accordance with general usage, they would confine the address on the back of their rolls to the fewest possible words. In the papyrus letters that have come down to us, this consists as a rule of nothing but the name of the person addressed, with sometimes a descriptive epithet added. A letter of introduction which recalls the commendatory letters (συστατικαὶ ἐπιστολαί) of 2 Cor. iii. 1, is inscribed simply 'To Philoxenus' (Φιλοξένωι):[1] another of a similar character bears the address 'To Tyrannus, the Procurator' (Τυράννωι διοικ(ητῇ).[2] Sometimes the name of the place where the person addressed resided was added, as in the letter 'To Stotoëtis, chief priest, at the island of . . . ,' the name of the particular island unfortunately being lost.[3] And sometimes, though so rarely as to be exceptional, the writer inserted his own name. A good example is afforded by an Oxyrhynchus letter of B.C. 1 (see further, p. 116 n[3]), where the address runs 'Hilarion to Alis, deliver' (Ἱλαρίων Ἅλιτι ἀπόδος).

[1] *Greek Papyri from the Cairo Museum*, ed. Goodspeed (Chicago, 1902), p. 8 (= *Selections from the Greek Papyri*[2], No. 8).

[2] *The Oxyrhynchus Papyri*, edd. Grenfell-Hunt, ii. p. 292, No. 292 (= *Selections*, No. 14).

[3] Στοτόητι λεσώνῃ εἰς τὴν νῆσον τ . . . : see *Berliner Griechische Urkunden*, i. p. 52, No. 37 (A.D. 50); and cf. Deissmann, *Light from the Ancient East*, p. 157 ff.

THE ORIGINAL MANUSCRIPTS 19

We must not, therefore, think of the New Testament autographs bearing any such full addresses, as we have become accustomed to in the headings of the different books in our English version: these, like the subscriptions, are the work of later scribes.[1] The original titles must have run much as they appear in the Greek text of Westcott and Hort, πρὸς Ῥωμαίους, πρὸς Ἑβραίους, 'To the Romans,' 'To the Hebrews,' any difficulty as to the exact destination of the books being removed by the fact that they were entrusted to private messengers for delivery, who would be fully instructed as to their writers and recipients (cf. p. 30 f.).

The σίλλυβοι, or small strips of papyrus or vellum, containing the title, which was frequently attached to literary works for the purpose of identification,[2] would be wanting in the first instance at any rate in the more occasional writings of the New Testament. Nor is there any reason to believe that these last would be enclosed in the coverings, in which the sacred books of the Jews were, as a rule, preserved.[3] The ordinary rolls of the period at any rate, such as those discovered at Herculaneum, had no such protection. But it is at least an interesting conjecture whether it was not to some such satchel or wrap,

---

[1] See Additional Note B, 'The Titles and Subscriptions of the New Testament Writings.'

[2] Cf. Cicero, *ad Attic.* iv. 4. 1, and for recently recovered specimens of these σίλλυβοι, see *The Oxyrhynchus Papyri*, edd. Grenfell-Hunt, ii. pp. 303, 313, Nos. 301, 381.

[3] Blau, *Studien*, p. 173.

rather than to his travelling cloak, that St. Paul refers in the φελόνης of 2 Tim. iv. 13: 'The book-cover that I left at Troas with Carpus, bring when thou comest, and the books, especially the parchments.'[1] In any case, the latter words recall an important distinction to which attention has already been drawn, for by 'the books' (τὰ βιβλία) the Apostle probably meant certain papyrus sheets or notes, possibly writings of his own, which he regarded as of little importance compared with 'the parchments' (τὰς μεμβράνας), copies of certain portions of the Old Testament Scriptures.

5. Preservation of rolls.

5. For preservation rolls were fastened together in bundles, and laid in arks or chests,[2] a practice which enables us to understand how unsigned rolls, laid up in the same place, and dealing with cognate subjects, would come in some instances to be joined together as if they formed parts of one work,[3] while in the case of others, errors regarding authorship and destination might readily arise.[4]

[1] The word φαινόλης (*paenula*) is often written by transposition of ν and λ, φαιλόνης or φελόνης. For its use as a book-wrap, see Hesychius' *Lexicon*, where it is defined as εἰλητάριον μεμβράϊ(ν)ον ἢ γλωσσόκομον, and cf. Birt, *Das antike Buchwesen*, p. 65.

[2] Cf. *The Oxyrhynchus Papyri*, ed. Hunt, viii. p. 254, No. 1153³ᵇ·ᶠ· (i/A.D.): [ἐ]κομισάμην διὰ Ἡρακλᾶτος τὰς κίστας [σὺν] τοῖς βιβλίοις.

[3] See further, p. 173 f.

[4] 'Die darin vereinigten Rollen bildeten ein σύνταγμα, *corpus* u.s.w. Manche irrige Zuweisung einer Schrift an einen falschen Autor mag in ihrer Zusammenstellung mit inhaltlich verwandten Schriften in der gleichen *capsa* ihren Grund haben.' Dziatzko, art. 'Buch' in Pauly-Wissowa, iii. p. 970.

III. From the outward appearance and form of the New Testament autographs, we pass to consider the manner in which they were written. And in lack of any definite information as to the circumstances under which they were composed—information which, if it were available, would go far to set at rest many vexed questions of Biblical criticism—we are again led to fall back on the ordinary practice of the time. In accordance with this, and in agreement with various hints thrown out in the New Testament books themselves, there is every reason to believe that they were in many instances at any rate originally written to dictation. *III. The manner in which the books of the New Testament were written.*

1. In support of this conclusion appeal is sometimes made to the note appended to countless papyrus documents and letters to the effect that they were written by so-and-so on behalf of so-and-so, 'seeing that he does not know letters.'[1] But of even the most 'unlettered'[2] of the New Testament writers that could hardly be said. And it is better rather to think of the instances where the services of a scribe are requisitioned, owing to the fact that the original author could himself only write slowly or with difficulty. A good example is afforded by a marriage contract of the early second century dis- *1. Dictation.*

---

[1] *E.g. The Oxyrhynchus Papyri*, edd. Grenfell-Hunt, ii. p. 262 ff., No. 275⁴³ (= *Selections*, No. 20) (A.D. 66): Ζωίλος . . . ἔγραψα ὑπὲρ αὐτοῦ μὴ ἰδότος γράμματα.

[2] The adjective ἀγράμματος in Acts iv. 13 (cf. xxvi. 24, John vii. 15) is probably = 'unacquainted with literature or Rabbinic teaching.'

covered at Oxyrhynchus, where, with reference to one of the signatories at the end, it is stated, 'I write on his behalf seeing that he writes slowly' (ἔγραψα ὑπὲρ αὐτοῦ βραδέα γράφο[ντος]).[1] And even more significant is the statement in connexion with the enrolment as an ephebus of a certain Ammonius in A.D. 99. By trade a river fisherman (ἁλιεὺς ποτάμι⟨ο⟩ς), Ammonius can only write 'slowly' (βραδέως). Consequently a friend writes the body of the document for him, leaving him to add the signature at the end.[2]

In view of such instances, and the evidence might easily be multiplied, it does not need any great exercise of imagination to realize that the Galilean fishermen, Peter and John, might well find the actual task of writing both irksome and tedious, and would gladly take advantage of skilled assistance when opportunity offered.

In the case of the First Epistle of St. Peter, indeed, this seems to be distinctly stated, for the words διὰ Σιλουανοῦ, 'by Silvanus,' in c. v. 12, are best understood as implying that Silvanus was not only the bearer, but the actual scribe of the Epistle.[3] And in the same way an interesting tradition, which

---

[1] *The Oxyrhynchus Papyri*, edd. Grenfell-Hunt, iii. p. 212 ff., No. 497[24] (early ii/A.D.).

[2] *The Tebtunis Papyri*, edd. Grenfell-Hunt-Goodspeed, ii. p. 118 f., No. 316, col. iv[100 ff.] (A.D. 99).

[3] For a similar use of διά, cf. Ign. *Rom.* x. 1, γράφω δὲ ὑμῖν ταῦτα ἀπὸ Σμύρνης δι' Ἐφεσίων τῶν ἀξιομακαρίστων, with Lightfoot's note *ad l.*

finds pictorial representation in many mediaeval manuscripts of the Fourth Gospel, says that St. John dictated his Gospel to a disciple of his named Prochorus.[1]

Even an educated man, like St. Paul, amidst the pressure and anxieties of his daily work, was glad, as several indications in his Epistles imply, to follow the same practice. Thus, when in one of the earliest of the Epistles that have come down to us, the Apostle sets his authenticating signature at the end in apparent contrast with what had preceded, the natural conclusion is that the body of the Epistle was written by some one else (2 Thess. iii. 17, 18; cf. also 1 Cor. xvi. 21, Col. iv. 18). And the same appears still more strongly in the greeting of Tertius in Rom. xvi. 22, ἀσπάζομαι ὑμᾶς ἐγὼ Τέρτιος ὁ γράψας τὴν ἐπιστολὴν ἐν κυρίῳ, 'I Tertius, who write the Epistle, salute you in the Lord'; where, unless we are to think of Tertius as having made a copy of the letter which the Apostle had penned, we can only regard him as the original scribe.[2]

It is sometimes thought that the Epistle to the Galatians formed an exception to this general practice on St. Paul's part, the 'with how large

---

[1] Cf. p. 160 f., and see Plate V.

[2] An interesting parallel to Tertius's postscript is afforded by an Oxyrhynchus letter of the third century from a certain Helene to her brother, to which their father Alexander adds—κἀγὼ Ἀλέξανδρος ὁ π[α]τὴρ ὑμῶν ἀσπάζομαι ὑμᾶς πολλά. As, however, there is no change of hand, in this case both Helene and her father would seem to have employed an amanuensis: see Hunt, *The Oxyrhynchus Papyri*, vii. p. 221 f., No. 1067[25] note.

letters I have written unto you with mine own hand' (πηλίκοις ὑμῖν γράμμασιν ἔγραψα τῇ ἐμῇ χειρί) of Gal. vi. 11 being taken as pointing back to what had preceded. If so, may we not suppose that in this so severe letter St. Paul, with his exquisite tact, may have preferred to make use of no intermediary between himself and those whom he was obliged to warn in such strong terms? On the other hand, if the 'how great letters' refer rather to what follows, then they may be understood either of the large, irregular handwriting of the man who wrote but little, as compared with the more flowing hand of his practised amanuensis, or as by their size intended to draw special attention to the importance of the contents.

<small>Autographic conclusions.</small> In any case, we have abundant evidence of autographic conclusions both in the literature of the day,[1] and, what is more to the point in the present connexion, in the non-literary Egyptian papyri, where the signature is frequently in a different hand from the body of the document, and serves to confirm and authenticate the whole. When, for example, in the year A.D. 50 the Egyptian olive-planter Mystarion writes to commend his messenger Blastus to Stotoëtis, a chief priest, the change of handwriting in the closing salutation ἔρρωσο, 'Farewell,' seems to indicate that it was written by Mystarion himself.[2] And

[1] Cf. *e.g.* the letter of Pompey, of which Cicero, *ad Attic.* viii. 1. 1, speaks 'in extremo ipsius manu.'

[2] *Berliner Griechische Urkunden*, i. p. 52 (cf. p. 353), No. 37[8]. For facsimile see Deissmann, *Light from the Ancient East*, p. 157, Fig. 20.

the same practice is expressly vouched for in an Oxyrhynchus letter of A.D. 95, where the original sender authenticates the contents, which were doubtless written by one of his clerks, by adding at the end Ἡρακλ(ᾶς) σεση(μείωμαι), 'I, Heraclas, have signed.'[1]

Before leaving the question of handwriting it is of importance to point out that, as the New Testament amanuenses would not be professional scribes, but educated friends or companions of the authors, the writing would be of the ordinary non-literary character, though doubtless more than the usual care would be taken in view of the importance of the writings' contents.[2] The words would as a rule be closely joined together, though occasionally in doubtful instances they might be separated by dots. Contractions, especially in the leaving out the last syllables of familiar words, would be frequent, while accents and breathings would be very sparingly employed. And there would be no punctuation, unless it might be the occasional insertion of a dot above the line to divide words, or a slight space to mark an important break in the sense. These paragraphs were also divided from one another by a short horizontal line (παράγραφος) *below* the line in which the pause occurs.[3]

Character of the handwriting.

---

[1] *The Oxyrhynchus Papyri*, edd. Grenfell-Hunt, i. p. 101 ff., No. 45[18].

[2] See especially Kenyon, *Palaeography of the Greek Papyri*, p. 9 ff. for the distinction between the book hand and the common hand, and Plate I. for the probable character of the handwriting of the New Testament autographs.

[3] Cf. Kenyon *Palaeography of the Greek Papyri*, p. 27.

The task of punctuating the New Testament manuscripts fell accordingly for the most part to the later copyists and editors, with the result that there is often a wide difference of opinion as to how particular words are to be connected, or as to whether a sentence is to be understood interrogatively or indicatively.[1]

<small>The amount of liberty left to the New Testament scribes.</small> Another inquiry of great interest with regard to our New Testament autographs is the amount of liberty which their authors left to their amanuenses. What, for example, was St. Paul's practice? Did he dictate his letters word for word, his scribe perhaps taking them down in some form of shorthand, and then rewriting them?[2] Or was he content to supply a rough draft of what he wished to be said, leaving the scribe free to throw it into more formal and complete shape?

It is true that to these questions no definite answer can be given. In all probability the Apostle's practice varied with the special circumstances of the case, or the particular scribe whom at the time he was employing. More might be left to

---

[1] A good example of the former difficulty is afforded by the famous text Rom. ix. 5, where at least three of the principal interpretations are dependent on the particular punctation adopted.

[2] On the practice of shorthand amongst the ancients, see Additional Note C, where reference is made to the contract, belonging to the year A.D. 155, in which an ex-cosmetes of Oxyrhynchus apprentices his slave to a shorthand writer (σημιογράφῳ) for two years to be taught to read and write shorthand (πρὸς μάθησιν σημείων) (*The Oxyrhynchus Papyri*, edd. Grenfell-Hunt, iv. p. 204 f., No. 724).

the discretion of a Timothy than of a Tertius. And if in one case the Epistle as dictated underwent a close revision and correction at the Apostle's own hands, at another he might allow it to go out practically unchanged.

2. All this is, however, matter of conjecture, and we are on surer ground in pointing out that the mere fact of the employment of a scribe would help to impart to St. Paul's Epistles some of that vividness and directness of language by which they are distinguished. In dictating the Apostle would have clearly before his mind's eye the actual persons and circumstances of those to whom he was writing, and the broken constructions and sudden changes of subject prove how often the eager rush of his words overmastered the grammatical and orderly sequence of his thought. *2. General results from the use of dictation.* *(1) Vividness of language.*

Nor can we marvel that even in the same Epistle there are often sudden changes in tone and expression, when we remember that it was in the spare moments of a laborious life that St. Paul's Epistles were written, and that the work of dictation must have been often interrupted by some unforeseen and pressing call, demanding the Apostle's immediate attention.

There are still other ways in which the practice of dictation may have affected the outward form of the Pauline Epistles. These Epistles, as we know, were frequently written to answer questions which had been addressed to the Apostle by Churches he had founded. What more natural, then, than that *(2) Quotations embodied from correspondents' letters.*

St. Paul, when dictating his answer, should have held in his hand the communications that had been addressed to him, and embodied quotations from them in his reply! In the absence of any method of distinguishing these quotations in the early manuscripts corresponding to our modern use of inverted commas, these can only be guessed at now from the general meaning and context. But there can be no doubt that the interpretation of many passages is made clearer by recognizing that not infrequently the Apostle throws back, as it were, their own words at those whom he is addressing.

A notable example of this has been found in 1 Thessalonians, where, on the strength of such a practice, Dr. Rendel Harris has ingeniously reconstructed the epistle from Thessalonica to which it was an answer.[1] And the same treatment can be applied with even greater success to 1 Corinthians, when the Apostle is avowedly dealing with a long series of questions addressed to him by the Corinthian Church, and naturally marks the different stages in his reply by pointed references to the Corinthians' own words. This comes out very clearly, as Dr. Lock has shown,[2] in the section 'Concerning things sacrificed to idols' (c. viii. 1-9), where the Apostle quotes, only to refute, the Corinthians' plea, 'We know that we have all knowledge,' and also sets aside their emphatic claim for liberty,

[1] *The Expositor*, V. viii. p. 161 ff., 'A Study in Letter-writing.'
[2] *The Expositor*, V. vi. p. 65 ff., '1 Corinthians viii. 1-9. A Suggestion.'

'But meat will not commend us to God; neither, if we eat not, are we the worse, nor, if we eat, are we the better,' on the ground that, while theoretically true, such an argument must not be allowed to interfere with their duty towards the weak.

And so, again, in the very personal Second Epistle to the same Church, such phrases as 'I who in your presence am lowly among you, but being absent am of good courage toward you,'[1] and 'being crafty, I caught you with guile,'[2] may well recall the actual taunts which his Jewish Christian opponents in Corinth had hurled against the Apostle.[3]

Or, once more, to appeal to what many regard as St. Paul's latest Epistle, when he writes to the Philippians, 'But I hope in the Lord Jesus to send Timothy shortly unto you, that I also may be of good comfort, when I know your state' (c. ii. 19), is not the 'also' due to the fact that St. Paul wishes the Philippians to know that he is as anxious to hear good news of them, as they had already professed themselves to be, to hear good news of him? Or when in c. iv. 10 he writes, 'But I rejoice in the Lord greatly, that now at length you have revived your thought for me; wherein you did indeed take thought, but you lacked opportunity,' have we not the fine courtesy which accepts, even while it

[1] c. x. 1. [2] c. xii. 16.
[3] 'Such phrases are wholly unintelligible unless we hear in the catchwords the language of the enemy' (Weizsäcker, *The Apostolic Age*, Eng. Tr. by Millar, ii. p. 102 f.).

30   THE NEW TESTAMENT DOCUMENTS

dismisses the need of, the apology with which the Philippians had admitted a certain remissness in attending to his wants?

3. Differences of style.

3. Similar considerations apply in the case of the other New Testament writings. The form which 1 Peter took, and the many Pauline echoes it contains, may be due to the fact that Peter employed as his scribe Silvanus, who had already acted in a similar capacity for Paul. And though it will hardly be accepted as an adequate explanation of the phenomena of the so-called Second Epistle of St. Peter, it is worth noting that, so far back as St. Jerome, the differences between it and 1 Peter were explained by the employment of different interpreters or scribes.[1] And it is at least possible that in the dictation and revision of the Fourth Gospel we may have a partial key to some of the vexed questions that have arisen regarding its authorship.[2]

IV. Delivery of the New Testament writings.

IV. The only other point that concerns us is the manner in which the New Testament writings would be delivered to their first readers. Considering the elaborate organization of the Roman Empire, it may seem somewhat surprising that nothing in the form of a general postal system had as yet been thought of. An Imperial post, based

---

[1] 'Denique et duae epistolae quae feruntur Petri stilo inter se et charactere discrepant structuraque verborum. Ex quo intellegimus, pro necessitate rerum diversis eum usum interpretibus.' (*Ep. ad Hedibiam*, 120, *Quaest.* xi.)

[2] See p. 159 ff.

THE ORIGINAL MANUSCRIPTS 31

apparently on the Persian model,[1] had indeed been instituted by Augustus, but its use was strictly limited to State purposes, and ordinary correspondence had to be carried by the favour of some friend or passing traveller.[2] Even had it been otherwise, it is obvious that the Apostolic communications could only be entrusted with safety to Christian messengers in full sympathy with their object, who would be able to reinforce and supplement the message they contained. Thus, Titus would seem to have played an important part in connexion with the correspondence with the Church at Corinth,[3] while in the case of the Epistle to the Ephesians, the lack of personal references may be explained, not only by the Epistle's circular character, but also by the fact that St. Paul had charged his messenger Tychicus to supply orally all needed information, and to comfort his readers' hearts.[4]

_{Use of private messengers.}

---

[1] The institution of the State post in Persia is ascribed to King Darius, and in keeping with this is the belief that his wife Atossa invented the form of the letter.

[2] Cic. *ad Attic.* i. 9. 1; Pliny, *Epist.* vii. 12; Mart. iii. 100, and cf. Friedländer, *Darstellungen aus der Sittengeschichte Roms*[8] (Leipzig, 1910), I. ii. p. 19 ff.

[3] Cf. 2 Cor. ii. 13, vii. 6, 13 f.

[4] Cf. Eph. vi. 21 f. An interesting example of a similar practice is afforded by a letter of B.C. 103, in which the writer enjoins his messengers to 'greet kindly' (ἀσπάσεσθαι φιλοφρόνως) those to whom he was writing. (*An Alexandrian Erotic Fragment, and other Greek Papyri chiefly Ptolemaic*, ed. Grenfell, p. 59 f. No. 30.)

The permanent value of the New Testament writings.

Here then, in the meantime, we must leave our New Testament autographs. The details with which we have been engaged may in themselves, as I have already hinted, seem very trivial as compared with the absorbing interest of their contents, and the influence which they have exerted in the world. And yet they will not have been without their use, if they have succeeded in bringing home to us the fact that we are dealing with real documents, born amidst 'the toil and moil' of life, and for the most part intended in the first instance to meet only immediate and local needs. For the more clearly we realize this, the more certain does it become that 'that which was in origin most casual became in effect most permanent by the presence of a divine energy,' and that 'the most striking marvel in the scattered writings of the New Testament is the perfect fitness which they exhibit for fulfilling an office of which their authors appear themselves to have had no conception.'[1]

---

[1] Westcott, *An Introduction to the Study of the Gospels*⁶ (London, 1881), p. 167.

LECTURE II.

THE LANGUAGE OF THE NEW TESTAMENT WRITINGS.

'Nam si quis minorem gloriae fructum putat ex Graecis versibus percipi quam ex Latinis, vehementer errat, propterea quod Graeca leguntur in omnibus fere gentibus, Latina suis finibus, exigue sane, continentur.'

CICERO, *Pro Archia*, 23.

II.

THE LANGUAGE OF THE NEW TESTAMENT WRITINGS.

Καὶ ὁ πολὺς ὄχλος ἤκουεν αὐτοῦ ἡδέως.
Mark xii. 37.

Τὰ ῥήματα ἃ ἐγὼ λελάληκα ὑμῖν πνεῦμά ἐστιν καὶ ζωή ἐστιν.
John vi. 63.

Οὐ γράμματος ἀλλὰ πνεύματος· τὸ γὰρ γράμμα ἀποκτείνει, τὸ δὲ πνεῦμα ζωοποιεῖ.
2 Cor. iii. 6.

I. WE have seen that the original manuscripts of the New Testament were written on papyrus sheets or rolls, and that in the actual work of transcription their authors largely availed themselves of the assistance of trusted friends, who were practised in the art of writing. We have now to consider the language that was made use of. And when we remember that, with the exception of St. Luke, the New Testament writers were all Jews, and that through the influence of the Old Testament Scriptures Hebrew was regarded as essentially the sacred language, we might naturally have expected that recourse would again have been had to it.

1. The linguistic conditions of Palestine.

Various circumstances, however, prevented this.

36   THE NEW TESTAMENT DOCUMENTS

To have employed the sacred language of Judaism for the new records' might have seemed to the disciples to invest these with an authority to which at first at any rate they laid no claim. Nor must we forget that Hebrew by this time had largely passed out of general knowledge and use, and given place to the more popular Aramaic.[1]

<small>Wide-spread use of Aramaic.</small>

We are not specially concerned at present with the history of Aramaic, but it may be well to guard against the common error which looks upon it as a mere dialect of Hebrew, and not as an independent, though allied, language which, as Zahn has shown, had spread gradually throughout Western Asia during the five hundred years preceding the advent of Christianity.[2] How widely, indeed, it was known is shown by the fact that Josephus expressly states that he wrote his *History of the Jewish War* originally in Aramaic in order that it might be understood by the Asiatics, the Parthians, the Babylonians, and the Arabs.[3]

Certain portions of the Old Testament itself were written in Aramaic,[4] and, though this is not universally admitted, there can be little doubt that in their ordinary teaching both our Lord and His disciples

---

[1] The Ἑβραϊστί in which the title on the Cross was written (John xix. 20) and the Ἑβραῒς διάλεκτος of St. Paul's speech at Jerusalem (Acts xxi. 40) refer to Aramaic and not to Hebrew.

[2] *Introduction to the New Testament*, Engl. Trans., Edinburgh, 1909, i. p. 4 ff.

[3] *Bellum Judaicum, proem.* 1 f.

[4] Ezra iv. 8–vi. 18, vii. 12-26, Dan. ii. 4–vii. 28.

LANGUAGE OF THE NEW TESTAMENT

employed the same language. For proofs of this we are generally referred to the existence in our Gospels of certain Aramaic words and expressions, directly attributed to Christ Himself, like the cry on the Cross, Ἐλωί Ἐλωί λαμὰ σαβαχθάνει, 'My God, My God, why hast Thou forsaken me?' (Mark xv. 34); or such phrases as Ταλειθά κούμ, 'Damsel, arise' (Mark v. 41), and Ἐφφαθά, 'Be opened' (Mark vii. 34), though it must not be forgotten that their retention in this form can also be explained on the ground that they were exceptional. On the whole, however, in view of the generally Aramaic background of the Gospels, on which Dalman[1] and Wellhausen[2] amongst others have recently laid such stress, combined with the inherent probabilities of the case, we may take it that Jesus, while able on occasion, as in His interview with Pilate, to speak Greek, as a rule employed the more indigenous and familiar Aramaic.[3]

There would have been nothing astonishing, then, if the New Testament books which appeared in Palestine had been written in Aramaic, and, as a matter of fact, our first three Gospels are in part at least based on earlier Aramaic documents (see further, p. 139). But no one of them in its present

Use of Greek by the New Testament writers.

---

[1] *Die Worte Jesu*, i., Leipzig, 1898; Engl. Trans. by Kay, Edinburgh, 1902.

[2] *Einleitung in die drei ersten Evangelien*[2], Berlin, 1911.

[3] The opposite view is maintained by Roberts, *Discussions on the Gospels*, London, 1862, and *A Short Proof that Greek was the Language of Christ*, Paisley and London, 1893.

form is a direct translation from Aramaic.[1] And there is again practical unanimity amongst scholars that the New Testament Epistles have all come down to us in the language in which they were first written. Attempts indeed have been made to revive the view held both by Clement of Alexandria and St. Jerome that our present Epistle to the Hebrews is a translation from Hebrew or Aramaic,[2] but the purity and elegance of the language, to say nothing of the fact that the quotations in the Epistle are taken from the Septuagint, and not from the Hebrew text, point conclusively to a Greek original.[3] And the same holds true of the Epistle of St. James. That an Epistle emanating from such a source should contain Aramaisms is only what we should expect, but, regarded as a whole, it exhibits none of the ordinary signs of a translation, and 'is written in strong, simple Greek, used with no slight rhetorical skill by one who has

---

[1] On the view to be taken of Papias' statement that 'Matthew composed the *Logia* in the Hebraic dialect,' see p. 137 f. As regards the Second Gospel, Allen suggested so far back as 1902, that St. Mark wrote it in Aramaic (*The Expository Times*, xiii. p. 328 ff.), and in a more recent study he again emphasizes its Aramaic background (*Studies in the Synoptic Problem*, Oxford, 1911), x. p. 298. Wellhausen has also declared strongly for an original Aramaic document, based on oral tradition (*Einleitung*[2], p. 38).

[2] *E.g.* by Biesenthal, *Das Trostschreiben des Apostels Paulus an die Hebräer* (Leipzig, 1878), p. 43 ff.

[3] See further the present writer's *Theology of the Epistle to the Hebrews* (Edinburgh, 1899), p. 16 f.

something of his own to say, and says it with perfect freedom.'[1]

Nor need this preference for Greek over Aramaic on the part of the New Testament writers cause us any surprise. Largely through the conquests of Alexander the Great, Greek had come into ever-increasing use throughout the East. It would be the one language generally understood by the different bodies of soldiers of which his armies were composed, and in which alone the administrative work of his widely spread Empire could be carried on. *Reasons for their preference for Greek.*

This would apply with even greater force to the state of things under the Diadochi. And when eventually the Romans united East and West in one great Empire, it was naturally in Greek that they continued to rule their Eastern subjects.

We need not wonder then that even in Palestine, notwithstanding the national prejudices which excluded everything un-Jewish from education, Greek speedily gained a strong footing.[2] The cities of

---

[1] J. B. Mayor, *The Epistle of St. James*[2] (London, 1897), p. ccxxxiv. See further, p. 111 of the present volume.

[2] The fact that Josephus found it necessary to translate his *History of the Jewish War* from Aramaic (cf. p. 36) into Greek is alone proof of this, especially when combined with the fact that his *Antiquities of the Jews* were originally composed in the latter language. Any deficiencies that it might exhibit in Greek learning he is careful to put down to the fact that his own nation did nothing to encourage those who learned the language of many nations (παρ' ἡμῖν γὰρ οὐκ ἐκείνους ἀποδέχονται τοὺς πολλῶν ἐθνῶν διάλεκτον ἐκμαθόντας, *Antt. Jud.* xx. 264, ed. Niese).

Pella and Dion in Eastern Palestine with their Macedonian names were probably founded by Alexander's soldiers, and when we come down to Roman times we are at once met with the Decapolis, a League of Greek cities specially formed perhaps to oppose 'the various Semitic influences east and west of Jordan, from which Rome had freed them.'[1] One thing is certain, that the religion of the Decapolis, as distinguished from that of the surrounding district, was thoroughly Hellenic. And Principal George Adam Smith has drawn a striking picture of the influence which this Greek life in Palestine could not fail to have on the beginnings of Christianity.

'The Decapolis,' he writes, 'was flourishing in the time of Christ's ministry. Gadara, with her temples and her amphitheatres, with her art, her games and her literature, overhung the Lake of Galilee, and the voyages of its fishermen. A leading Epicuraean of the previous generation, the founder of the Greek anthology, some of the famous wits of the day, the reigning emperor's tutor, had all been bred within sight of the homes of the writers of the New Testament. Philodemus, Meleager, Menippus, Theodorus, were names of which the one end of the Lake of Galilee was proud, when Matthew, Peter, James and John, were working at the other end. The temples of Zeus, Pallas, and Astarte crowned a height opposite to that which gave its name to the

[1] G. A. Smith, *The Historical Geography of the Holy Land* (London, 1897), p. 596.

Sermon on the Mount. . . . We cannot believe that the two worlds, which this one landscape embraced, did not break into each other.'[1]

Similar influences were everywhere at work, and may be said to have reached their height in the reign of Herod the Great, who, as Josephus records, was in the habit of boasting that he was more nearly related to the Greeks than to the Jews.[2] And when we add to this, that under the Roman system of rule by Procurators residing at Caesarea, Greek became the recognized official language, as the only language intelligible alike to the governors and the governed, its increasing hold upon all classes of the population becomes at once intelligible.

Nor in estimating the place which Greek had come to occupy in Palestine, must we forget the influence exercised by the Jews of the Dispersion. From long residence abroad they had ceased to use their native language to any extent, and for the old Hebrew Scriptures had substituted the Greek translation which we know as the Septuagint. They continued, however, to attend the great feasts at Jerusalem, 'the metropolis of Judaism the world over,' where for convenience they had their own synagogues (Acts vi. 9), and where eventually not a few finally settled, perhaps from a wish to end their days and be buried in the Holy Land (cf. Acts ii. 5).

[1] *Ibid.* p. 607 f.
[2] *Antt. Jud.* xix. 329, ed. Niese: Ἕλλησι πλέον ἢ Ἰουδαίοις οἰκείως ἔχειν ὁμολογούμενος.

However vigorously, therefore, Palestinian Jewish teachers might combat the Greek spirit as a menace to orthodox Judaism, they would be powerless to prevent the spread of the Greek tongue. It was the language of government, of the army, of business, and even of religion, in the case of a large and influential section of the population. While, as showing how far it had penetrated amongst all classes, it is sufficient to point to the striking scene in Acts xxi. 40 ff., where it is obvious that the Jerusalem mob whom St. Paul addressed from the stairs of Antonia expected that he would have addressed them in Greek, and that it was his falling back on their native Hebrew or Aramaic that led to their being 'the more quiet.'[1]

How long this bilingual state of things continued in Palestine it is not easy to determine, but it would certainly be well over the period covered by our New Testament writings. And enough, I trust, has been said to show that during that period even the native Jews might very naturally fall back upon Greek for religious purposes.[2] And when we pass

---

[1] Dr. T. K. Abbott quotes an interesting parallel from a bilingual district of Ireland, where at a public discussion between a Protestant and a Roman Catholic champion any approach to a disturbance was at once quelled by a few words in Irish. 'The people were listening to English speeches, but the Irish touched their hearts more nearly' (*Essays chiefly on the Original Texts of the Old and New Testaments* (London, 1891), p. 164).

[2] Schürer, while holding that 'Aramaic was in the time of Christ the sole popular language of Palestine,' nevertheless admits 'that a slight acquaintance with Greek was pretty widely diffused,

LANGUAGE OF THE NEW TESTAMENT 43

outside of Palestine and think of St. Paul and other of the Apostles addressing their letters to scattered communities throughout the Graeco-Roman world, it is obvious that Greek was the one language in which they could hope to be understood. We are even met with the apparent paradox that an Epistle intended specially for 'Hebrews,' readers who, whatever their exact habitat, were certainly Jewish Christians, was written not in Hebrew but in Greek, and by one who made use of the Greek version of the Old Testament Scriptures.

II. This raises the question, What was the character of this Greek? *II. The character of New Testament Greek.*

1. Here let me say at once that the discussion of the real character of the Greek of the New Testament has in recent years entered on an entirely new phase. *1. Use of the common Greek of the day.* The old controversy between the 'Purists,' who endeavoured to bring all its peculiarities under the strict rules of Attic usage, and the 'Hebraists,' who magnified these peculiarities in the interests of a distinctively 'Biblical Greek,' or even 'language of the Holy Ghost,' is now completely a thing of the past.[1] And there is wide-spread agreement that the New Testament writers made use of the ordinary

---

and that the more educated classes used it without difficulty' (*Geschichte des Jüdischen Volkes im Zeitalter Jesu Christ*³ (Leipzig, 1898), ii. pp. 19, 63 f.: cf. Engl. Trans. II. i. pp. 9, 48).

[1] For the literature of this controversy, see Winer-Schmiedel, *Grammatik des neutestamentlichen Sprachidioms* (Göttingen, 1894-), p. 4 ff.

Greek of their own time, and that, too, in its more vulgar or colloquial form.

New light on this Greek. The confidence with which this conclusion is held is largely due to the new light which recent discoveries have thrown upon the true character of this Greek. For our knowledge of it in the past we were dependent upon its literary memorials, which betray a constant tendency, both conscious and unconscious, on the part of their writers to imitate the great Attic models of the classical period. But there have now come into our hands a large number of more popular or vernacular texts in the form of inscriptions, and especially of ostraca and papyri recovered from the sands of Egypt, in which we can see Greek, as it were, in undress, as it was spoken and written by the men and women of the day, with no thought of their words ever reaching the eyes of others than those to whom they were originally addressed. And the striking fact for our present purpose is, as I have just indicated, that these non-literary texts prove incontestably that it was in this same colloquial Greek, the Κοινή or common tongue of their day—to limit for convenience a term that is sometimes applied to Hellenistic Greek as a whole [1]—that the writers of the New Testament for the most part composed their books. Themselves sprung from the common people, the disciples of One whom the common people heard gladly, they in their turn wrote in

---

[1] See J. H. Moulton, *A Grammar of New Testament Greek*, i. *Prolegomena*[3] (Edinburgh, 1908), p. 2 f. This book is hereafter cited simply as *Prolegomena*[3].

that common tongue to be 'understanded of the people.'

The wonder, indeed, is not that this fact is now so generally admitted, as that it has been so long in being recognized. For while we gratefully acknowledge, and we can hardly do so with sufficient emphasis, the giant strides which the study of Papyrology has made in recent years through the almost phenomenal labours of Dr. Grenfell and Dr. Hunt in this country, to say nothing of their foreign compeers, we must not forget that for the earliest papyrus discoveries in Egypt we have to go back as far as the year 1778. It is true that for a time the finds were comparatively few and unimportant, but by the middle of the following century quite a number of documents had been made available in connexion with the collections in Turin, London, Leyden, and Paris.[1] And yet full of varied significance as many of these *documents humains* were, they evoked comparatively little interest even amongst palaeographers and historians, while their bearing upon the Greek of the Biblical writings passed practically unnoticed. The earliest hint in this direction that I have been able to discover is afforded by a passage in Peyron's Introduction to his edition of the Turin papyri in 1826, in which he states that in order to understand the meaning of some of their unusual words, he had consulted 'the contemporary writers, especially the translators of

[1] The Turin Papyri were published in 1826-27, the London (by Forshall) in 1839, the Leyden in 1843-85, and the Paris in 1865.

the LXX, the writers of the New Testament, Polybius, and Aristeas.'[1] But no one seems to have thought of reversing the process, and of examining the papyri for illustrations of LXX or New Testament Greek.

One can hardly help wondering what they might have yielded in this direction in the hands of Dr. Hort, who included Peyron's book in his library, but there is no evidence that he had ever thought of examining it in this connexion. Nor does it seem to have been different in the case of either of the other two members of the great Cambridge triumvirate, though a striking prophecy attributed to Bishop Lightfoot in 1863 shows how keenly alive he was to the importance of such evidence, should it ever present itself—as indeed it had already done.

Speaking of some New Testament word which had its only classical authority in Herodotus, he is reported to have said: 'You are not to suppose that the word had fallen out of use in the interval, only that it had not been used in the books which remain to us: probably it had been part of the common speech all along. I will go further, and say that if we could only recover letters that ordinary people

---

[1] 'Nec praetermittendum est, Papyros puram putamque dialectum referre, quae per ora vulgi volitabat.... Maior difficultas oritur a potestate verborum, quae quandoque Graecis prorsus inaudita, propria erat Aegyptiorum. Quare consului affines scriptores, praesertim LXX Interpretes, Scriptores Novi Testamenti, Polybium, atque Aristeam' (*Papyri Graeci Regii Taurinensis Musei Aegyptii* (Turin, 1826), i. p. 21).

LANGUAGE OF THE NEW TESTAMENT

wrote to each other without any thought of being literary, we should have the greatest possible help for the understanding of the language of the New Testament generally.'[1]

Twenty-one years later, an admission to the same effect, based this time on actual evidence, was made by Dean Farrar, and his words deserve to be recalled, as probably the first direct recognition in this country of the value of the papyri for New Testament study. In a note to the chapter on the 'Form of the New Testament Epistles,' in his volume on *The Messages of the Books*,[2] Dr. Farrar remarks with reference to the general identity of structure in the Pauline Epistles : 'It is an interesting subject of inquiry to what extent there was at this period an ordinary form of correspondence which (as among ourselves) was to some extent fixed. In the papyrus rolls of the British Museum (edited for the trustees by J. Forshall [in 1839]) there are forms and phrases which constantly remind us of St. Paul' (p. 151). But he does not seem to have pursued the inquiry further, and it was left to Adolf Deissmann, now Professor of New Testament Exegesis in the University of Berlin, to write as a Privatdocent at Marburg, and to publish as a pastor at Herborn, the *Bibelstudien* first issued in 1895, and followed by the *Neue Bibelstudien* in 1897, which were virtually to inaugurate

---

[1] From notes of Bishop Lightfoot's lectures supplied by the Rev. J. Pulliblank to Dr. J. H. Moulton: see *Prolegomena*[3], p. 242.

[2] London, 1884.

a new movement in the linguistic study of our Greek Bible.¹

For, whatever judgment may be passed on some of the conclusions arrived at by Deissmann and his subsequent fellow-workers, this at least is certain, that they have succeeded in lifting the so-called Biblical Greek completely out of the isolation in which hitherto it had been believed to stand, and exhibiting it as 'neither an example of "Jewish-Greek"' (which is nowhere demonstrable) nor of a specific "Christian Greek," but rather a monument of the *Koinē* as a whole—the first earnest and really magnificent attempt to employ the spoken language of the time for literary purposes.'²

<small>General uniformity of the Κοινή.</small>

It is no part of my present purpose to discuss in detail the proofs which Deissmann and Thumb in Germany, and J. H. Moulton in England, have brought forward to establish this conclusion. Nor is it possible at present to attempt any philological discussion of the exact nature of this Κοινή, or common Greek. It must be enough that though it is frequently spoken of as debased, or even as bad, Greek, in itself it marks a distinct stage in the

---

¹ The two volumes are combined in the English translation by the Rev. A. Grieve under the title *Bible Studies. Contributions chiefly from Papyri and Inscriptions to the History of the Language, the Literature, and the Religion of Hellenistic Judaism and Primitive Christianity*, 2nd edit., Edinburgh, 1903. See further for Deissmann's works, Additional Note A, 'Some Books for the Study of the Greek Papyri.'

² A. Thumb, art. 'Hellenistic and Biblical Greek' in *A Standard Bible Dictionary* (London, 1909), p. 331.

history of the language. Standing midway in point of time between classical and modern Greek, it presents all the marks of a living tongue, which, while wanting in many of the niceties by which classical Greek was distinguished, was nevertheless governed by regular laws of its own. Its main basis was Attic, with an intermingling of not a few Ionic elements. And though in its spoken form this common speech would naturally exhibit other dialectic differences in view of the wide area over which it was used, these differences disappear to a surprising extent in the written texts. And the consequence is, that we are able to appeal with confidence to documents emanating from different countries and different circumstances in support and illustration of each other on the linguistic side. An Egyptian papyrus letter and a New Testament Epistle may be widely separated alike by the nationality and habitat of their writers, and by their own inherent characters and aims, but both are written in substantially the same Greek.

2. On the richness of the field of illustration thus opened up in New Testament lexicography, I shall have something to say directly; but meanwhile it seems necessary to safeguard and limit the conclusions thus reached in one or two directions. In the not unnatural recoil from the old position of treating the Greek of the New Testament as an isolated language, a tendency has shown itself in various quarters to lose sight of certain distinctive features by which it is none the less marked, and

2. Influences affecting the Greek of the New Testament.

which, notwithstanding all the linguistic and stylistic parallels that have been discovered, impart a character of its own to the language of our New Testament writings.

(1) Hebraisms. (1) This applies, in the first place, to the over-eagerness which many advocates of the new light display in getting rid of the 'Hebraisms' or 'Semitisms,' which have hitherto been regarded as a distinguishing feature of the Greek New Testament.

That the number of these has been greatly exaggerated in the past, and that there is now ample evidence for looking on many of them as 'true Greek,' I should be amongst the first to admit. When, for example, in a letter of A.D. 41, a man counsels a friend who was in money difficulties, βλέπε σατὸν ἀπὸ τῶν Ἰουδαίων, 'Beware of the Jews,' apparently as money-lenders, and if so, probably the first reference to them in that character,[1] there is no longer any need of finding a Hebraistic construction in our Lord's warning, Mark xii. 38, βλέπετε ἀπὸ τῶν γραμματέων, 'Beware of the scribes,' or again, of regarding the use of ἐν in such a passage as 1 Cor. iv. 21, ἐν ῥάβδῳ ἔλθω πρὸς ὑμᾶς; 'Shall I come to you with a rod?' as 'an after effect of the Hebrew בְּ,' in view of the half-dozen instances of a similar usage which the editors cite from Tebtunis Papyri 'free from all suspicion of Semitic influence.'[2]

---

[1] *Berliner Griechische Urkunden*, iv. p. 123 f. No. 1079[24 f.] (= *Selections from the Greek Papyri*[2], No. 15).

[2] *The Tebtunis Papyri*, edd. Grenfell-Hunt-Smyly, i. p. 86, note on No. 16[14]: cf. *e.g.* No. 41[8 ff.] (*c.* B.C. 119): πυκνότερον Μαρρείους

In the same way the use of such a word as ἀναστρέφομαι in the sense of 'behave oneself,' which Grimm compares with the moral signification of הלך 'walk,' can now be readily paralleled from a Fayûm petition complaining of an assault committed by certain persons οὐ ἀπὸ τοῦ βελτ[ί]στου ἀναστρεφομένων, 'of the less reputable class' (Edd.).[1] Nor need we any longer appeal to the Hebrew שאל as determining the New Testament meaning of 'ask' for ἐρωτάω, when we find the word constantly so used in the ordinary Greek of the time, as, for example, in the second century letter in which a certain Antonius ἐρωτᾷ, 'invites,' a friend to dine with him, 'at the table of the lord Serapis.'[2] Apart from its lexical interest, this last document is very significant as giving an actual instance of those banquets held in honour of a god and in his temple, against which St. Paul pointedly warns the Corinthian Christians in 1 Cor. x. 21 : 'You cannot drink the cup of the

τοπογραμματέως σὺν ἄλλοις πλείοσι ἐν μαχαίραις παρ[α]γινομένου εἰς τὴν κώμην, 'Marres the topogrammateus is in the habit of coming to the village with numerous others armed with swords.'

[1] *Fayûm Towns and their Papyri*, edd. Grenfell-Hunt-Hogarth, p. 103 ff. No. 12⁶ᶠ· (c. B.C. 103). For numerous examples from the inscriptions, see Deissmann, *Bible Studies*, pp. 88, 194, and add from the *Inschriften von Priene*, ed. H. von Gaertringen (Berlin, 1906), No. 115⁵ (i/B.C.), ἀναστρεφόμενος ἐν πᾶσιν φιλ[ανθρώπως]—a good parallel to Heb. xiii. 18, ἐν πᾶσιν καλῶς θέλοντες ἀναστρέφεσθαι.

[2] *The Oxyrhynchus Papyri*, edd. Grenfell-Hunt, iii. p. 260, No. 523 (= *Selections from the Greek Papyri*², No. 39).

Lord, and the cup of demons: you cannot partake of the table of the Lord, and of the table of demons.'

Even after, however, we have disposed of these and a number of similar instances, it still remains true that it is impossible to remove genuine 'Semitisms' from the New Testament altogether, or to the extent that is sometimes demanded. Why, indeed, should there be any undue anxiety to do so? The presence of a few 'Semitisms' more or less does not prevent our recognizing that the general language of the document in which they occur is Greek, any more than the Scotticisms, into which a North Briton shows himself so ready to fall, exclude the possibility that all the time he is doing his best to talk English. And it is surely wiser to attribute these Semitic-seeming words and constructions at once to their natural source, the more especially when they occur in circumstances which make their presence not only explicable but inevitable.

The mother-tongue of almost all the New Testament writers was Aramaic, and although, in keeping with the general practice of the time, they had learned to use Greek freely as a subsidiary language, their native upbringing would constantly assert itself in the choice of particular words and phrases. In the case of the Evangelists this tendency would be still further encouraged by the fact that not merely Aramaic traditions, but Aramaic documents, lay at the basis of their writings; while even St. Paul, to whom Greek had been all along a second language, constantly shows signs of his Jewish upbringing in the arrangement and construction of his sentences.[1]

This was due, doubtless, in no small degree to the influence which the translation-Greek of the Septuagint had come to exercise over him. Whatever may have been the case in his earlier years, the Greek Old Testament was undoubtedly the Bible of St. Paul's manhood and ministry, and not only its thoughts but its actual phraseology had passed *in sucum et sanguinem*. What more natural, then, than that when he himself came to write on cognate themes, he should almost unconsciously fall into the same mode of speech, much as a modern preacher or devotional writer is tempted to imitate the archaic English of the Authorized Version.

It is quite possible that too much has been made in the past of the translation-Greek of the Septuagint, and that its writers by no means betray throughout the literal, almost slavish, following of the Hebrew original that is sometimes alleged against them. Still the fact remains that the Septuagint *is* a translation which bears, though in varying degrees in its different parts, the marks of its source,

[1] 'Ebensowenig als die Septuaginta darf das Neue Testament sprachlich isoliert werden. Wir treffen auch hier die Umgangssprache der Zeit. Sie ist stark mit Semitismen versetzt, wo der aramäische Originale zugrunde liegen oder die Septuaginta nachwirkt. Aber z.B. Paulus hat zwar in der Wortfügung manchmal, dagegen im Wortschatz sehr wenig hebraisiert' (Wackernagel, 'Die Griechische Sprache,' p. 309, in *Die Kultur der Gegenwart*[2], I. viii. Berlin, 1907).

and which therefore in its turn could not fail to influence the Greek of those who were nurtured upon it.[1]

It is not so easy to determine the exact limits of another consideration which must be kept in view in estimating the 'Semitisms' of the New Testament. We have seen that many of these are disposed of on the ground that they can be paralleled from the Greek papyri found in Egypt. But what, pertinently ask Dr. Swete and others, if these parallels are themselves due to Semitic influence? We know that from an early date there were large numbers of Jewish settlers in Egypt, and these may easily have affected the Greek of the surrounding population.[2] To this it is generally answered that in many instances we can support the papyri by evidence drawn from vernacular inscriptions found in widely distant regions, where it is impossible always to postulate an influential Ghetto, and that even in Egypt, outside the larger cities, there is no evidence of a Jewish element strong enough to affect the

---

[1] Cf. Thackeray, *A Grammar of the Old Testament in Greek* (Cambridge, 1909), i. p. 29: 'Notwithstanding that certain so-called "Hebraisms" have been removed from that category or that their claim to the title has become open to question, it is impossible to deny the existence of a strong Semitic influence in the Greek of the LXX.' As bearing this out, it is interesting to find that Psichari's important *Essai sur le Grec de la Septante* (Extrait de la *Revue des Études juives*, Avril, 1908) turns round the two points 'hébraïsmes à écarter, hébraïsmes à reconnaître' (cf. p. 207).

[2] Swete, *The Apocalypse of St. John*, p. cxx.

local speech to the extent demanded.¹ The answer may well seem to be conclusive. At the same time, without fuller information than is at present available regarding the position and power of these Jewish colonies, it would be unwise to deny altogether the possibility of some such influence, more particularly as exercised on a language which was neither the Jews' nor the Egyptians' native speech, but a medium of communication adopted by both alike, and on that very account more open to modification at the hands of all who used it.²

(2) A second feature of our New Testament writings which is apt to be ignored, or at any rate under-estimated, in view of the generally popular Greek in which they are written, is their literary character. *(2) Certain literary tendencies.*

I do not of course for a moment mean that any part of the New Testament is 'Kunstprosa' in the ordinary sense of that term, or that the literary character of its different books stands on the same footing throughout. At the same time, leaving out of sight meanwhile the Gospels, where the question is complicated by the writers' relation to their sources, we cannot deny to the historian of the Acts of the Apostles, to St. Paul, and to the author of the Epistle to the Hebrews, a command over the Greek language, and a power in using it, which

---

¹ *E.g.* J. H. Moulton, *Cambridge Biblical Essays* (London, 1909), p. 468 f.

² This point is well stated by G. C. Richards in the *Journal for Theological Studies*, x. p. 289 f.

entitle them to rank amongst the greatest writers as well as the greatest teachers.

In the case of St. Luke we are prepared for this not only by the instinct for style, which would belong to him in virtue of his Greek birth, but also by his medical training, which enriched his vocabulary with many scientific and quasi-scientific terms:[1] while, whatever the view taken of the relation of the different factors which combined to form the Lucan account of the Pauline speeches in the Book of Acts, none can fail to recognize with Professor Percy Gardner in his recent study of them, that 'as a man of letters' their compiler is 'highly gifted,' and brings to his difficult task extraordinary versatility and literary skill.[2]

The same holds true *mutatis mutandis* of St. Paul, to whom from the circumstances of his birth and upbringing Greek was virtually a second mother-tongue.[3] That he was imbued with its culture and literature to the extent that some of his modern biographers would have us believe may well seem doubtful: it is at least not borne out by his vocabulary, which is in the main thoroughly popular and in

---

[1] These can still be most conveniently studied in Dr. Hobart's well-known Essay on *The Medical Language of St. Luke*, Dublin and London, 1882. See also Knowling, 'The Medical Language of St. Luke and Recent Criticism' in *Messianic Interpretation and other Studies* (London, 1910), p. 113 ff.

[2] *Cambridge Biblical Essays*, pp. 387, 394.

[3] On the probability that St. Paul was able also to speak Latin, see the interesting paper by Professor A. Souter, *The Expositor*, VIII. i. p. 337 ff.

accord with the living speech of his day.¹ At the same time, it is undeniable that the Apostle could, when necessary, fall back on the philosophic language of the day, and employ it in such a way as would be appreciated by thinking and educated men. Obvious examples are his use of αὐτάρκεια in its subjective sense of 'self-sufficiency,' and of συνείδησις, which, though not unknown in the Jewish Apocrypha, first gains its full introspective moral importance in the teaching of the Stoics.²

The same τέχνη is seen still more markedly, I need hardly say, in the Epistle to the Hebrews. Even those who are most anxious to emphasize the generally 'popular' character of the New Testament writings admit that we have here an exception.³

¹ 'P. spricht nicht anders als die lebendige Sprache seiner Zeit.' Nägeli, *Der Wortschatz des Apostels Paulus* (Göttingen, 1905), p. 42—an important contribution to the study of the Pauline vocabulary (in so far as it falls under the first five letters of the alphabet), more particularly in its relation to the Κοινή.

² Upon the necessity of the study of such writers as Musonius and Epictetus for a complete insight into the language and style of St. Paul, see J. Weiss, *Die Aufgaben der Neutestamentlichen Wissenschaft in der Gegenwart* (Göttingen, 1908), p. 10 f. Cf. also R. Bultmann, *Der Stil der paulinischen Predigt und die Kynisch-stoische Diatribe* (Göttingen, 1910), A. Bonhöffer, *Epiktet und das Neue Testament* (Giessen, 1911), and the articles by these two writers in the *Zeitschrift für die neutestamentliche Wissenschaft* for 1912.

³ Deissmann describes the Epistle to the Hebrews as 'historically the earliest example of Christian artistic literature,' and again as 'like an intruder among the New Testament company of popular books' (*Light from the Ancient East*, pp. 237, 243).

And I refer to it now only for the purpose of again emphasizing that even if it stood alone in this matter of artistic force, and we have seen already that it does not, we should still have to admit that with all its 'splendid simplicity and homeliness,' the New Testament contains elements of a distinctively literary character—that it is itself literature.

(3) The transforming power of Christianity. (3) There is still a third consideration that must not be lost sight of in estimating the true character of the New Testament vocabulary, and that is the deepening and enriching which it has received through Christian influences.

The common language of the time has been 'baptized' into new conditions; and only by a frank recognition of these conditions can we hope to fix the full connotation of many of our most characteristic New Testament words and phrases. The point has been well put by Sir William M. Ramsay: 'Even though the same words were used by the pagans, it may be the case—I would go so far as to say it certainly was so—that there were some, perhaps many, which acquired a special and distinct meaning to the Christians, as suited to express certain ideas of the Christian religious thought, and which thus immediately became characteristic and almost positive marks of Christian writing.'[1]

A familiar instance is afforded by the word ἀγάπη. It would be going too far to say that the word has been actually 'born within the bosom of revealed religion,' though it is somewhat remarkable that no

[1] *The Expositor*, VII. vii. p. 6.

absolutely clear instance of its use in profane Greek has been discovered;[1] at the same time, it is so characteristic of the Biblical writings that it may be regarded as peculiar to them in the full sense which they have taught us to ascribe to it.

The use of ἀδελφοί, again, to describe the members of a guild, or the 'fellows' of the Serapeum at Memphis, may prepare us for, but does not exhaust, its definite Christian significance. And the same may be said of παρουσία, which our new authorities exhibit as a kind of *terminus technicus* to describe the visit of a king or great man.[2] Very suggestive, too, is the light which these throw upon the original associations of such words as αἰώνιος, ἀπόστολος, ἐπίσκοπος, θρησκεία, πρεσβύτερος and σωτήρ, to name a few almost at random,[3] but it is certainly not light of a character that enables us to dispense with the light derivable from within the New Testament itself.

[1] The nearest approach of which I am aware is in a Pagan inscription of the Imperial period from Tefeny in Pisidia, giving the mantic significance of various throws of the dice: πένψει δ' εἰς ἀγά[πη]ν σε φιλομμειδὴς Ἀφροδείτη (*Papers of the American School of Classical Studies at Athens*, ii. 57, cited by Hatch, *Journal of Biblical Literature*, xxvii. 2 (1908), p. 134 ff.).

[2] On these two words, see my edition of *St. Paul's Epistles to the Thessalonians*, pp. 21, 145 f.

[3] For a discussion of these and many similar terms reference may be made to the 'Lexical Notes from the Papyri' contributed by Professor Moulton and the writer to *The Expositor*, VII. v. — It is hoped soon to republish a first instalment of these 'Notes' in an enlarged and revised form.

It may seem, perhaps, as if all this tends to disparage somewhat the aid we are likely to receive in the work of interpretation from our new sources. But this is very far indeed from being my intention. All that I wish to insist upon is, that in using these sources we must not lose sight of other evidence which has at least an equal right to be heard, and that loss rather than gain will result from calling them in to decide questions which lie outside their distinct province. Within that province, however, their value is undoubted, and will, I am confident, be increasingly recognized as their contents become more generally known and studied.

<small>III. Recent gains to our knowledge of the Greek New Testament.</small>

III. Let me indicate a few of the directions in which these spoils from the ancient East have already thrown light on the text and diction of our New Testament writings.

<small>1. Direct additions to our New Testament texts.</small>

1. In the matter of text, it may be a disappointment to some that hitherto comparatively few Biblical texts of any importance have been recovered. This doubtless arises from the fact that while casual letters and papers that were no longer required were thrown out on the village dustheaps, there to be preserved by the kindly protection of the desert sand for the instruction of future generations, the more valued texts and documents continued to be treasured and used, until gradually through the frailty of the papyrus leaves they crumbled away.[1]

[1] Birt calculates that if a papyrus roll reached the age of a hundred years it did well, seeing that even the lying in a chest

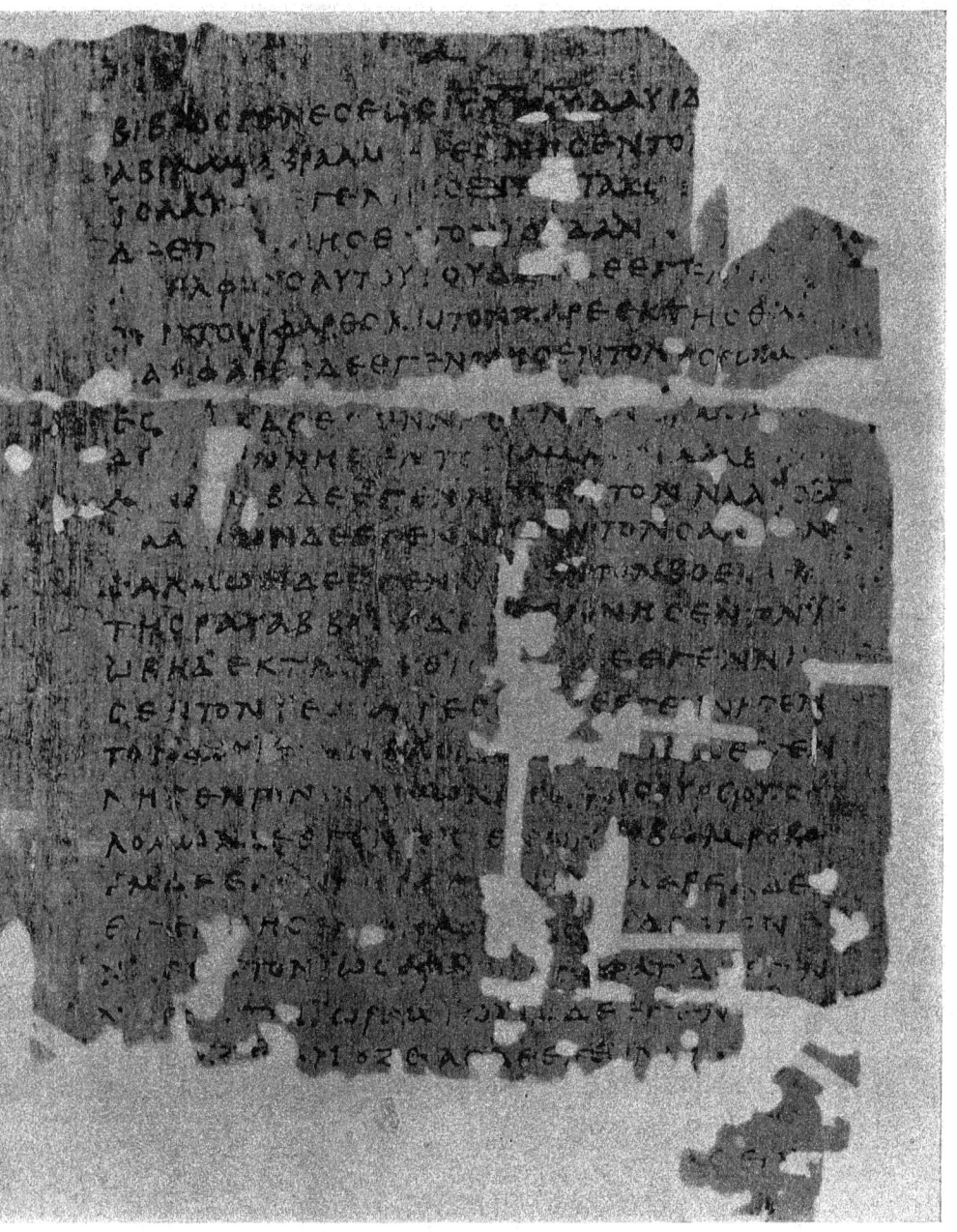

LEAF FROM A PAPYRUS BOOK, CONTAINING PART OF ST. MATTHEW i.

rd Century. Discovered at Oxyrhynchus, and now in the Museum of Science and Art, University of Pennsylvania, U.S.A. By permission of the Egypt Exploration Fund.

To face p. 61.

The probability, therefore, of finding any large number of Biblical manuscripts of great antiquity on papyrus may be at once discounted, though it is impossible to say what treasures may still be lurking in some unrifled tomb or sealed jar. And yet, even as it is, we cannot forget that, apart from many important manuscripts of parts of the Greek Old Testament, we owe to the sands of Egypt the oldest original manuscripts of the Greek New Testament in existence, namely, fragments of the Gospels of St. Matthew and of St. John, belonging to the third century, as well as a fourth century manuscript of nearly one-third of the Epistle to the Hebrews.

We shall return to these and similar documents in connexion with the transmission of our New Testament writings.[1] In the meantime they are only mentioned as examples of the additions which recent discoveries have made to our textual authorities.

2. But valuable as the papyri are in this direction, the indirect aid which they afford to the New Testament student is still more significant. It may well seem absurd that these fragmentary leaves, in themselves often of the most trivial and occasional character, should have anything to teach us regarding the language and meaning of the most significant Greek writings in the world. But so it

2. Indirect gains as affecting

---

injured it: see *Die Buchrolle in der Kunst*, p. 24, and cf. the same writer's *Das antike Buchwesen*, p. 364 ff.

[1] See p. 189, and cf. Additional Note D, 'New Testament Texts on Papyrus.'

62   THE NEW TESTAMENT DOCUMENTS

is, and in the remainder of this lecture I shall try to show you how.

(1) Orthography and accidence.

(1) We may begin with Orthography and Accidence.

In these particulars the New Testament writings have not yet been subjected to the same searching comparison with the new evidence which Helbing and Thackeray have already accomplished in the case of the Greek Old Testament,[1] but enough has already been done by Blass,[2] Schmiedel,[3] Moulton,[4] and Deissmann,[5] following on the notable work already done in this direction by Westcott and Hort,[6] to show that we are in a better position to-day for recovering the *ipsissima verba* of the New Testament autographs than many modern textual critics are ready to admit.

Thus, when we remember the constant tendency on the part of the later copyists to improve on the 'vulgarisms' or 'colloquialisms' of the original, it cannot but help us to determine what is due to this

---

[1] Helbing, *Grammatik der Septuaginta, Laut- und Wortlehre*, Göttingen, 1907; Thackeray, *A Grammar of the Old Testament in Greek*, i. *Introduction, Orthography and Accidence*, Cambridge, 1909.

[2] *Grammatik des Neutestamentlichen Griechisch*[2] (Göttingen, 1902), pp. 1-74; Eng. Trans. by Thackeray (London, 1905), pp. 1-71.

[3] Winer's *Grammatik des neutestamentlichen Sprachidioms neu bearbeitet* (Göttingen, 1894-), pp. 31-144.

[4] *Prolegomena*[3], p. 42 ff.   [5] *Bible Studies*, pp. 181-193.

[6] *Introduction to the New Testament in the Original Greek*[2] (London, 1896), p. 302 ff., and Appendix, p. 148 ff.

refining process when we have such abundant evidence now in our hands as to how the common people of the time actually wrote and spelt. The form γένημα, for example, which Westcott and Hort prefer for the five occurrences of this word in the New Testament (Matt. xxvi. 29, Mark xiv. 25, Luke xii. 18, xxii. 18, 2 Cor. ix. 10), as against the γέννημα of the *Textus Receptus* (except in Luke xii. 18), is now fully established on the evidence both of the Ptolemaic papyri, and of those belonging to the first four centuries after Christ, and the aspirated σφυρίς for σπυρίς (Matt. xv. 37, xvi. 10, Mark viii. 8, 20, Acts ix. 25) is again amply, though not universally, attested in the vernacular documents.

The very indifference, indeed, of the writers of these documents to symmetrical forms or to unified spelling may in itself be taken as a warning against the almost feverish haste with which a 'redactor,' or later author, is sometimes brought in to explain similar phenomena in the different parts of a New Testament book.

In the same way, when we pass to morphology, it is again to discover that many verbal forms with which our best New Testament texts have made us familiar can again be illustrated. One of the commonest of these is the attaching 1st aorist forms to the 2nd aorist, as when in Matt. x. 13 we read ἐλθάτω for ἐλθέτω, and in Mark iii. 8 ἦλθαν for ἦλθον— a practice abundantly confirmed by the papyri, as well as by late Hellenistic writers generally, while the γέγοναν for γέγονασι which Westcott and Hort

Morphology.

read in Rom. xvi. 7 in accordance with B ℵ A receives frequent corroboration, as, for example, from an almost contemporary papyrus letter from the Fayûm.[1]

An interesting form, which may cause trouble if it is not watched, is the substitution of ἐάν for ἄν after ὅς, ὅπου, etc., which the same editors have faithfully reproduced from the leading manuscripts in such passages as Matt. xii. 32, ὃς ἐὰν εἴπῃ, and Mark xiv. 9, ὅπου ἐὰν κηρυχθῇ. Professor J. H. Moulton has carefully examined the evidence of the papyri on this point, and has found that in the first and second centuries of the Christian era ἐάν greatly predominated, but that, as a form of ἄν, it had almost died out in ordinary usage before the great Uncials were written. The fact, therefore, that their scribes preserved ἐάν may be taken as showing that they 'faithfully reproduce originals written under conditions long since obsolete.'[2]

One other example, which has an important bearing on the interpretation of a famous passage, must suffice. In John i. 14, the reading πλήρης (πλήρη D) χάριτος καὶ ἀληθείας is practically certain, and the question arises with what does πλήρης agree. Treating it as a nominative, Bishop Westcott[3] connects it directly with the principal subject of the sentence ὁ λόγος, making the words καὶ ἐθεασάμεθα τὴν δόξαν αὐτοῦ, δόξαν ὡς μονογενοῦς παρὰ πατρός a parenthesis (as in A.V., R.V), and this undoubtedly

---

[1] *Berliner Griechische Urkunden*, ii. p. 241, No. 597¹⁹ (A.D. 75).
[2] *Prolegomena*³, p. 42 f.
[3] *The Gospel according to St. John* (edit. 1908), i. p. 18 f.

yields good sense. But when we remember that in the papyri from the first century after Christ onwards πλήρης is treated as indeclinable,[1] and that this usage is confirmed on the evidence of the Septuagint, and of many good manuscripts on its various occurrences in the New Testament,[2] the probability is that πλήρης is to be similarly treated in the passage before us, as in reality an accusative referring to δόξαν. It will then be the 'glory," or the self-revelation, of the Word, that is 'full of grace and truth.'

(2) This last example may fittingly introduce us to the field of Syntax, and to Dr. Moulton's brilliant *Prolegomena*, where at every turn the evidence of the newly discovered vernacular documents is called in to decide corresponding usages in the New Testament writings. One or two examples will show how rich and suggestive that evidence is.

(2) Syntax.

Take, for instance, the prepositions, and an impartial survey can hardly fail to lead us to the conclusion that the laxer usage which is everywhere observable in later Greek hardly justifies many of the

Examples of laxer usage in the case of prepositions,

---

[1] Only one instance B.C. has as yet been found, Μαρσείπειον πλήρης (= πλήρες) in *Papyri Graeci Musei Antiquarii Publici Lugduni-Batavi*, ed. Leemans, i. p. 118, C col. 2¹⁴ (B.C. 160).

[2] For the Septuagint evidence, cf. Thackeray i. p. 176 f., and for the New Testament, see especially Mark iv. 28, where Hort (*Notes on Select Readings*², p. 24) thinks that an original πλήρης σῖτον best explains the confusion of readings, and Acts vi. 5, where the best manuscripts (except B) read ἄνδρα πλήρης πίστεως. See further, Blass, *Grammar*, p. 81; Moulton, *Prolegomena*³, p. 50, and two notes by C. H. Turner, *The Journal of Theological Studies*, i. pp. 120 ff., 561 f.

overniceties of interpretation in which New Testament expositors have been apt to indulge. The free interchange of εἰς and ἐν is a case in point. This may be carried back to the fact that both words are originally forms of the same root; but what we are specially concerned with is that they are largely interchanged in ordinary usage, as when in a letter of A.D. 22 the writer tells us that when he came to Alexandria (ἐπὶ τῷ γεγονέναι ἐν Ἀλεξανδρίᾳ), he learnt so and so from certain fishermen at Alexandria (εἰς Ἀλεξάνδρι[αν]).[1] When, then, in commenting on John i. 18, ὁ ὢν εἰς τὸν κόλπον τοῦ πατρός, Bishop Westcott speaks of the phrase as implying 'the combination (as it were) of rest and motion, of a continuous relation, with a realization of it,'[2] is he not pressing the phraseology further than contemporary evidence warrants, however doctrinally true the deduction may be?

Nor, similarly, can those who advocate the rendering 'immersing them into the name of the Father and of the Son and of the Holy Spirit' for the baptismal formula in Matt. xxviii. 19, do so on the ground that the more familiar rendering is philologically inaccurate. Without entering on the question as to the exact shade of meaning underlying βαπτίζοντες, it is clear that εἰς τὸ ὄνομα may be understood as practically equivalent to ἐν τῷ ὀνόματι, the new light thus joining hands with, and lending

---

[1] *The Oxyrhynchus Papyri*, edd. Grenfell-Hunt, ii. p. 294 ff., No. 294[3 and 6] (= *Selections from the Greek Papyri*[2], No. 13).

[2] *The Gospel of St. John*, i. p. 28.

support to, the almost unanimous tradition of the Western Church.[1]

A corresponding caution must be observed in connexion with the construction of ἵνα. Classical Greek has taught us to expect that ἵνα construed with the subjunctive must denote purpose, but in Hellenistic Greek this has been extended to include a consecutive usage, and sometimes, as in modern Greek, a simple statement of fact. When, therefore, in John xvii. 3, the Fourth Evangelist writes: 'And this is life eternal, that they should know Thee (ἵνα γινώσκωσί σε) the only true God, and Him whom Thou didst send, Jesus Christ,' it is of course possible that by the latter clause he means us to understand our Lord as pointing to the knowledge of God as the aim and end of eternal life. But it is equally permissible, and more in accord with contemporary usage, to interpret the words as defining the contents of the life eternal: this life is a life consisting in, and maintained by, the knowledge of God, and of Him whom God had sent. *and in the construction of ἵνα.*

It may seem, perhaps, from these and similar instances that the niceties of construction which we are accustomed to look for in Greek writers are wanting in the New Testament, but this is far from being the case. And many passages, especially in the more literary parts of the New Testament, can *Grammatical niceties in the New Testament.*

---

[1] See the interesting discussion between Bishop Chase and Dean Armitage Robinson in *The Journal of Theological Studies*, vi. p. 481 ff., vii. p. 186 ff., and viii. p. 161 ff., and on the phrase generally, cf. Heitmüller, *Im Namen Jesu*, Göttingen, 1903.

be adduced where only by a close observance of the distinctions of tense and case construction can the writers' full meaning be grasped.

Tense construction. In 1 Cor. xv., for example, the whole force of the argument rests on the fact that the Lord Jesus Christ who died and was buried is now risen, and continues unchangeably the same. And accordingly, after using aorists to denote the two former acts, ἀπέθανεν and ἐτάφη, St. Paul in v. 4 changes to the perfect ἐγήγερται in speaking of the resurrection. Christ not merely 'rose again,' as in the rendering of the Authorized Version, but 'hath been raised,' and consequently, by implication, lives for ever, the earnest of His people's resurrection.

Case construction. Changes in case construction are often equally suggestive. When in Heb. vi. the verb 'taste' is construed with the genitive in v. 4, γευσαμένους τε τῆς δωρεᾶς τῆς ἐπουρανίου, 'as touching those who tasted of the heavenly gift,' and in the following verse with the accusative, καλὸν γευσαμένους θεοῦ ῥῆμα, 'tasted the word of God that it is good,' this can hardly be explained in the case of so careful a writer as the author of this Epistle as an example of the well-known encroachment of the accusative on the genitive in late Greek, but as due rather to the fact that in the first instance the verb is simply a verb of sense (cf. c. ii. 9), whereas in the second the thought of experience is added—those spoken of had not merely tasted, but recognized, the goodness of the word of God.

Still more exegetically important are the different

constructions of the verb πιστεύω 'believe,' the simple dative giving place to εἰς with the accusative, when it is desired to bring out the deliberate effort of faith, by which one man, as it were, puts himself into another's power, and surrenders his 'self' to him. It is this attitude which is predicated of the 'many' in John viii. 30, πολλοὶ ἐπίστευσαν εἰς αὐτόν, 'many believed on Him,' in distinction from the Jews of the following verse, whom Jesus can only address as τοὺς πεπιστευκότας αὐτῷ, 'those who have believed Him.' These last are as yet only on the way—the perfect tense is again significant—to the higher faith, but, as Jesus proceeds at once to remind them, if they continue to abide in His word, that word will gradually exercise its power over them, until they too become His disciples in truth (ἀληθῶς).

It would carry us altogether beyond our immediate object if I were to go on multiplying examples in this direction, but I have thought it right to bring these before you to make perfectly clear that while the syntax of the New Testament is not modelled on strictly classical rules, many of its writers were by no means wanting in literary skill, and had the means at their disposal of drawing the suggestive, and sometimes subtle, distinctions which were demanded by the character of the new thoughts and ideas they desired to express.

(3) In passing to the vocabulary of the New Testament, the same thing meets us. *(3) Vocabulary.*

With all its native simplicity and directness, the New Testament exhibits a wonderfully rich and varied vocabulary, and many of its words, occurring as they do at a late stage in the development of the Greek language, have a very interesting history behind them. To trace that history, and to show the changes that time and circumstances have wrought upon their meaning, will be the task of the next New Testament lexicographer. And it is good news, therefore, to learn that one who possesses such outstanding qualifications as Professor Deissmann is already engaged on this all-important task. In his hands, we may be sure, the new Lexicon 'will bring out once more'—to borrow his own description of what such a work should be—'the simplicity, inwardness, and force of the utterances of evangelists and apostles,' and 'will meet with that best of all rewards, far exceeding all scholarly recognition, the reward of exerting an influence in real life.'[1]

(a) Reduction in the number of 'Biblical' words.

(a) This result will be brought about by a large reduction in the number of so-called 'Biblical' words —words, that is, which have hitherto been regarded as the special property of the Biblical writers, seeing that no evidence of their use has hitherto been procurable from profane sources.

Thayer, at the end of his edition of Grimm's Lexicon, gives a long list of these ἅπαξ λεγόμενα, with the result that they help largely to confirm that feeling of the isolation or peculiar character of the New Testament writings to which reference has already been made. The list is unnecessarily long

[1] *Light from the Ancient East*, p. 418.

even from Thayer's point of view, as it includes not a few words for which in the body of his book he himself supplies references from pagan sources, which, though sometimes later in point of time than the New Testament itself, nevertheless show unmistakably that the words belong to the ordinary stock of the time. And now the new evidence comes in to extend these references in so many directions that Deissmann is able to reduce the number of words peculiar to the New Testament writers to something like fifty, or about one per cent. of the whole vocabulary.[1]

This will become clearer if we take two special instances.

In what are probably the earliest writings of the New Testament as it has come down to us, the two Epistles to the Thessalonians, there are in all 460 different words, of which twenty-seven are generally reckoned as ἅπαξ λεγόμενα. But if we exclude from this number the words which are found in the Septuagint, or in other late Greek writings, including the papyri, the twenty-seven can be reduced to two, θεοδίδακτος and συμφυλέτης, both of which St. Paul himself may very well have formed on the analogy of similar compounds.[2]

Or to turn to the latest book in the New Testament Canon, the so-called Second Epistle of St. Peter, the peculiarities of whose style have led to its being

[1] *Light from the Ancient East*, p. 73.
[2] For further particulars, see the writer's edition of *St. Paul's Epistles to the Thessalonians* (London, 1908), p. lii. f.

described as 'Baboo Greek,'[1] we are here confronted with the long list of fifty-six ἅπαξ λεγόμενα. The process of reducing this list has not been so successful as in the case of the Thessalonian Epistles, as there are still twenty words which have not as yet been found anywhere else; but, after all, that is little more than one-third of the earlier calculation, and any day a newly discovered inscription or papyrus letter may reduce the proportion still further.

(b) Confirmation of traditional meanings.

(*b*) Nor do our new sources only thus reduce the number of words hitherto regarded as peculiar to the New Testament writings, they also confirm the meanings that have been traditionally assigned to others, sometimes on somewhat slender grounds.

A familiar example is the Pauline word λογεία. According to Grimm-Thayer, the word is 'not found in profane authors,' but for its meaning in 1 Cor. xvi. 1 f., the only places where it occurs in the New Testament, the translation 'a collection' is suggested. Such a translation is in harmony with the context, and is now conclusively established by the fact that from the second century B.C. the word is found in the papyri in this sense. It is sufficient to refer to a curious letter from Tebtunis, in which a tax-gatherer, after naïvely describing his unprincipled efforts to defeat a rival in the collection of a certain tax, adds, 'I bid you urge on Nicon regarding the collection (περὶ τῆς λογε⟨ί⟩ας).'[2]

[1] E. A. Abbott, *From Letter to Spirit* (London, 1903), 1121-1135.
[2] *The Tebtunis Papyri*, edd. Grenfell-Hunt-Smyly, i. p. 168 ff., No. 58⁵⁵ (B.C. 111).

Along with λογεία, although derived from a different root, may be mentioned the verb ἐλλογάω, which St. Paul uses with such effect in the Epistle to Philemon, when he bids Philemon put down to his account (v. 18, τοῦτο ἐμοὶ ἐλλόγα) any loss he may have suffered at the hands of Onesimus. For this usage Thayer can only supply two parallels from the inscriptions; but the verb, at any rate in the form ἐλλογέω, is now proved to have been the regular *terminus technicus* in this sense, as when in a Strassburg papyrus a man is called upon to render his account ἵνα οὕτως αὐτῷ ἐνλογηθῇ, 'that so a reckoning may be made with him,'[1] or as when provision is made in hiring certain dancing-girls for a village festival that they are to receive so much 'as earnest money to be reckoned in the price (ὑπὲρ ἀραβῶνος [τῇ τ]ιμῇ ἐλλογουμέν[ο]υ).'[2]

Or, to take a wholly different example, when in the letter already referred to (p. 50) his friend counsels a man in money difficulties to plead with one of his creditors μὴ ἵνα ἀναστατώσῃς ἡμᾶς, 'do not unsettle us,' that is, 'drive us out from hearth and home,'[3] he little

[1] *Griechische Papyrus der Kaiserlichen Universitäts- und Landesbibliothek zu Strassburg im Elsass*, ed. Preisigke (Strassburg im Elsass, 1907), i. p. 119 f., No. 32^{10} (A.D. 261).

[2] *Greek Papyri*, edd. Grenfell-Hunt, ii. p. 101 ff., No. 67$^{17f.}$ (= *Selections from the Greek Papyri*^{2}, No. 45). It may be noted that the use of ἀρ[ρ]αβών in the above quotation shows that in 2 Cor. i. 22, v. 5, Eph. i. 14, the word is to be understood not as a 'pledge,' but an 'earnest,' a part given in advance of what will be fully bestowed afterwards.

[3] *Berliner Griechische Urkunden*, iv. p. 123 f., No. 1079^{20} (A.D. 41).

thought that he would supply future students of the New Testament with an apt parallel for the metaphorical use of the same verb in Gal. v. 12, where St. Paul expresses the hope that οἱ ἀναστατοῦντες, 'those who are unsettling' his Galatian converts, 'would even mutilate themselves,' any more than the naughty boy's admission from Oxyrhynchus that his mother complains 'that he is upsetting me' (ὅτι ἀναστατοῖ με)[1] throws light upon the description of the Brethren at Thessalonica by their Jewish opponents, 'These that have turned the world upside down (οἱ τὴν οἰκουμένην ἀναστατώσαντες) have come hither also' (Acts xvii. 6).

(c) Choice of meanings.

(c) Similar aid is given in the choice of meaning, where more than one rendering is possible.

In Matt. vi. 27, for example, both the Authorized and Revised Versions agree in rendering ἡλικία by 'stature,' 'And which of you by being anxious can add one cubit unto his stature?' but the margin of the Revised Version has 'age,' and if we are to follow the almost unanimous testimony of the papyri, this latter sense should be adopted throughout the New Testament occurrences of the word, except in Luke xix. 3, where the context makes it impossible. Thus in the important verse, Luke ii. 52, καὶ Ἰησοῦς προέκοπτεν τῇ σοφίᾳ καὶ ἡλικίᾳ, the meaning is not that Jesus 'advanced in wisdom and stature,' that is 'in height and comeliness' (as Grimm-Thayer), but 'in wisdom and age,' a description to which it may be

[1] *The Oxyrhynchus Papyri*, edd. Grenfell-Hunt, i. p. 185 f., No. 119[10] (= *Selections from the Greek Papyri*[2], No. 42).

noted in passing a striking parallel is now afforded by a first century inscription, in which a certain Aristagoras is praised as ἡλικίᾳ προκόπτων καὶ προαγόμενος εἰς τὸ θεοσεβεῖν.[1]

Or, to turn to a much discussed passage, though I tried elsewhere,[2] a number of years ago, to defend the translation of διαθήκη by 'covenant' in Heb. ix. 16, 17, I now recognize that it is impossible any longer to confine the word to that sense. Its regular use for 'will' in the ordinary documents of the day makes it practically certain that it would be so understood by the first readers of the Epistle, and that it is only by admitting a *play* on the word that the meaning of 'covenant' can be imported into the passage at all.

In the same way, if we take account of contemporary usage, it seems practically certain that ἀπάτη in its New Testament occurrences (*e.g.* Matt. xiii. 22, 2 Pet. ii. 13) can only have the popular Hellenistic meaning of 'pleasure,' and that ἀρχηγός, both in the Book of the Acts of the Apostles (iii. 15, v. 31) and in the Epistle to the Hebrews (ii. 10, xii. 2), is best understood as 'author,' or 'founder,' rather than 'leader.'

(*d*) Again, in not a few instances, our new documents supply us with the true meaning of words only imperfectly understood before.

(*d*) Suggestion of new meanings.

---

[1] Dittenberger, *Sylloge Inscriptionum Graecarum*², Leipzig, 1898, No. 325¹⁸ (i/B.C.).

[2] *The Theology of the Epistle to the Hebrews*, Edinburgh, 1899, p. 166 ff.

In commenting on 1 Pet. i. 7, ἵνα τὸ δοκίμιον ὑμῶν τῆς πίστεως πολυτιμότερον χρυσίου τοῦ ἀπολλυμένου διὰ πυρὸς δὲ δοκιμαζομένου εὑρεθῇ εἰς ἔπαινον καὶ δόξαν καὶ τιμὴν ἐν ἀποκαλύψει Ἰησοῦ Χριστοῦ, Dr. Hort saw that the meaning required was 'the approved part or element of the faith,' that is, the pure faith that remained when the dross had been purged away by fiery trial; but unable to find any warrant for this sense of δοκίμιον, he was driven to suspect that the true reading was δόκιμον.[1] There was no need, however, for any such conjecture. Ever since Deissmann[2] first drew attention to the importance of the evidence of the papyri in this connexion, examples have been rapidly accumulating to show that δοκίμιος, as well as δόκιμος, means 'proved,' 'genuine,' as in such phrases as χρυσοῦ δοκιμίου, 'tested gold,' and we need no longer have any hesitation in so translating the word both in the Petrine passage and in Jas. i. 3.

Or, to take another example, where a hitherto unestablished usage has again done away with the need of textual emendation. In Acts xvi. 12, ἥτις ἐστὶν πρώτη τῆς μερίδος Μακεδονίας, the reading μερίδος was objected to by Dr. Hort, on the ground that μερίς never denotes simply a region or province, and he proposed accordingly to read Πιερίδος in its stead, 'a chief city of Pierian Macedonia.'[3] But while it is true that μερίς in the sense of a geographical division does not occur in classical writers, it is regularly so

---

[1] *The First Epistle of St. Peter*, i. 1–ii. 17 (London, 1898), p. 41 f.
[2] *Bible Studies*, p. 259 ff.
[3] *Notes on Select Readings*[2], p. 96 f.

used in documents of the Apostolic Age, so that the rendering 'district' in the Revised Version, however arrived at, need no longer raise any qualms.

(e) It is, however, especially by imparting a fresh life and reality to many of our most ordinary New Testament terms that the new authorities render their most signal service. *(e) Fresh life and reality imparted to familiar phraseology.*

We know how our very familiarity with Scriptural language is apt to blind us to its full significance. But when we find words and phrases, which we have hitherto associated only with a religious meaning, in common, everyday use, and employed in circumstances where their meaning can raise no question, we make a fresh start with them, and get a clearer insight into their deeper application.

The 'sincere milk' by which our Authorized Version renders the ἄδολον γάλα of 1 Pet. ii. 2 may be taken as an example. Every one supposes that he knows what is meant by that, but if he were closely pressed, his explanation might be somewhat hazy.[1] Nor can it be said that the Revisers have helped him much with their literal etymological translation, 'milk which is without guile.' But when in scores of papyrus documents we find the adjective

---

[1] It ought to be noted that this ambiguity would not exist when the Authorized Version was made, as 'sincere' was then used in the sense of 'unmixed,' 'pure,' as when the translators of the Rhemish New Testament tell us in their Preface: 'We translate that text which is most sincere, and in our opinion, and as we have proved, incorrupt' (p. 16). But we are dealing with the impression the phrase conveys to the ordinary student of to-day.

applied to corn in the sense of 'pure,' 'unadulterated,' we see that this is exactly what is intended with reference to the 'spiritual milk' of the Petrine passage. Unlike the falsified teaching renounced by St. Paul in 2 Cor. iv. 2, μηδὲ δολοῦντες τὸν λόγον τοῦ θεοῦ, 'nor adulterating the word of God,' it is unmixed with any strange or foreign elements, and comes directly from God Himself.

The use of ἀπέχω, again, in connexion with receipts on countless ostraca and papyri lends fresh point to St. Paul's assurance to the Philippians, ἀπέχω δὲ πάντα καὶ περισσεύω (c. iv. 18), that is not merely, 'I have all things and abound,' but almost 'I am prepared to give you a receipt for all things' (as showing how completely your bounty has repaid all that you owed me), and may even, as Deissmann has suggested, impart a pungent irony to our Lord's condemnation of the hypocrites who disfigure their faces that they may be seen of men to fast: 'I tell you, they can sign the receipt of their reward (ἀπέχουσιν τὸν μισθὸν αὐτῶν)' (Matt. vi. 16)—'their right to receive their reward is realised, precisely as if they had already given a receipt for it.'[1] And similarly, when we find those who 'checked' or 'verified' an account using the term ἐπηκολούθηκα to describe the result, much as we should write 'Found correct,' we can understand that more than at once meets the eye underlies such a passage as [Mark] xvi. 20, τοῦ κυρίου . . . τὸν λόγον βεβαιοῦντος διὰ τῶν ἐπακολουθούντων σημείων: the signs did not merely

[1] *Bible Studies*, p. 229.

accompany or follow, they acted as a kind of authenticating signature to the word.[1]

How vividly, too, Bishop Lightfoot's translation of προεγράφη in Gal. iii. 1, 'was posted up, placarded,' stands out when we find the same verb used of the public notice which, according to a papyrus now in Florence, certain parents caused 'to be posted up' ([π]ρογραφῆναι) to the effect that they would no longer be responsible for their son's debts, seeing that he had squandered all his own property 'by riotous living' (ἀσωτευόμενος, cf. Luke xv. 13).[2] While another papyrus in the same collection provides a striking parallel to Mark xv. 15, 'And Pilate, wishing to content the multitude, released unto them Barabbas, and delivered Jesus, when he had scourged Him, to be crucified,' in the words addressed by the Egyptian governor, C. Septimius Vegetus, to a certain Phibion whom he was trying: 'Thou hadst been worthy of scourging... but I will give thee to the people' (ἄξιος μ[ὲ]ν ἦς μαστιγωθῆναι... χαρίζομαι δέ σε τοῖς ὄχλοις).[3]

[1] Cf. the signatures to a series of tax receipts in the Tebtunis papyrus, No. 100[20 f.] (B.C. 117-6), Δρεῦος ἐπηκ⟨ο⟩λούθηκα, Ἀκουσίλαος ἐπηκολούθηκα (*The Tebtunis Papyri*, edd. Grenfell-Hunt-Smyly, i. p. 441 ff.), and the ratifying of an order by an official, ἐπακολουθοῦντος Γαίου Ἰουλίου Σαλουίου, in British Museum papyrus, 1213, A.D. 65-66 (*Greek Papyri in the British Museum*, edd. Kenyon-Bell, iii. p. 121).

[2] *Papiri Greco-Egizii pubblicati dalla R. Accademia dei Lincei*, i. *Papiri Fiorentini*..., ed. G. Vitelli (Milan, 1906), p. 188 f., No. 99 (i./ii. A.D.) (= *Selections from the Greek Papyri*[2], No. 27).

[3] *Ibid.*, p. 113 ff., No. 61[59 ff.] (A.D. 85). The parallel is noted by Vitelli: cf. also Deissmann, *Light from the Ancient East*, p. 266 f.

It would be easy to go on multiplying examples, but these must suffice as at least indicating what are some of the gains which we owe to the new light from the Ancient East—gains, I venture to predict, which will be enormously increased when there has been time to investigate fully the ever-increasing store of papyrus and other texts, which year by year are being brought within our reach by the industry of discoverers and editors.

The ultimate aim of New Testament study

Meanwhile it may be well to remind ourselves that though we have been engaged on a linguistic survey, and that too in connexion with the more external features of our New Testament vocabulary, the ultimate aim and goal of all our studies lies elsewhere.

The New Testament is more than a book : it is the record of life, of *the life which is life indeed.* And all our study of its words will be in vain, unless they are the means of conducting us to Him Who is the Word. But the more earnestly we devote ourselves to that study with the best aids which modern discovery and research have placed within our reach, and the more loyally we follow the leading of the Spirit who has been sent to guide us into *all the truth,* the more fully we shall recognize with Origen, the first great Biblical critic, that 'there is not one jot or one tittle written in Scripture, which does not work its own work for those who know how to use the force of the words which have been written.'

LECTURE III.

THE LITERARY CHARACTER OF THE NEW TESTAMENT WRITINGS—THE EPISTLES AND THE APOCALYPSE.

Ἐπιστολὴ μὲν οὖν ἐστὶν ὁμιλία τις ἐγγράμματος ἀπόντος πρὸς ἀπόντα γινομένη καὶ χρειώδη σκοπὸν ἐκπληρουσα, ἐρεῖ δέ τις ἐν αὐτῇ ἅπερ ἂν παρών τις πρὸς παρόντα.

[Pseudo-]PROCLUS, *De Forma Epistolari* (ed. Hercher, p. 6).

III.

THE LITERARY CHARACTER OF THE NEW TESTAMENT WRITINGS—THE EPISTLES AND THE APOCALYPSE.

Αἱ ἐπιστολαὶ μέν, φησίν, βαρεῖαι καὶ ἰσχυραί, ἡ δὲ παρουσία τοῦ σώματος ἀσθενὴς καὶ ὁ λόγος ἐξουθενημένος.
2 Cor. x. 10.

Καθὼς καὶ ὁ ἀγαπητὸς ἡμῶν ἀδελφὸς Παῦλος κατὰ τὴν δοθεῖσαν αὐτῷ σοφίαν ἔγραψεν ὑμῖν, ὡς καὶ ἐν πάσαις ἐπιστολαῖς λαλῶν ἐν αὐταῖς περὶ τούτων, ἐν αἷς ἐστὶν δυσνόητά τινα.
2 Pet. iii. 15, 16.

Μακάριος ὁ ἀναγινώσκων καὶ οἱ ἀκούοντες τοὺς λόγους τῆς προφητείας καὶ τηροῦντες τὰ ἐν αὐτῇ γεγραμμένα, ὁ γὰρ καιρὸς ἐγγύς.
Rev. i. 3.

FROM the language in which the books of the New Testament were written we pass to their general form and literary character. In doing so it is not easy to determine the order in which they should be considered. Much might be said for beginning with the books that stand first in our collected New Testament, the Gospels, both as the record of the historical facts of which the remaining books are the interpretation, and also because they have imbedded in them the earliest fragments of Christian tradition,

The earliest books of the New Testament were epistles.

both oral and written. At the same time in their completed form the Gospels are undoubtedly later than many of the Pauline Epistles, and in an historical inquiry like the present, it will be well to commence with these, and to associate with them certain other writings of an epistolary character which the New Testament contains.

<small>I. The Pauline Epistles. Their authenticity.</small>

I. Of Epistles ascribed to St. Paul, thirteen survive in the New Testament, and though for a time the authenticity of several of these was strongly attacked, recent years have seen a marked reaction in their favour.[1] To the four principal Epistles, Galatians, Romans, and 1 and 2 Corinthians, which were alone admitted as genuine by Baur, the great majority of critics are now prepared to add 1 Thessalonians, Philippians, Philemon, and (with doubts in certain quarters) Colossians. The once much attacked 2 Thessalonians has been accepted as the work of St. Paul by its latest commentators, von Dobschütz, Moffatt, and Frame, while Harnack defends it on the ingenious, though hardly convincing, hypothesis that it was addressed to the Jewish minority at Thessalonica at the same time that 1 Thessalonians was sent to the Gentile section of the Church.[2] And

---

[1] The extravagances of certain Dutch and Swiss critics, who do not leave a single New Testament writing to its traditional author, may safely be left out of account: see, as regards the Pauline Epistles, Knowling, *The Witness of the Epistles*, London, 1892, pp. 133-243, and more recently, *The Testimony of St. Paul to Christ*[2], London, 1911.

[2] *Sitzungsberichte der Königlich Preussischen Akademie der Wissenschaften zu Berlin, philosophisch-historische Classe*, 1910, p.

LITERARY CHARACTER OF THE EPISTLES 85

though Ephesians is still widely regarded as sub-Pauline, the advocacy of Hort, Armitage Robinson, and Westcott has done much in this country at any rate to confirm the belief in the traditional authorship.[1]

There remain only the Pastoral Epistles, and in view of their general language and style, of the advanced state of ecclesiastical organization which they presuppose, and of the difficulty of finding a suitable period in the Apostle's life for their writing, we can hardly wonder that many scholars refuse to regard them as the work of St. Paul. On the other hand, there is such wide-spread agreement that they embody not a little genuine Pauline material (*e.g.* 2 Tim. iv. 9-22) that, for our present purpose, we may continue to refer them, along with the Epistles already mentioned, to St. Paul, even though other hands may have given them their final form.

1. The general mould in which all these Pauline writings are cast is that of an epistle or letter, and in adopting this the Apostle made use of a mode of

1. The epistolary form. Antiquity of letters.

560 ff. On the whole question of the literary relation of the two Epistles, see the present writer's commentary on *St. Paul's Thessalonians*, p. lxxx ff.

[1] Harnack now indentifies the Epistle with the Epistle to the Laodiceans, mentioned in Col. iv. 16, and ingeniously conjectures that the erasion of the original words ἐν Λαοδικίᾳ from c. i. 1. may have been due to the ill-repute into which Laodicea had fallen (cf. Rev. iii. 14 ff.), comparing the 'tituli erasi' of unworthy persons from the inscriptions and papyri (*Sitzungsberichte, ut supra*, p. 705 ff.).

composition which had already a long history behind it. The earliest mention of the art of writing in the *Iliad* (vi. 168 ff.) is in connexion with a letter, and we actually possess an original Greek letter inscribed on a leaden tablet, which dates from the fourth century before Christ.[1]

<small>Classical collections of letters.</small>

Amongst later instances it is sufficient to recall the letters of Aristotle, of Cicero, and of Seneca, and the correspondence, dealing apparently with philosophical and scientific subjects, which Epicurus addressed to various companies of his friends.[2] Still more important for our purpose, as showing how the epistolary form had penetrated into the literature of Hellenistic Judaism, is the well-known letter in which the Pseudo-Aristeas describes how the Septuagint, or Greek translation of the Old Testament came to be written.[3]

<small>Letters in the Old Testament and the Apocrypha.</small>

The same tendency to enlarge the scope of the letter from private purposes to a medium of im-

---

[1] For a description of this letter with facsimile, see Deissmann, *Light from the Ancient East*, p. 148 f.

[2] The extant titles of some of the letters of Epicurus are interesting in connexion with the titles of our New Testament Epistles, *e.g.* Πρὸς τοὺς ἐν Αἰγύπτῳ φίλους, Πρὸς τοὺς ἐν Μυτιλήνῃ φιλοσόφους ἐπιστολή : see Usener, *Epicurea*, Leipzig, 1887, p. 135 f.

[3] The Greek text of this letter, edited by H. St. John Thackeray, will be found as an Appendix to Swete's *Introduction to the Old Testament in Greek*, Cambridge, 1900. The same editor supplied an English translation to the *Jewish Quarterly Review*, April, 1903, which has since been separately reprinted, London, Macmillan, 1904. See also Wendland's Teubner edition, *Aristeae ad Philocratem Epistula*, Leipzig, 1900, with its valuable collection of *Testimonia* and useful lexical and grammatical Indices.

LITERARY CHARACTER OF THE EPISTLES 87

parting knowledge is traceable within the Old Testament itself. The first letter mentioned there is the letter which David addressed to Joab with reference to Uriah (2 Sam. xi. 14 f.), a purely personal communication, but this is followed by the open letter of Sennacherib to Hezekiah (2 Kings xix. 14) and by Jeremiah's letter to the captives at Babylon (Jerem. xxix.), in which the prophet has definitely in view their religious instruction. And with this last there may be compared the Epistle of Jeremy appended to the apocryphal book of Baruch, and the Epistles at the beginning of 2 Maccabees.[1]

2. The way was thus prepared for the use of the epistle or letter for the purposes of edification in the first Christian age, and we can readily understand how gladly St. Paul would avail himself of a form of composition so admirably adapted in its simplicity and directness to the immediate and practical ends he had in view, and yet capable of being employed as a vehicle for the conveyance of the deepest and most far-reaching truths.[2] And only as we keep in view both purposes, personal and homiletic, can we understand the form which his Epistles assumed in the Apostle's hands.

2. The adoption of the epistolary form by St. Paul.

---

[1] Renan, *Saint Paul*, Paris, 1869, p. 229 n^2, compares the communications which passed between Jewish synagogues with reference to debated points of doctrine and practice; but he gives no references.

[2] Cf. Renan, *op. cit.* p. 230: 'L'épître fut ainsi la forme de la littérature chrétienne primitive, forme admirable, parfaitement appropriée à l'état du temps et aux aptitudes naturelles de Paul.'

(1) The personal side of the Pauline Epistles illustrated from contemporary papyrus letters.

(1) Thus, to look at them first of all from their more personal side, the fact that they were intended to serve as a substitute for St. Paul's own presence, and to say in writing what he would gladly have said by word of mouth, prepares us for the fact that in their general structure and tone they constantly recall the ordinary letters of the day. Such a comparison has been rendered possible by the stores of private letters of all kinds recently recovered from the sands of Egypt, from which, according to Professor Deissmann, the Pauline letters differ 'not as letters, but only as the letters of *Paul*.'[1] And though, as we shall see later, the comparison may easily be pushed too far, especially in view of the great variety in character and aim by which the Pauline correspondence is marked, it certainly helps to bring out the direct and living nature of the Apostle's methods.

The best way to show this is by giving a few specimens of these letters.

A commendatory letter.

We may begin with a first-century letter, in which Theon writes to his brother Heraclides to introduce the bearer Hermophilus. The letter thus belongs to the class of commendatory letters (ἐπιστολαὶ συστατικαί) to which St. Paul refers in 2 Cor. iii. 1. It runs as follows in the translation of Dr. Grenfell and Dr. Hunt:[2]

'Theon to Heraclides his brother, many greetings and wishes for good health.

[1] *Bible Studies*, p. 44.

[2] For the Greek text of this and the following letters, see Additional Note E, 'Greek Papyrus Letters.'

LITERARY CHARACTER OF THE EPISTLES

Hermophilus the bearer of this letter is (the friend or relative) of .. erius, and asked me to write to you. Hermophilus declares that he has business at Kerkemounis. Please therefore further him in this matter, as is just. For the rest take care of yourself that you may remain in good health.
      Good-bye.
The 3rd year of Tiberius Caesar Augustus, Phaophi 3 (= September 30).'

The letter is addressed on the back:

'To Heraclides, basilicogrammateus of the Oxyrhynchite and Cynopolite nomes.'

This gives us a Greek private letter in its simplest form, and as showing how readily the same form was extended even to official communications, we may take next a document in which Phanias and two other inspectors report to the authorities the cession of certain arourae of corn land by a sister to her brother (?). The document is dated in the month of August, A.D. 95, according to our mode of reckoning. I give it again in the original editors' rendering. *[An official letter.]*

'Phanias, Heraclas, and Diogenes also called Hermaeus, officials employed in land distribution, to the agoranomi, greeting. Diogenes, son of Ptolemaeus, has had ceded to him by Tapotamon, the daughter of Ptolemaeus, son of Kolylis, acting with her guardian who is her grandson Plutarchus, son of Plutarchus, son of Plutarchus, in accordance with the terms of a contract executed this day, a square piece of allotment corn land ready for sowing, the property of Tapotamon, situated near the village of Korobis and forming part of the lot of Menoetius, in size $1 + \frac{1}{2} + \frac{1}{3} + \frac{1}{12}$ arourae. We therefore write to inform you. Farewell.'

The date follows, and the letter is then endorsed by Heraclas, one of the senders, in his own hand :

'I Heraclas have signed'

with a twice-repeated note regarding the amount of land concerned, first in ordinary script and then in the contracted symbols of the time, and a statement to the effect that the signature is of the same date as the rest of the document.

Family letters. More interesting in themselves, and still more significant for our purpose, are the large number of family letters which have been recovered. The very artlessness of their contents marks them out as obviously never intended for other eyes than the eyes of those to whom they were first addressed, while their frank expression of personal feeling recalls the self-revealing glimpses which even the most impersonal of the Pauline Epistles give into the depth of the writer's longings for the welfare of his readers.

A daughter to her father The following, for example, is a letter addressed by a daughter to her father, rejoicing over the tidings of his escape, apparently from some serious danger, and concluding, after certain messages of a purely personal character, with those greetings from others, which bulk so largely in the Pauline correspondence. The letter is very illiterate, the original Greek abounding in false concords. It belongs to the second century of the Christian era.

'Ammonous to her sweetest father, greeting.

When I received your letter, and recognized that by the will of the gods you were preserved, I rejoiced greatly. And as at the same time an opportunity has presented itself, I am writing you this letter, being very anxious to pay my respects to you. Attend as quickly as possible to the matters that are pressing. Whatever the little one asks shall be done. If the bearer of this letter hands over a small basket to you, it is I who send it. All your friends greet you by name. Celer greets you and all who are with him.

I pray for your health.'

A somewhat similar example from the recently published volume of Giessen papyri bears striking testimony to a slave's affection for her master. The mention of 'dying' because she cannot see him 'daily,' and the longing to 'fly' that she might reach him as quickly as possible are specially noteworthy. Like the foregoing, the letter belongs to the second century, probably to the time of Hadrian. It runs as follows:

A slave to her master.

'Tays to the lord Apollonius, many greetings.

Above all I greet you, master, and am praying always for your health. I was distressed, lord, in no small measure, to hear that you were sick; but thanks be to all the gods that they are keeping you from all harm. I beseech you, lord, if you think it right, to send to us; if not, we die, because we do not see you daily. Would that we could fly and come and pay our reverence to you. For we are distressed . . . Wherefore be reconciled to us, and send to us. Goodbye, lord . . .

All is going well with us.

Epeiph 24 (= July 18).'

92   THE NEW TESTAMENT DOCUMENTS

  The letter is addressed on the back:

   'To Apollonius, strategus.'

<small>A prodigal son to his mother.</small> An even deeper note is struck in the well-known letter which about the same time a prodigal son writes to his mother asking her forgiveness. As the accompanying facsimile (Plate IV.) shows, the concluding part of the original letter has been much mutilated. But it is not difficult for us to fill up the blanks for ourselves, though perhaps the broken lines testify even more forcibly than if they were complete to the depth of the writer's emotion.

 'Antonis Longus to Nilus his mother, heartiest greetings. Continually I pray for your health. Supplication on your behalf I direct each day to the lord Serapis. I wish you to know that I had no hope that you would come up to the metropolis. On this account neither did I enter into the city. But I was ashamed to come to Karanis, because I am going about in rags. I wrote you that I am naked. I beseech you, mother, be reconciled to me. But I know what I have brought upon myself. Punished I have been in any case. I know that I have sinned. I heard from Postumus who met you in the Arsinoite nome, and unseasonably related all to you. Do you not know that I would rather be a cripple than be conscious that I am owing anyone an obolus ... Come yourself ... I have heard that ... I beseech you ... I almost ... I beseech you ... I will ... not ... otherwise ...'

 On the back is the address:

  'To ... his mother from Antonius Longus her son.'

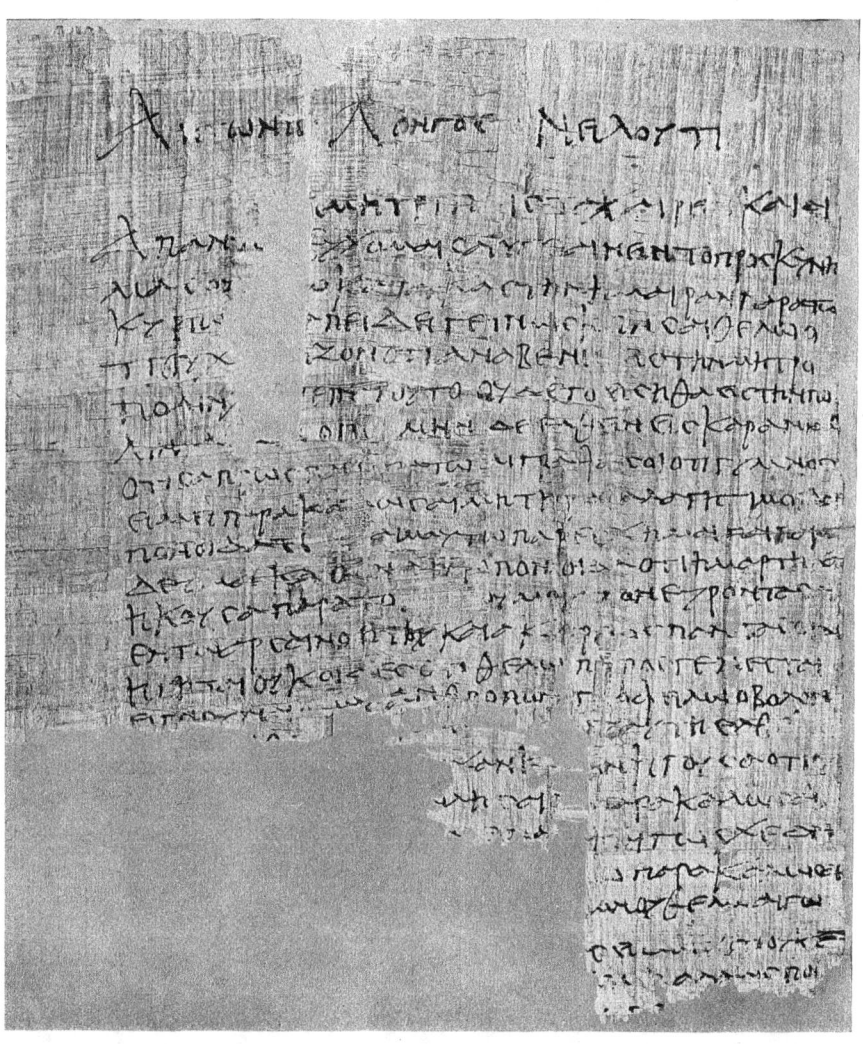

LETTER FROM A PRODIGAL SON TO HIS MOTHER.

From the Fayûm. Second Century A.D. Now in the Berlin Museum.
By permission of the Directors of the Royal Museums.

Nothing would be easier than to multiply similar examples, but these must suffice to illustrate the light which the ordinary letters of the time throw upon the outward form of the Pauline Epistles. All are constructed, it will be noticed, on a general model which, at least in the case of the longer letters, embraces Opening Address or Greeting, Thanksgiving and Prayer, Special Contents, Closing Salutations and Valediction—just the features, that is, which in a more elaborate form are found in the Apostle's writings.

Nor is this all, but it will be also apparent how frequently St. Paul avails himself of the current epistolary phraseology of the day in the more formal parts of his Epistles. Obviously that phraseology as amongst ourselves had become stereotyped, and writing as he did with a definite class of readers clearly in view in the first instance, the Apostle naturally fell back upon it, even when he read into it a new and deeper meaning. The point did not escape the notice of the older commentators as when, with reference to the opening of St. Paul's First Epistle to the Thessalonians, Theodore of Mopsuestia remarks: 'As we are accustomed to place χαίρειν ("Greeting" or "Rejoice") in the forefront of our letters, so he [St. Paul] places χάρις ὑμῖν ("Grace to you"), adding ἐν θεῷ πατρί ("in God the Father"), just as we write ἐν κυρίῳ ("in the Lord")'.[1]

[1] *Theodori Episcopi Mopsuesteni in Epistolas B. Pauli Commentarii*, ed. Swete, Cambridge, 1882, ii. p. 2.

(2) The literary side of the Pauline Epistles.

(2) But while this is so, and we are thus reminded in a most significant way of the personal character of the Pauline writings, as distinguished from the literary essay or the theological treatise, we must not forget that in other respects these writings are widely separated from an ordinary letter. The short Epistle to Philemon may approach very nearly to this,[1] though even in it the 'Church' in Philemon's house is included in the address, and the Apostle is careful throughout to base his request on the loftiest and most far-reaching grounds, but in other instances the Epistles, however occasional in origin and in the circumstances with which they deal, bear traces of much anxious preparation and thought, while some of them, such as the Epistles to the Romans and to the Ephesians, may well have been written from the first with a view to wider circles than those to which they were originally addressed.[2]

The fact is that Deissmann, in his eagerness to rescue the Pauline writings from the category of literature, and to emphasize the definite, historical surroundings in which they first arose, has carried his thesis too far, and has insisted on the distinctive

[1] In this connexion it is interesting to compare the private letter which Papa Kaor addresses to the Roman prefect Abinnaeus regarding a run-a-way soldier, Paulus: see *British Museum Papyrus* 417, ed. Kenyon, ii. p. 299 f. (= *Selections from the Greek Papyri*[2], No. 51).

[2] Cf. Tertullian, *c. Marcionem*, v. 17: 'Cum ad omnes apostolus scripserit, dum ad quosdam.'

letter or epistle in a way which in the present connexion can hardly be made good.¹ The letters of St. Paul may not be epistles, if by that we are to understand literary compositions written without any thought of a particular body of readers. At the same time, in view of the tone of authority adopted by their author, and the general principles with which they deal, they are equally far removed from the unstudied expression of personal feeling, which we associate with the idea of a true letter. And if we are to describe them as letters at all, it is well to define the term still further by the addition of some such distinguishing epithet as 'missionary' or 'pastoral.' It is not merely St. Paul the man, but St. Paul the spiritual teacher and guide who speaks in them throughout.

3. Passing from the general form of the Pauline writings, we are prepared from what has just been said to find that, as regards manner and style, St. Paul stands midway between the literary and non-literary writers of his day, and further that the special circumstances under which the different Epistles were written largely determined their several characters. The Epistles addressed to individuals stand in a different category from those to Churches,² while in the case of the Churches he himself had

<small>3. The style of the Pauline Epistles. Variety of style according to address and circumstances.</small>

---

¹ *Bible Studies*, p. 3 ff.; *Light from the Ancient East*, p. 217 ff.; *Paulus, Eine kultur- und religionsgeschichtliche Skizze*, Tübingen, 1911, p. 4 ff. (Engl. Trans. p. 9 ff.).

² Cf. Cicero, *ad Fam.* xv. 21. 4: 'Aliter enim scribimus quod eos solos quibus mittimus, aliter quod multos lecturos putamus.'

founded the Apostle naturally adopts a warmer and more direct tone than when writing to those whom he knows only by report.

It is no part of my present purpose to discuss the Pauline Epistles in detail, but a few remarks of a general character may help to bring out the variety in style and manner which exists amongst them.

1, 2. Thessalonians. The Epistles to the Thessalonians, which are very generally reckoned as the earliest Epistles that have come down to us, may be taken as specimens of St. Paul's normal mode of writing. In them he conveys his message to his friends at Thessalonica simply and directly, in for the most part smooth and well-ordered sentences, which, however, never fail to let us feel the affectionate man behind, to whom his converts were in very truth his greater 'self.'[1]

Galatians. But when we pass to the great controversial Epistles we are in a wholly different atmosphere. In the first of these, the Epistle to the Galatians, the Apostle has been stirred to the quick by the dangers confronting his beloved converts, whether these dangers be due to their own laxity, or to the insidious attacks of false teachers. And the result is that his words dart forth 'flames,'[2] while the depth of his emotion leads to those broken constructions and sudden changes of subject, which often make it so hard to follow the exact course of the argument.

[1] Cf. 1 Thess. iii. 8 : ὅτι νῦν ζῶμεν ἐὰν ὑμεῖς στήκετε ἐν κυρίῳ.

[2] Luther, *in Gal.* i.: 'Paulus meras flammas loquitur tamque vehementer ardet ut incipiat etiam quasi Angelis maledicere.'

The same features appear, though with a differ- *Romans.*
ence, in the Epistle to the Romans. By this time
the storm has spent itself, or rather there is nothing
in the circumstances of the Roman Church to arouse
the more combative elements in St. Paul's nature.
He writes, therefore, still with deep earnestness, but
more dispassionately and calmly, and takes advantage of the general and cosmopolitan character of
the address to develop and extend the arguments of
the earlier Epistles, so that we have now 'the
finished statue,' of which the Epistle to the Galatians
was 'the rough model.'[1]

It is vain indeed—let it be said once more—to
attempt to understand this or any Pauline Epistle,
without the constant effort to picture to ourselves the
person and the feelings of the writer—the eager and
impulsive Paul, overflowing with love and tenderness,
as he conjures up the needs of those to whom he is
writing, and yet so bold and resolute, as he presses
home upon others with relentless logic and keen irony
the convictions that have completely mastered himself.

Both these aspects of the Apostle's character *1, 2. Corin-*
appear very clearly in the Epistles to the Corinthians. *thians.*
Written in the main to answer inquiries which had
been addressed to him by the Corinthian brethren,
the First Epistle is perhaps the finest example we
possess of St. Paul's tact and argumentative skill,
while in such passages as the glorious Hymn in
praise of Love (c. xiii.) it touches the heights of

---

[1] Lightfoot, *Saint Paul's Epistle to the Galatians*[10], London, 1892, p. 49.

rhythmical beauty. But in the Second Epistle we are once more back in the region of keen feeling, as, in view of the calumnies with which he has been assailed, 'the Apostle of Christ Jesus through the will of God' (2 Cor. i. 1) pens the *Apologia pro Vita Sua*, and in words of mingled humility and boldness lays bare the inmost secrets of his mind and heart, not so much for his own defence, as for the sake of the cause to which his whole life was pledged.

Ephesians. Similar considerations must weigh with us when we pass to the Epistles of the Captivity. That these differ greatly in style from many of the earlier writings must be obvious to every careful reader. Take, for example, the Epistle to the Ephesians, in which perhaps this appears most noticeably. The words peculiar to the Epistle need not detain us, for they are neither so numerous nor so important as many of those who attack the Epistle's authenticity would like to make out.[1] But the style as a whole is certainly very different from what we have been accustomed to in the earlier Pauline writings. The old, crisp sentences have given place to long, involved paragraphs, in which clause follows clause, and thought is drawn out of thought, as if the writer did not know how to come to an end.[2]

[1] Cf. Nägeli, *Wortschatz des Apostels Paulus*, p. 85: 'Im ganzen scheint mir der Wortschatz dieses Briefes . . . eher eine Instanz für als gegen die Echtheit zu sein.'

[2] The whole of the opening Thanksgiving—c. i. 3-14—is really one sentence, and with it may be compared the involved structure of the succeeding vv. 15-23, and of c. iii. 1-13.

The change, as we have already seen, may be partly due to the employment of a different amanuensis,[1] but also arises very naturally from the surroundings in which St. Paul was writing, and the new themes that were occupying his thoughts. He is now far advanced in years and experience; the old controversies are for the time being forgotten or left out of sight, and in the solitude of his Roman prison the great Apostle is wrapped up 'in the heavenlies' and in all their far-reaching applications to our present and future destinies.[2] The very magnitude of his themes appears for the moment to crush him, and to prevent his finding suitable language in which to express his thoughts. Hence the involved and laboured sentences, the constant going off at a word, as if in the attempt to make the meaning clearer—in a word, a general diffusiveness

---

[1] See p. 26 f., and cf. Sanday, *Inspiration*, p. 342: 'I have sometimes asked myself whether this [the relation of Ephesians to some of the other Epistles] may not be due to the degree of expertness attained by the scribe in the art of shorthand. We know that this art was very largely practised; and St. Paul's amanuenses may have had recourse to it somewhat unequally. One might take down the Apostle's words *verbatim*; then we should get a vivid, broken, natural style like that of Romans and 1, 2 Corinthians. Another might not succeed in getting down the exact words; and then when he came to work up his notes into a fair copy, the structure of the sentences would be his own, and it might naturally seem more laboured.' See also Additional Note C, 'Dictation and Shorthand.'

[2] The expression ἐν τοῖς ἐπουρανίοις occurs five times in this Epistle (i. 3, 20; ii. 6; iii. 10; vi. 12), and nowhere else in this exact form.

of style far removed from the eager rush of the earlier writings. It is often, no doubt, very perplexing, and makes the interpretation of many parts of the Epistle exceedingly difficult. But after all, it is a phenomenon by no means unknown in the case of other writers, and in itself, unless supported by other and far stronger arguments, cannot be allowed to turn the scale against the Epistle's authenticity.

<small>The literary relation of Ephesians and Colossians.</small>
It is unnecessary to refer to the other Epistles of the Captivity separately, but, before we leave them, attention may be drawn to the interesting literary problem that has been raised by the close verbal affinity between the Epistle to the Ephesians and the Epistle to the Colossians. Various theories have been advanced as to how this could have happened, the most elaborate of which has been worked out with great elaborateness by Holtzmann.[1] Starting with Colossians, he has argued that even that Epistle does not exist now in the form in which it originally left its author's hand. There was a brief Pauline Epistle, which formed the foundation on which the writer of the Ephesian Epistle based his work. And then this writer—not St. Paul—turned back to the original Colossian Epistle, and enlarged it to the form in which we have it now. The only genuine Pauline writing was thus the shorter Colossian Epistle, from which a later hand developed both Colossians and Ephesians in their present form.

But the very complexity of this theory is against

[1] *Kritik der Epheser- und Colosserbriefe*, Leipzig, 1872.

it. And, after all, why resort to elaborate and subtle explanations when none are required? Is there any real reason why the same writer dealing with strictly cognate subjects at a very short interval of time—'probably in the same week'[1]—should not repeat himself to a large extent, especially if we can think of him as reading over an abstract or copy of the earlier letter to the Colossians, before commencing his letter to the Ephesians?

And when we add to this that in dealing with new and great themes St. Paul, in common with all the early Christian writers, would have constant difficulty in finding adequate expression for his thoughts, what more likely, as Dr. Sanday has suggested, than that he should show a readiness to fall back on expressions which he had once reached, and which were again suitable for his purpose? 'It was not poverty of mind—far from it—but only a natural expedient to relieve an unwonted strain.'[2]

The case of the Pastoral Epistles suggests questions of a more complicated kind. We have seen already the difficulties which many feel regarding

The Pastoral Epistles.

---

[1] A. Souter, *The Expositor*, VIII. ii. p. 136 ff. where interesting textual evidence is adduced against the 'secondary' or 'sub-Pauline' character of the Ephesians, as against Moffatt, *Introduction to the Literature of the New Testament*, p. 375 ff. See Moffatt's reply to the same magazine, p. 193 ff., with Souter's rejoinder, p. 321 ff.

[2] Art. 'Colossians, Epistle to the,' in Smith's *Dictionary of the Bible*[2], London, 1893, i. p. 630. See also Paley's remarks, distinguished by his usual robust commonsense, *Horae Paulinae*, ch. vi.

their direct Pauline authorship, but it is right to notice here that they have recently found a warm advocate in Sir William M. Ramsay, who, to refer at present only to the linguistic argument, has pointed out that 'the marked change of language and the number of new words' which these Epistles exhibit is due to the fact that St. Paul had to 'create' a new terminology to correspond with the new ecclesiastical situation with which he found himself confronted. 'Many of his new words are the brief expression of something which in his earlier letters he describes as a process, but which had now become so common a phenomenon in the practical management of a congregation that it demanded a special name.' And he instances by way of illustration the very first peculiar word that occurs in them, ἑτεροδιδασκαλεῖν, 'to teach a different doctrine' (1 Tim. i. 3), whose occurrence to describe a danger that had become very pressing in the early Church, he regards as 'not only not un-Pauline,' but as 'thoroughly true to Paul's mind and character.'[1]

Whether this explanation will cover the whole of the peculiarities in the Epistles' diction may be questioned, but taken in conjunction with the marked variations of language which even the earlier and acknowledged Epistles exhibit, and the possibility that in the case of the Pastorals the Apostle's amanuensis may have been a man of wider culture,[2]

---

[1] *The Expositor*, VII. vii. p. 488 ff.

[2] Nägeli, *Wortschatz*, p. 88, regards the vocabulary peculiar to the Pastorals as pointing to a larger acquaintance with profane

and have been left a freer hand than usual,[1] it certainly helps to support the positive arguments which can be brought forward from other sources in favour of the Pauline authorship of these Epistles.

4. Before leaving the Pauline Epistles, there are one or two points of a more general character that demand attention.

4. Some general points regarding the Pauline Epistles.

(1) The first is that, as these Epistles were originally written to dictation, and always with a definite audience before the composer's eye, they may, from this point of view, be regarded as speeches almost as much as letters. And just as the speech of a great orator becomes the more vivid and real when we hear it read aloud, or read it aloud to ourselves, so in the very act of reading aloud the Pauline Epistles, we often see more clearly where the true emphasis is to be laid, or catch some of the subtler distinctions that their speech-form carries with it.

(1) Their speech-character.

---

literature than we are accustomed to ascribe to St. Paul, and similarly Wendland, *Die Urchristlichen Literaturformen*[2], (in *Handbuch zum Neuen Testament*, I. iii.), Tübingen 1912, p. 364, n⁵, describes it as drawn 'fast durchweg aus der literarischen Oberschicht der Sprache.'

[1] 'The Pastorals leave us wondering how much St. Paul actually dictated ... and how far he may have given his amanuensis general directions' (J. Armitage Robinson in a paper on 'Pauline Thought,' read before the Church Congress at Swansea in 1907, *Official Report*, p. 319). On the possibility that they may have been written by friends and disciples of the Apostle, who adopted his name 'without any fraudulent intent,' see some good remarks in Simcox, *The Writers of the New Testament*, London, 1890, p. 38.

104 THE NEW TESTAMENT DOCUMENTS

(2) Their artistic and rhetorical character.

(2) And this leads us to ask how far this speech-form may have been moulded by the ordinary methods of contemporary rhetoric.

Blass has probably found few followers in the theory that in this respect St. Paul was not above making use of 'Asiatic rhythm' for the embellishment of some of his most eloquent passages,[1] and even the stylistic and rhetorical parallels which Johannes Weiss is so fond of discovering may easily be carried too far.[2] But the very fact that such suggestions have been made, and made too in such influential quarters, is in itself a proof of the literary tact and skill that the Pauline writings undoubtedly display. The art may be $\tau\acute{\epsilon}\chi\nu\eta$ $\ddot{\alpha}\tau\epsilon\chi\nu o s$, as Heinrici well describes it,[3] but it is nevertheless $\tau\acute{\epsilon}\chi\nu\eta$, and forms a fitting frame for the wisdom and grandeur of the Apostle's thoughts.[4]

(3) Their relation to Jewish literature.

(3) Nor must these traces of Hellenic training in

---

[1] *Die Rhythmen der asianischen und römischen Kunstprosa*, Leipzig, 1905. For a detailed criticism of Blass's hypothesis, see Deissmann in the *Theologische Literaturzeitung*, 31 (1906), cols. 231 ff.

[2] *Beiträge zur Paulinischen Rhetorik* (reprinted from *Theologische Studien D. B. Weiss gewidmet*), Göttingen, 1897; *Die Aufgaben der Neutestamentlichen Wissenschaft in der Gegenwart*, Göttingen, 1908, p. 11 ff.

[3] *Der litterarische Charakter der neutestamentlichen Schriften*, Leipzig, 1908, p. 69.

[4] For an elaborate attempt to trace the Greek influences of Tarsus on St. Paul, see Böhlig, *Die Geisteskultur von Tarsos im augusteischen Zeitalter mit Berücksichtigung der paulinischen Schriften*, Göttingen, 1913.

St. Paul lead us to forget how still more markedly he is influenced by Jewish methods of expression and reasoning. Whatever the Greek atmosphere in which so much of his life was passed did for the Apostle, it never obliterated the Jew that was in him. All through his life, he was 'Jew' not only in nationality and education, but in language and tradition. And we are not surprised therefore to find him, more particularly in his controversies with his Jewish opponents, constantly falling back upon their methods, and meeting their arguments with their own weapons.

An obvious instance is afforded by Gal. iii. 16, where St. Paul seeks to draw a Messianic reference out of a well-known verse in Genesis from the fact that the word 'seed' is there employed in the singular: 'To Abraham were the promises spoken and to his seed (τῷ σπέρματι αὐτοῦ): he saith not, And to seeds (τοῖς σπέρμασιν), as of many, but as of one, And to thy seed (τῷ σπέρματι σου), which is Christ.' But as a matter of fact, in ordinary usage, the plural neither of the Greek word σπέρμα, nor of the Hebrew זֶרַע which it represents, could be used of human progeny, and, consequently, on strict grammatical grounds, the Apostle's argument loses its force. Only when we interpret it *more Rabbinico*, and from a singular *form* draw a singular *sense*, irrespective of all other considerations, can we see how the Apostle's reasoning would appeal to his Jewish readers.[1]

---

[1] Deissmann discovers a very early Christian protest against St. Paul's insistence on the singular σπέρμα in the substitution of σπορά

The same may be said of the manner in which St. Paul constantly clothes his thought in figures drawn from the later Jewish literature, which has been made so accessible to English readers by the labours of Dr. R. H. Charles and others.[1] But interesting though the parallels suggested undoubtedly are, care must be taken not to exaggerate their importance, at any rate to the extent of losing sight of the far more significant debt which the Apostle owes to the canonical books of the Greek Old Testament. The Septuagint, as we have had occasion to notice before, was St. Paul's Bible, and the number of his quotations from it, and still more the ever-recurring and almost unconscious reminiscences of its language and imagery show how largely it had taken possession of him.[2]

(4) Their originality.

(4) And yet with all this, the final impression which the Pauline writings leave upon us is that of their outstanding originality. Nothing exactly like them had appeared before, or has appeared since. And when, to meet the special circumstances in which he found himself, St. Paul struck out this happy combination of the letter with the epistle, of

---

for σπέρμα in a recently discovered parchment fragment of the fifth century, containing a Greek translation of Gen. xxvi. 3, 4 (*Light from the Ancient East*, p. 35, n[4]).

[1] Special reference may be made to H. St. John Thackeray's interesting Essay, *The Relation of St. Paul to Contemporary Jewish Thought*, London, 1900.

[2] Cf. H. Vollmer, *Die Alttestamentlichen Citate bei Paulus*, Freiburg i. B., 1895.

the frankly personal message with the most far-reaching exposition of Christian truth, he invented a form of composition which in its every line bears witness to the commanding personality and genius of its author.[1]

II. In all these circumstances it is not to be wondered at that the Pauline method should furnish a model for subsequent writers. It is indeed probably going too far to say that, left to themselves, these last would hardly have thought of adopting the epistolary form at all, when we remember the prevalence of that form for literary purposes at the beginning of the Christian era.[2]

<small>II. The other Epistles of the New Testament.</small>

---

[1] Cf. U. von Wilamowitz-Moellendorf, *Die griechische Literatur des Altertums*, p. 159 (in *Die Kultur der Gegenwart*[2], i. 8, Berlin, 1907): 'Als einen Ersatz seiner persönlichen Wirkung schreibt er seine Briefe. Dieser Briefstil ist Paulus, niemand als Paulus; es ist nicht Privatbrief und doch nicht Literatur, ein unnachahmliches, wenn auch immer wieder nachgeahmtes Mittelding'; and Wendland, *Die Urchristlichen Literaturformen*[2], p. 358: 'Der Stil ist so original wie die Persönlichkeit. Und der persönliche Gehalt hat den Briefen eine literarische Wirkung gesichert, wie sie dem professionellen Literatentum, das sich an ein Allerweltspublikum wendet, versagt zu sein pflegt.'

[2] To what is said in this connexion on p. 85 ff., may be added the words of Norden: 'The epistolary literature, even in its artless forms, had a far greater right to exist, according to the ideas of the age, than we can understand at the present day. The epistle gradually became a literary form into which any material, even of a scientific nature, could be thrown in a free and easy fashion' (*Antike Kunstprosa*[2], ii. p. 492).

108 THE NEW TESTAMENT DOCUMENTS

Their general, and yet personal, character.

At the same time it is impossible to doubt that in seeking the fittest expression for their own teaching they would be much influenced by the example of the great Apostle. And this all the more, because notwithstanding the more general character of their contents, the later Epistles of the New Testament are never wholly wanting in the personal note. The Epistle to the Hebrews, for example, while describing itself as a 'word of exhortation' (c. xiii. 22) or a homily, shows by the direct tone of praise and blame adopted throughout (cc. v. 12, vi. 9, x. 32, xii. 4), no less than by the closing salutations (c. xiii. 22-25), that its author has in view a definite circle or community of readers.[1] Similarly the carefully arranged list of the Provinces of Asia Minor with which the First Epistle of St. Peter opens enables us to follow the bearer step by step on his journey, as he carries the Apostolic message to the different Christian communities north of Taurus, and thereby lends local colouring and warmth to the otherwise markedly catholic nature of the Epistle.

Even the First Epistle of St. John is very insufficiently described as an encyclical or manifesto addressed to Christendom as a whole. Though 'it

---

[1] This comes out very clearly if we can think of the Epistle as addressed originally, not to any general body of Hebrew Christians, either at Jerusalem or elsewhere, but to a small community of Jewish believers, almost a 'Church in the house,' at Rome: see the critical introduction to my *Theology of the Epistle to the Hebrews*, p. 34 ff.

does not contain a single proper name (except our Lord's), nor a single definite allusion, personal, geographical, or historical,' it is still, as one of the ablest of its recent expositors has pointed out, a true letter. 'From beginning to end the writer shows himself in close contact with the special position and immediate needs of his readers. The absence of explicit reference to either only indicates how intimate was the relation between them.'[1]

Passing from the general character of these Epistles to their language and style, and turning first of all to the Epistle to the Hebrews, we are immediately struck by the excellence of the Greek in which it is written, and the care that has been bestowed upon its composition. It is an aspect of the Epistle which from the time of Origen[2] has occupied the attention of critics, and recently has led Blass, with greater excuse than in the case of the Pauline letters, to discover a rhythmical principle running throughout it.[3]

The Epistle to the Hebrews. Its language and style.

---

[1] Law, *The Tests of Life*², Edinburgh, 1909, pp. 39, 41.

[2] *Apud* Euseb. *Hist. Eccles.* vi. 25. 11 ff.

[3] *Brief an die Hebräer, Text mit Angabe der Rhythmen*, Göttingen, 1903: cf. *Grammatik des Neutestamentlichen Griechisch*², p. 304 f.

It is worth noting that the text of the two recently discovered papyrus fragments of Hebrews, belonging to the fourth century, published by Grenfell and Hunt in *The Oxyrhynchus Papyri*, iv. p. 36 ff. No. 657, and vii. p. 11 f. No. 1078, is divided by means of double dots into a series of στίχοι, which frequently coincide with Blass's arrangement.

Apart, however, from its over-artificial character, it is obvious that such a theory may easily be pressed to the serious loss of the writer's meaning, as when in the very opening verse the omission of the definite article before υἱῷ, 'Son,' is traced to metrical considerations, instead of to the writer's desire to lay stress on the nature or character rather than on the personality of the Son. It is in 'a Son,' 'one that is Son,' that God is speaking to us as distinguished from 'the prophets,' in whom He spoke to the fathers.

This, however, is far from denying that the Epistle does show more signs of artistic structure than any other writing of the New Testament. Every sentence is carefully finished, every period exactly balanced. And the orderly plan of the whole, the springing of each step from what immediately precedes, and the use of such aids to style as full-sounding phrases, rhetorical questions, explanatory parentheses, and vivid, pictorial images, sometimes condensed into a single word, all betray the conscious stylist, who in the interests of his theme does not neglect any advantage that attention to phraseology and order can bring.[1]

Bearing of these considerations on authorship.

That all this has an important bearing on the vexed question of authorship is obvious. For one thing it practically excludes St. Paul, even if he were not excluded on other grounds. And if we are to conjecture at all, our choice must fall on some such

[1] For particulars, see *Theology of the Epistle to the Hebrews*, p. 20 f.

man as Joseph, whose surname Barnabas was popularly identified with exhortation or comfort,[1] or the 'eloquent' Apollos, if not, as Harnack has suggested,[2] on an authoress Prisca who, according to the description in Acts xviii. 26, was able, along with her husband Aquila, to expound the word of God ἀκριβέστερον, that is, 'with marked accuracy and precision.'

The general excellence of the Greek in which it is written is again a distinguishing feature of the Epistle of St. James. And so varied is its vocabulary, and so forcible and epigrammatic its style, that many scholars have found it difficult to ascribe it to its traditional Palestinian author. But in view of the wide-spread diffusion of Greek in Palestine at the time, and the impossibility of determining the extent of St. James's proficiency in it, there is nothing actually to prevent his having written it. *The Epistle of St. James. Its language*

Nor can we forget that, apart from its Greek dress, the form and atmosphere of the Epistle are thoroughly Hebraic, much of its teaching being cast in the gnomic or aphoristic utterances, so characteristic of the wisdom-literature of the Jews. Spitta indeed has gone the length of describing it as originally a Jewish, possibly pre-Christian document, *and form.*

---

[1] Acts iv. 36. For the true etymology of Barnabas = 'son of Nebo,' see Deissmann, *Bible Studies*, p. 307 ff., and G. B. Gray in *The Expository Times*, x. p. 233 f.

[2] *Zeitschrift für die neutestamentliche Wissenschaft*, i. (1900) p. 16 ff. The name of Aquila had already found favour with Bleek, *Der Brief an die Hebräer*, Berlin, 1828-40, i. p. 421 f.

into which a Christian admirer inserted the name of Christ in cc. i. 1, ii. 1, in order that the Epistle might be admitted into the New Testament.¹ But if so, it is hardly likely that such an interpolator would have contented himself with inserting so little; while Harnack's view that it is made up of a collection of fragments and discourses, which as late as the end of the second century were combined by an unknown hand into their present form,² fails to account for the unity of language and thought by which the Epistle as a whole is distinguished.

More might be said on general grounds for Professor J. H. Moulton's interesting suggestion that James of Jerusalem composed the Epistle for the benefit of Jews rather than of Christians, and consequently avoided specific reference to Christ and to His Cross in order to avoid giving unnecessary offence,³ were it not for the difficulty of imagining a Christian teacher of James's position suppressing his distinctive beliefs under any circumstances whatsoever. Besides, what comes on this showing of the important passage, c. ii. 14-26, where faith—obviously Christian faith—is assumed as the starting-point of justification (v. 24, οὐκ ἐκ πίστεως μόνον)?

1 Peter. Its authorship

Reference has already been made to the important part which Silvanus played in the production of the

---

¹ 'Der Brief des Jacobus,' in *Zur Geschichte und Litteratur des Urchristentums*, Göttingen, 1896, ii. p. 1 ff.

² *Die Chronologie der altchristlichen Litteratur,* Leipzig, 1897, i. p. 487 f.

³ *The Expositor*, VII. iv. p. 45 ff.

LITERARY CHARACTER OF THE EPISTLES 113

First Epistle of St. Peter.[1] And if, as is most probable, this Silvanus is to be identified with Silas, the friend and companion of St. Paul, we have an additional ground for the many affinities of language and thought between the Epistle and certain Pauline writings, notably the Epistles to the Romans and the Ephesians.

The writer's vocabulary is a large one, including not a few classical words, as well as words for which there is little or no attestation elsewhere. And his style, while simple, is marked by close attention to grammatical rules, and by a suggestive order and balance in the arrangement of his words. His dependence on the Septuagint is very marked, as in the case of the other New Testament writers.[2] *and literary character.*

The so-called Second Epistle of St. Peter raises a wholly different set of questions, and whether we look to its language, which shows a tendency, unobservable elsewhere, of imitating the great Attic models,[3] or to its dependence upon the Epistle of *The pseudonymous character of 2 Peter.*

---

[1] See p. 22, and cf. Zahn, *Introduction to the New Testament*, Engl. Tr., ii. p. 150: 'It purports to be a letter of Peter's; and such it is, except that Peter left its composition to Silvanus, because he regarded him as better fitted than himself, indeed as better fitted than any one else, to express in an intelligible and effective manner the thoughts and feelings which Peter entertained toward the Gentile Christians of Asia Minor.'

[2] On these and similar points, see Bishop Chase's classical article, 'Peter, First Epistle of,' in Hastings' *Dictionary of the Bible*, iii. p. 779 ff.

[3] Cf. Moulton, *Prolegomena*³, p. 97, *Cambridge Biblical Essays*, p. 484.

St. Jude,[1] we are led to think of it not as an original work of the Apostle whose name it bears, but rather as a pseudepigraph written in the second century by an unknown author, who desired to gain credit for his work by issuing it under the great name of St. Peter.

In itself there was nothing unusual in this, nor anything contrary to the literary canons of the time. The later Jewish Apocalypses were almost all *pseudepigrapha*, issued as the work of some Old Testament lawgiver or prophet, and receiving thereby the authority of his name. And in thus adopting the name of St. Peter, the author of our Epistle had no intention of deceiving, but desired simply to express his own sense of personal indebtedness to the Apostle, and to extend the influence of his teaching.[2] That in the judgment of the Early Church he succeeded in this may be taken as proved by the eventual inclusion of his book in the Sacred Canon.

[1] See J. B. Mayor, *The Epistle of St. Jude and the Second Epistle of St. Peter*, London, 1907, p. i ff., where the priority of Jude is maintained against Spitta, Zahn, and Bigg.

[2] Other pseudonymous works associated with the name of the same Apostle are the Preaching, the Gospel (see p. 281 ff.), and the Apocalypse of Peter, the last of which stands in such close literary relationship to the Second Epistle as to suggest a common authorship. Even Zahn, who stoutly maintains the Apostolic authorship of the Epistle, nevertheless admits that it is 'entirely comprehensible that the name of the chief of the apostles should be misused in the writing of a spurious letter,' and that 'the mere occurrence of Peter's name in an ancient writing is no proof of authorship.' (*Introd. to the New Testament*, Engl. Tr., ii. p. 270 f.).

There remain still the three Epistles attributed to St. John, and without entering at present into the vexed question as to whom we are to understand by this John, we may take it as practically certain that he is to be identified with the author of the Fourth Gospel. In the case of the First Epistle, in particular, this comes out very clearly. And whether we think of the Epistle as written at the same time as the Gospel, to serve as a kind of covering-letter to it, as Bishop Lightfoot suggests,[1] or some time later, as an appeal to the Church to abide by the spiritual teaching of the Gospel, as its latest commentator the Rev. A. E. Brooke prefers,[2] the close association between the two books in language and thought bears unmistakeably the impress of one mind. *The Johannine Epistles. 1 John. Authorship*

Of the distinctive features of the writer's Greek, it will again be more convenient to speak later (see p. 154 f.), but before leaving his First Epistle it may be well, as in the case of the Epistle of St. James, to draw attention to its markedly Hebraic colouring. 'One has only to read the Epistle,' says Professor Law, 'with an attentive *ear* to perceive that, though using another language, the writer had in his own ear, all the time, the swing and the cadences of Old Testament verse. With the exception of the Prologue and a few other periodic passages, the majority of sentences divide naturally into two or three or *and Hebraic colouring.*

---

[1] *Biblical Essays*, London, 1893, pp. 63, 99, 198.

[2] *The Johannine Epistles* (in the *International Critical Commentary*), Edinburgh, 1912, p. xix ff.

four στίχοι.' 'It is not suggested,' he continues, after illustrating these particulars, 'that there is in the Epistle a conscious imitation of Hebraic forms; but it is evident, I think, that no one could have written as our author does, whose whole style of thought and expression had not been unconsciously formed upon Old Testament models.'[1] And, further on, he describes St. John's 'mode of thinking and writing' in this Epistle as 'spiral. The course of thought does not move from point to point in a straight line. It is like a winding staircase—always revolving around the same centre, always recurring to the same topics, but at a higher level.'[2] That is excellently said, and affords a valuable clue for tracing the progress of the Apostle's thought with the constant appearance and reappearance of the same leading themes.

2, 3 John. The two shorter Epistles need not detain us. One of them, which we know as the Third Epistle of St. John, is obviously a private letter, addressed to the writer's friend Gaius, in order to commend to his good services certain travelling missionaries who were about to visit the Church of which he was a member. But the destination of the Second Epistle is not so clear. In view of the fact that κυρία (see v. 1) is a common form of address in the ordinary letters of the time, many think that the Epistle was originally sent to an individual lady, Electa.[3] But

[1] *The Tests of Life*[2], pp. 2, 4.   [2] *Op. cit.* p. 5.

[3] Cf. *e.g.* a papyrus letter of B.C. 1 which Hilarion addresses Βερούτι τῇ κυρίᾳ μου, 'to my dear Berous' (*The Oxyrhynchus*

the contents of the Epistle are against this view, and the probability is that the author was addressing a Church,[1] very likely the Church of which the Gaius of the Third Epistle was a member (cf. 3 John 9). As to where this Church was situated, we have no means of determining: it may have been in Rome, or, as others think with more reason, in Asia, perhaps at Pergamum or Thyatira. But whatever the exact *locale*, the writer is evidently in anxiety regarding certain new movements which had been asserting themselves, and accordingly writes with all the authority belonging to him as 'the Elder' to encourage his readers to continue 'walking in truth,' if they are to enjoy 'a full reward' of the work he has 'wrought' amongst them (vv. 4, 8).

III. There remains still one writing of the New Testament, which may be considered in the present connexion if only because of its epistolary address (c. i. 4) and conclusion (c. xxii. 21), and because of the Seven Letters to the Seven Churches in Asia

---

Papyri, edd. Grenfell-Hunt, iv. p. 243 f., No. 744 = *Selections from the Greek Papyri*[2], No. 12).

In an article in *The Expositor*, VI. iii. p. 194 ff., on 'The Problem of the Address in the Second Epistle of John,' Dr. Rendel Harris argues with customary ingenuity that St. John's 'dear' friend was a Gentile proselyte of the tribe of Ruth, and like Ruth a widow!

[1] Cf. 1 Pet. v. 13, ἡ ἐν Βαβυλῶνι συνεκλεκτή.

with which it opens. It is not, however, these Letters which have given its ordinary title to the book as a whole, nor even the writer's own account of it as a 'prophecy' (cc. i. 3, xxii. 7, 10, 18 f.), but rather the fact that he directly ascribes its contents to an 'apocalypse' or 'revelation,' given by Jesus Christ to His servant (c. i. 1).

In this way the book is at once linked with a widely-spread form of writing of the time. In the books of the earlier Old Testament prophets we have frequent traces of apocalyptic writing; and outside the Canon we are in possession of a large number of Jewish apocalypses, which both in general aim and literary form exhibit certain well-marked characteristics which reappear in the book before us. In one important particular, however, they differ from it. They are pseudonymous, written in the name and under the shelter of some great figure in the past, such as Enoch, Moses, Isaiah, Baruch, whereas the writer of the New Testament Apocalypse names himself in such a way as to suggest that he was its real author, and was contemporary with the events he records.[1]

Its Hebraic Leaving aside in the meantime the question of the exact identity of this 'John,' and turning to some of the more external features of his book, we are at once struck by the extent of its dependence on the Jewish Scriptures. Not indeed that its writer ever directly quotes them, or, except in rare instances,

[1] Cf. Swete, *The Apocalypse of St. John*, London, 1906, p. clxx f.

LITERARY CHARACTER OF APOCALYPSE 119

employs the *ipsissima verba* of the Old Testament. It is rather that his whole mind is so steeped in its vocabulary that almost unconsciously he makes use of it as the best means for the conveyance of his own message.[1]

But along with this Hebraic background the Apocalypse possesses also a distinctly Greek side, as shown by the facts that not only is it 'linguistically deep-rooted in the most popular colloquial language'[2] of the day, but that many of its allusions and figures are clearly due to a close first-hand acquaintance with the customs and beliefs of the Greek East.[3]

and its Hellenic sides.

This latter consideration only makes the more astonishing the character of the writer's language and grammar. Genders, numbers, and cases are frequently at fault; different tenses and moods are joined by a copula without any obvious reason for the changes; adjectives and verbs are made to govern unusual cases.[4]

Its barbarous Greek

The phenomena are unique, so far as the New Testament writings are concerned, unique, we may

---

[1] According to the convenient list appended to Westcott and Hort's edition of the Greek New Testament, the Apocalyptist is influenced by Old Testament writings in 278 out of the 404 verses, into which his work is now divided.

[2] Deissmann, *Light from the Ancient East*, p. 63.

[3] Cf. W. M. Ramsay, *The Letters to the Seven Churches of Asia*, London, 1904, where the suggestive illustrations in the text are specially selected with the view of showing that the Apocalypse 'was written to be understood by the Graeco-Asiatic public' (p. viii f.).

[4] Particulars will be found in Swete, *Apocalypse*, p. cxviii f.

say, in literature. Can any explanation of them be offered?

<small>due to its being written in an acquired tongue,</small> Some, no doubt, may be set down as Semitisms, or Aramaisms, due to the writer's nationality and his close dependence on the Old Testament Scriptures already referred to. And in the same connexion it is not out of place to point out that if Greek was a secondary language to the author, it is not to be wondered at that he should not always hit upon the right constructions. His vocabulary might not cause him much difficulty, but when it came to framing sentences in an acquired tongue, governed by different grammatical rules, he may well be pardoned if occasionally he stumbles.

On the other hand, some of the lapses are of such a character as to suggest intention rather than ignorance. When, for example, in his opening greeting to the Churches in Asia, the seer construes the preposition ἀπό with the nominative ὁ ὢν καὶ ὁ ἦν καὶ ὁ ἐρχόμενος, 'He Who is and Who was and Who is to come' (c. i. 4), this cannot have been because he did not know that ἀπό was regularly followed by the genitive, but because for the moment he regarded the whole phrase as an indeclinable noun; just as later in the same sentence he treats the threefold description of Jesus Christ as ὁ μάρτυς ὁ πιστός, ὁ πρωτότοκος τῶν νεκρῶν καὶ ὁ ἄρχων τῶν βασιλέων τῆς γῆς, 'the faithful witness, the firstborn of the dead, and the ruler of the kings of the earth,' as a kind of parenthetical addition, and consequently is not afraid to leave it in the nominative, though strictly it is in apposition with the genitive Ἰησοῦ Χριστοῦ.¹

And in these whole circumstances it may well be asked whether apocalyptic writing is to be judged on the rules of strict grammar, or whether it may not claim a character and licence of its own. For the time being the seer is, as it were, lifted out of himself, and in his eagerness to find expression for the thoughts and longings by which his whole being is dominated, he does not stop to weigh his words, but pours them forth as they come. His grammatical lapses thus become, as Dr. Moulton remarks from a somewhat different standpoint, 'the sign-manual of a writer far too much concerned with his message to be conscious of the fact that he is writing literature which after ages will read with a critical eye.'² *and in an apocalyptic style.*

A similar consideration, arising from the general character of apocalyptic writing, may help us when we pass from the language to the structure of the Apocalypse. Ever since, in 1886, Vischer suggested that the peculiar character of the Apocalypse was to be explained by the fact that it was fundamentally a Jewish writing worked over by a Christian hand,³ *The structure of the Apocalypse.*

---

[1] For a further attempt to reduce the number of grammatical peculiarities in the Apocalypse by the theory that the Seer frequently interjected comments or explanations, which would now find their place in footnotes or marginal abstracts, see Archbishop Benson, *The Apocalypse*, Essay. V. 'A Grammar of Ungrammar,' p. 131 ff.

[2] *Cambridge Biblical Essays*, p. 490.

[3] *Texte und Untersuchungen*, ii. 3, *Die Offenbarung Johannis, eine jüdische Apocalypse in christlicher Bearbeitung. Mit Nachwort von* Adolf Harnack. Cf. now Harnack, *Chronologie*, i. p. 675, n¹.

122   THE NEW TESTAMENT DOCUMENTS

Use of older apocalyptic material,

source-theories of the most varying kinds have been brought forward. The very number of these theories is against them, nor as yet has any of them succeeded in winning general acceptance. But one service at least they have performed. They have drawn attention to the large amount of material common to the general apocalyptic thought of the time. And without attempting to follow those who have tried to trace this material back to Babylonian or Persian sources,[1] we can at least notice how natural it was for the New Testament seer to avail himself of it for his own purposes, as in his description of the first wild Beast (cc. xiii.-xx.), or how in certain cases (*e.g.* cc. vii. 4-8, xi. 1-13, and xii.) he may even have taken over whole passages from the Jewish apocalypses of his day, which seemed to him capable of a Christian interpretation.[2]

but essential unity.

Notwithstanding, however, this use of earlier sources, the Apocalypse must be clearly recognized as no mere literary conglomerate, no 'compound of shreds and patches,' but a compact unity. Only a real author, as distinguished from a compiler or editor, could have so stamped the impress of his personality upon the book as a whole. And the longer it is studied, the closer is found to be the interrelation between its different parts, and the more

[1] *E.g.* Gunkel, *Schöpfung und Chaos*, Göttingen, 1895; Bousset, *Der Antichrist in der Überlieferung des Judentums, des Neuen Testaments und der alten Kirche*, Göttingen, 1895 (Eng. Tr., London, 1896).

[2] See further 'The Biblical Doctrine of Antichrist' in my edition of *St. Paul's Epistles to the Thessalonians*, p. 158 ff.

clearly does 'the presence of the same creative mind' make itself felt throughout.[1]

Bearing of language and date on the question of authorship.

In asking in which particular 'John' this 'creative mind' is to be found, we at once raise a question of deep interest, but one which cannot adequately be discussed without entering on historical and theological inquiries which lie altogether outside our present scope. This only can be said, that if the question is to be settled on literary grounds alone, the Apocalypse can hardly be put down to the same hand that wrote the Fourth Gospel.

The difficulty was felt as early as the middle of the third century by Dionysius of Alexandria († A.D. 265), and is stated by him in a passage to which recent research has been able to add little or nothing. After showing that the Gospel and the First Epistle of John present marks of agreement which suggest a common authorship, he goes on to argue that the Apocalypse differs widely from both in its ideas and in its way of expressing them, and more particularly in its diction. 'For they [the Gospel and First Epistle] were written not only without error as regards the Greek language, but also most artistically in their expressions, in their reasonings, and in the arrangements of their explanations': whereas the 'dialect and language' of the Apocalypse 'are not accurate Greek,' but disfigured by 'barbarous idioms, and, in some places, solecisms.'[2]

---

[1] Swete, *Apocalypse*, p. 1; cf. W. Milligan, *Discussions on the Apocalypse*, London, 1893, ii. 'The Unity of the Apocalypse.'

[2] *Apud* Euseb. *Hist. Eccles.* vii. 25. See further p. 262 ff.

With this position the latest English commentator on the Apocalypse, Professor Swete, is in substantial agreement when he writes that in the matter of style the Evangelist 'stands at the opposite pole to the eccentricities, the roughnesses, the audacities' of the Apocalyptist.[1] And in a subsequent section dealing directly with the question of authorship, he is even more emphatic. 'It is incredible that the writer of the Gospel could have written the Apocalypse without a conscious effort savouring of literary artifice.... The writer of the Apocalypse may not have been either more or less of a Greek scholar than the writer of the Gospel; but in their general attitude towards the use of language they differ fundamentally. The difference is due to personal character rather than to relative familiarity with Greek.'[2]

These are strong words, especially as coming from one who has made so close a study of the book before us on its linguistic side, and 'the relative familiarity with Greek' which Professor Swete here mentions as an explanation of the difference between the books, only to set it aside, is rendered still more unlikely by the change of attitude in recent years with regard to the date of the Apocalypse. So long as it was dated in the reign of Nero, the interval that elapsed before the appearance of the Gospel might have counted for something in the improvement of the writer's Greek. But the return to the

[1] *The Apocalypse of St. John*, p. cxxiv.
[2] *Ibid.* p. clxxviii.

traditional date under Domitian, which is now so generally accepted, no longer allows a sufficient interval of time for this.[1] And if we are to continue to regard the Fourth Gospel as the work of the Apostle, there seems nothing for it from the point of view of language except to assign the Apocalypse to some other John.

No sooner, however, has this been said than one begins to fear that one is wrong, and that the deep seated doctrinal harmony between the two books,[2] combined with the strong external evidence, can only be adequately explained by unity of authorship.

Beyond this indecisive position, I frankly confess that I am unable to advance in the meantime. And in asking to be allowed to keep an open mind on the question I am thankful that I can shelter myself under the example of so high an authority as Professor Swete. 'We cannot yet,' so he writes

[1] On the close relation between date and authorship Hort, who himself advocates the earlier date, is very clear: 'It is, however, true that without the long lapse of time and the change made by the Fall of Jerusalem the transition [from the Apocalypse to the Gospel] cannot be accounted for.... It would be easier to believe that the Apocalypse was written by an unknown John than that both books belong alike to St. John's extreme old age' (*The Apocalypse of St. John*, i.-iii., London, 1908, p. xl). On the evidence for the Domitianic date, see W. Milligan, *Discussions*, p. 75 ff.; W. M. Ramsay, *The Church in the Roman Empire*[5], London, 1897, p. 295 ff., and Swete, *Apocalypse*, p. xcv ff.

[2] Cf. W. Milligan, *Discussions*, v. 'The Apocalypse and the Fourth Gospel.'

in concluding the section on 'authorship' in the *Prolegomena* to his great edition of the Apocalypse, 'with safety go far beyond the dictum of Dionysius: ὅτι μὲν οὖν Ἰωάννης ἐστιν ὁ ταῦτα γράφων, αὐτῷ λέγοντι πιστευτέον· ποῖος δὲ οὗτος, ἄδηλον'—'But that he who wrote these things was called John must be believed, as he says it; but who he was does not appear.'

<small>Religious significance of the Apocalypse.</small>

In these circumstances it is well to keep in mind that all this is a matter of literary, rather than of religious or theological, interest. In whatever way the question of authorship is finally settled, nothing can rob us of the significance of the contents of this marvellous book, which was described by Milton long ago as 'the majestic image of a high and stately tragedy, shutting up and intermingling her solemn scenes and acts with a sevenfold chorus of hallelujahs and harping symphonies,'[1] and which finds its final interpretation in the triumphant assurance: 'The kingdom of the world is become the kingdom of our Lord and of His Christ: and He shall reign for ever and ever (c. xi. 15).'

[1] *The Reason of Church Government urged against Prelaty*, Bk. ii. *proem.*

LECTURE IV.

THE LITERARY CHARACTER OF THE NEW TESTAMENT WRITINGS—THE GOSPELS AND ACTS.

Τίς γὰρ ὀρθῶς διδαχθεὶς καὶ Λόγῳ προσφιλὴς γενηθεὶς οὐκ ἐπιζητεῖ σαφῶς μαθεῖν τὰ διὰ Λόγου δειχθέντα φανερῶς μαθηταῖς;
Ep. ad Diognetum, xi. 2.

'Quam scripturam [Acta Apostolorum] qui non recipiunt, nec spiritus sancti esse possunt, qui necdum spiritum sanctum possint agnoscere discentibus missum; sed nec ecclesiam se dicant defendere, qui, quando et quibus incunabulis institutum est hoc corpus, probare non habent.'
TERTULLIAN, *De Praescriptione Haereticorum*, c. 22.

IV.

THE LITERARY CHARACTER OF THE NEW TESTAMENT WRITINGS—THE GOSPELS AND ACTS.

Ἐπειδήπερ πολλοὶ ἐπεχείρησαν ἀνατάξασθαι διήγησιν περὶ τῶν πεπληροφορημένων ἐν ἡμῖν πραγμάτων, καθὼς παρέδοσαν ἡμῖν οἱ ἀπ' ἀρχῆς αὐτόπται καὶ ὑπηρέται γενόμενοι τοῦ λόγου, ἔδοξε κἀμοὶ παρηκολουθηκότι ἄνωθεν πᾶσιν ἀκριβῶς καθεξῆς σοι γράψαι, κράτιστε Θεόφιλε, ἵνα ἐπιγνῷς περὶ ὧν κατηχήθης λόγων τὴν ἀσφάλειαν.   Luke i. 1-4.

THE earliest Christian teaching, as we have already seen, was oral. It was from the living voice that men first heard the story of Christ. Nor can there be any doubt that this oral teaching would take varying forms according to the varying circumstances that called it forth. Frequently it would be of a very general character, the narrator's own reminiscences told in his own words of his Master's life and teaching. At other times, more particularly in connexion with the practice of catechizing which, following the Jewish model, had early been introduced to prepare converts for admission into the Christian Church, it would be more stereotyped and formal. *Oral teaching.*

The earliest Christian records.

It is obvious, however, that along with this oral instruction, the practice of committing the leading facts of the Christian revelation to writing must have arisen at a very early date. By way of proof we have only to appeal to the Preface or Prologue of St. Luke's Gospel (c. i. 1-4), for without pressing unduly the reference to the 'many' who had already taken in hand to draw up a narrative of the things that had happened, these narratives were obviously numerous, while the word used to describe them ($\delta\iota\eta\gamma\acute{\eta}\sigma\epsilon\iota\varsigma$) covers more than mere 'notes' or 'anecdotes,' and implies something in the nature of ordered accounts.

Their character and object.

Any attempt, however, to reconstruct the exact form of these narratives and the extent of their contents must be largely speculative. This only is certain, that their general character would be determined by the nature of the facts with which they dealt, and the special object they were intended to serve. These facts were matter not so much of literary or historic interest, as of saving power. And what primarily their writers had in view was the enabling of their readers to realize this saving power in its fullest extent.

The 'Gospel' name

Nothing could bring this out better than the new name which was eventually bestowed on the principal survivors of these early records. They were 'gospels,' 'good news,' a designation which in this connexion was practically a coinage of the first Christians, and defined their message as one

PLATE IV.

NEW "SAYINGS OF JESUS."

Papyrus from Oxyrhynchus, belonging to the Third Century A.D. Now in the British Museum. By permission of the Egypt Exploration Fund.

of forgiveness and comfort to a sinful and sorrowing world.[1]

And as the name was thus new, the form was new also. A certain prototype for the Gospels may no doubt be found in the narratives already referred to and in the collections of *Logia*, or Sayings, ascribed to Jesus, which we know to have been in existence at a very early date (see Plate IV.).[2] But at most these only supplied the rough materials which the Evangelists afterwards incorporated in their finished work, and, so far as our present evidence goes, the Gospels stand alone—a product of the Christian Church.[3]

The questions of language and composition, accordingly, that here meet us are principally concerned with the inter-relations of the Gospels

---

[1] For the history of the words εὐαγγέλιον, εὐαγγελίζομαι, see my edition of *St. Paul's Epistles to the Thessalonians*, Additional Note E, p. 141 ff.

[2] According to Professor Flinders Petrie, who draws special attention to the recently discovered *Logia* in this connexion, 'Between the *logia* and a gospel there is a difference like that between a note-book and a treatise' (*The Growth of the Gospels*, London, 1910, p. 3 f.). On the *Logia*, see further Additional Note G, 'The Oxyrhynchus "Sayings of Jesus."'

[3] Norden in emphasizing the newness of the Gospels, regarded simply as literary works, can find no nearer analogy to them than the eight books which in the beginning of the third century Philostratus wrote εἰς τὸν Τυανέα Ἀπολλώνιον, 'In Honour of Apollonius of Tyana,' in which he doubtless incorporated the earlier ἀπομνημονεύματα of Moiragenes (*Die Antike Kunstprosa*[2], Leipzig, 1909, ii. p. 480 f.: cf. Reitzenstein, *Hellenistische Wundererzählungen*, Leipzig, 1906, p. 40 ff.).

amongst themselves, and refer to the sources that lie behind our present Gospels, to the methods their writers followed in the use of these, and to the special characteristics of the individual Evangelists. No one can pretend that these are matters merely of speculative interest. They have obviously a very close bearing on the principles of interpretation that are to be applied to the Gospels, and the extent of the authority that is to be ascribed to them. Only by being satisfied that a writer has sufficient evidence at his disposal for the framing of his narrative are we prepared to lend credence to it, while any disadvantages under which he may have laboured, and to which the errors into which he has fallen are clearly due, so far from detracting from, in reality heighten, our sense of the general trustworthiness of the whole.

I. The Synoptic Gospels. (1) The character and complexity of the Synoptic Problem.

I. (1) We begin with the first three Gospels, and here the very name that is commonly given to them, the Synoptic Gospels—Gospels, that is, whose contents are capable of being viewed together in a tabular form—shows how close is the relation existing amongst them.[1] Of that relation it must be sufficient to recall generally that it consists, on the

---

[1] Apparently the earliest use of the *word* 'Synopsis' in this connexion occurs in the *Synopsis historiae Jes. Christi quemadmodum Matthaeus, Marcus, Lucas, descripsere informa tabulae proposita*, by Georgius Sigelius, Noribergae, 1585 (see Farrar, *The Messages of the Books*, p. 10, n²). But the real beginning of a scientific presentation of the evidence is to be found in J. J. Griesbach, *Synopsis Evangeliorum*, first published in 1774.

one hand, of resemblances of the most marked kind, as shown in their selection to a large extent of the same incidents out of the many other things which Jesus said and did, in their manner of presenting and grouping these incidents, and, notably, in their close and often exact verbal coincidences. And, on the other hand, of differences of the most marked kind in these same particulars.

Neither of these features in itself would have surprised us. Had we found the resemblances alone, we would naturally have thought of their writers as copying from each other, or from some common source. Nor again would there have been anything surprising in three independent narratives emanating from three independent writers showing marked dissimilarities both as to subject-matter and as to form. It is the combination of these qualities, this extraordinary mixture of likeness and of unlikeness, which constitutes what is known as the Synoptic Problem—a problem which has led to so much anxious investigation and to so many and varying solutions.

The very number, indeed, of these proposed solutions has often led to a feeling of despair as to the possibility of discovering *the* solution. At the same time there have been not a few signs in recent years of a marked advance towards this, and critics of all schools are now very generally agreed that the earliest of our present Gospels is St. Mark, and that from his Gospel, probably in a slightly modified form, and another document, largely made up of

The Two-Document Hypothesis.

Sayings and Discourses, which is best described by the non-committal symbol Q from the first letter of the German *Quelle*, or Source, the Gospels of St. Matthew and St. Luke are mainly derived. The name that is commonly given to this theory is the 'Two-Document Hypothesis,' and though taken by itself it cannot account for all the complex features which the Gospels exhibit, it certainly forms a convenient starting-point for all further investigation of them.

<small>The original Mark.</small>

Regarding the reconstruction of the first of these two sources we have the less difficulty, because, as has just been stated, it lies before us substantially in the canonical Gospel of St. Mark. And how closely it was followed by the later Evangelists is shown by the fact that all but at most some 50 of its 661 verses are incorporated in their Gospels.[1]

At the same time the large number of passages that have been collected occurring in all three Evangelists in which St. Matthew and St. Luke, instead of agreeing with their common source St. Mark, rather agree with each other as against him,[2] shows that it cannot have been St. Mark exactly in

---

[1] *Studies in the Synoptic Problem*, by Members of the University of Oxford, edited by W. Sanday, D.D., Oxford, 1911, p. 3. To this volume, referred to in future as *Synoptic Studies*, I desire to express my great indebtedness in all that relates to the Synoptic Problem in the present Lecture.

[2] Abbott, in *The Corrections of Mark adopted by Matthew and Luke* (being *Diatessarica*—Part II.), London, 1901, p. 307 ff., enumerates 230 of these passages.

its present form that they had before them. And this has led to the theory of an *Ur-Marcus* or primitive Mark, known to these Evangelists, out of which the canonical Mark was afterwards developed.[1]

But Dr. Sanday has recently shown that the character of the greater number of these coincidences of St. Matthew and St. Luke as against St. Mark points to a later rather than to an earlier form of text. And consequently he prefers to think not of an *Ur-Marcus*, or older form of the Gospel, but of a recension of the text of the original St. Mark, differing from that from which all the extant manuscripts of the Gospel are descended. This recension was evidently the work of a person of literary tastes who did not hesitate 'to improve the text before him and make it more correct and classical'; and its complete disappearance in a separate form is due to the fact that after St. Matthew and St. Luke came to be written with its help, it itself fell into comparative disuse owing to the greater value attached to the longer Gospels.[2]

---

[1] The designation *Ur-Marcus* is also applied sometimes not to an earlier form of our Second Gospel, but to the earlier sources out of which it was composed. The question of these earlier sources cannot be dealt with here, but for the efforts of various modern scholars such as Loisy, Wendling, and Bacon to disentangle them, see two papers by Professor Menzies in the *Review of Theology and Philosophy*, iv. p. 757 ff., v. p. 1 ff.

[2] *Synoptic Studies*, p. 21 ff. Cf. the brilliant discussion of the literary originality of St. Mark by F. C. Burkitt, *The Gospel History and its Transmission*, Edinburgh, 1906, p. 33 ff.

Reconstruction of Q.

The reconstruction or, as it is sometimes called in mathematical language, the evaluation of our second source is a more difficult matter, seeing that we have no longer an extant document, as was the case with St. Mark, to guide us. But confining ourselves meanwhile to the matter common to St. Matthew and St. Luke, but not found in St. Mark, that may be said for our present purpose to include 191 verses in St. Matthew's Gospel, and 181 verses in St. Luke's Gospel, or rather more than one-sixth of the former, and rather less than one-sixth of the latter.[1]

Included in these verses is a certain amount of narrative-matter, dealing with the preaching of John the Baptist, the Temptation of Jesus, and various incidents in the Public Ministry, such as the Healing of the Centurion's servant, and the Message of John from prison, but in the main, as has been stated, they are made up of a series of Sayings or Discourses—what the Germans call the *Lehrstoff*—of Jesus in their more primitive form.[2]

That the lost source originally contained more than this, it is of course impossible to deny. Why

---

[1] See Hawkins, *Horae Synopticae*[2], Oxford, 1909, p. 110. In *Synoptic Studies* (p. 111), the same writer gives a somewhat longer list of passages by including every exclusively Matthaeo-Lucan parallel, without reference to the probability of their having had a common written origin.

[2] For various attempted reconstructions of Q, see Moffatt, *Introduction to the Literature of the New Testament*, p. 197 ff., and cf. Streeter and Allen in *Synoptic Studies*, pp. 185 ff. and 235 ff.

should not St. Matthew have drawn from it material which suited his purpose in writing, but which fell outside St. Luke's scope, and was therefore discarded by him, or why should not St. Luke, in his turn, have acted in a similar way? Or why again may there not have been in it, that is in Q, material of which neither Evangelist availed himself, perhaps because he had it already before him in some other form? But whatever the answer given to these questions, everything points to this source as having been written at a very early date, if not during the lifetime of our Lord Himself,[1] then at latest within a generation after His death.[2]

Can we go a step further, and identify it with 'the logia' which, as Papias tells us in a well-known passage, 'Matthew composed in the Hebrew (*i.e.* Aramaic) dialect, and each one interpreted them as he was able'?[3] That this description can be applied to our present First Gospel is now generally admitted to be impossible, if only because, as we have seen, it draws its material from two main sources, of which St. Mark was one. But why should not this Papias-document be the other? It is just such

---

[1] W. M. Ramsay, *Luke the Physician*, London 1908, p. 89.

[2] Kirsopp Lake, *The Expositor*, VII. vii. p. 507 : 'It is probably not too much to say that every year after 50 A.D. is increasingly improbable for the production of Q.'

[3] *Apud* Euseb. *Hist. Eccles.* iii. 39. 16 : Ματθαῖος μὲν οὖν Ἑβραΐδι διαλέκτῳ τὰ λόγια συνετάψατο, ἡρμήνευσεν δ' αὐτά ὡς ἦν δυνατὸς ἕκαστος. See further Additional Note H, 'Papias and Irenaeus on the Origin of the Gospels.'

a document as St. Matthew might well have written, and as the genuine work of the Apostle would very readily give its name to the later Gospel, in which a subsequent and unknown editor incorporated it.

Before, however, it can have been so used, it must have been altered in one very important particular by being translated from the original Aramaic into Greek. Otherwise it is impossible to explain the closeness of the verbal parallels which the First Evangelist, whom for convenience I shall continue to describe as St. Matthew, and St. Luke exhibit in their reproduction of it.

Special Lucan source.

While, however, these two sources, a revised St. Mark and a collection of Sayings, probably a genuine Matthew-writing, go far to explain the common contents of our First and Third Gospels, there is still a considerable amount of material peculiar to St. Matthew and to St. Luke, notably in the case of the latter the great Peraean section c. ix. 51–xviii. 14, which remains unaccounted for. And for this last it is common to postulate another source known only to St. Luke, from which he was able to draw in the composition of this part of his Gospel.

The exact extent and character of this 'great insertion' is again uncertain, but we may take it that it was a written document of Palestinian origin, while the nature of the materials it embodies makes it very probable that they had been collected by St. Luke himself during his two years' stay at Caesarea,

LITERARY CHARACTER OF GOSPELS 139

perhaps from Philip the Evangelist.[1] These materials he would then keep by him, and, when he came to write his Gospel, incorporated them in it with little or no change.

Starting then from these three principal documents, a revised St. Mark, Q, and a special Lucan source, and keeping in view that the Evangelists would also have access to other narratives,[2] and would further be influenced frequently by the floating oral tradition of the day, we seem to have before us the main sources on which the Synoptists drew in the preparation of their Gospels.

(2) Of the manner in which they used these sources, something will have to be said directly, but meanwhile it is tempting to ask whether there is anything in the order in which these documents first appeared, which enables us to define more closely the different stages in our Gospels' composition and growth. The inquiry is a delicate one, and the evidence will appeal differently to different minds; but it has recently been made the subject of such an interesting study by Mr. Streeter, that

(2) The literary evolution of the Synoptic Gospels.

---

[1] Cf. Acts xxi. 8 f., and see Bartlet, *Synoptic Studies*, p. 350 ff., where, however, this special Lucan source (described as S) is fused with Q.

[2] Notably the birth-narratives incorporated in Matt. cc. i., ii., and Luke cc. i., ii. The latter chapters are described by Dr. Sanday as probably 'the oldest evangelical fragment or document' of the New Testament, and in any case 'the most archaic thing in the whole volume' (Hastings' *Encyclopaedia of Religion and Ethics*, art. 'Bible,' ii. p. 574).

I cannot do better than try to summarize his conclusions.[1]

First of all, then, according to his view, comes Q, written in Palestine, at a time when the leading facts of our Lord's Life and Passion were well known to all, and many witnesses to His Resurrection were still alive. And when, consequently, all that was required was to supplement this living tradition by recalling the relation of the Lord's teaching to the teaching of the Baptist and of the Pharisees.

It was different, however, a generation later in the Church at Rome. Something fuller was required in which not only the Lord's teaching but the leading events of His history should have a place. And this was supplied by St. Mark's writing down what he had heard in all probability from the lips of St. Peter himself.

The Marcan autograph was not allowed to remain unaltered, but with the literary freedom of the day was subjected to a thorough-going revision, and in its new form became the basis on which St. Matthew and St. Luke, working independently of each other, framed their Gospels, incorporating into it not only what they had learnt from Q, of which St. Mark had made but a sparing use, but also from other sources peculiar to themselves. Their aim was thus much wider than had been the case with any of their predecessors. And the skill with which they combined and arranged their sources, and systema-

[1] *Synoptic Studies*, p. 209 ff.; see also *The Interpreter*, viii. p. 37 ff.

LITERARY CHARACTER OF GOSPELS 141

tized the rough materials they found ready to their hands, proves them to have been practised writers.

In some such way as this then, according to Mr. Streeter, our present Gospels were developed. And however his account may be criticized in certain details, there can be no doubt that it presents us with what Dr. Sanday has described as 'a real evolution, and an evolution conceived as growth, in which each stage springs naturally, spontaneously, and inevitably out of the last.'[1]

(3) To complete our picture we have, however, still to think of the Evangelists actually at work, and of the conditions, external and internal, under which they wrote. And here again Dr. Sanday has given us the benefit of his invaluable guidance in the volume so often referred to.[2]   *(3) The conditions under which the Evangelists wrote,*

Thus, as regards the external conditions, he has shown us that, in using their sources, the Evangelists would not possess the advantage of having all their materials spread out before them in such a way as to make reference to them as easy as possible. On the contrary, as we have already seen, these sources would be contained in rolls placed, according to the general practice of the time, in a canister or box standing by the writer's side. The process of consultation would consequently be lengthy and cumbersome, and rather than be perpetually going through this the writers would on occasion be led to trust to their memories for the wording of a particular saying, or the description of a particular event.   *external*

[1] *Synoptic Studies*, p. xvi.   [2] *Ibid.* p. 3 ff.

and internal. Nor, strange though it may appear to us, would this freedom of reproduction seem at all out of place to the Evangelists themselves. No literary piety such as now exists would hamper them. And they would be satisfied that they had fully discharged their duty to their sources in giving a generally faithful account of the sense, as distinguished from the actual letter of their contents.[1]

In saying this, I am very far from disparaging the historical trustworthiness of the Synoptists. All that I am concerned to bring out is, that in their general methods they would naturally be influenced by the practices of their time, and that only by a frank recognition of this fact, can we hope to explain the selections and omissions, to say nothing of the undoubted inconsistencies and discrepancies which characterize their narratives.

General aim of the Evangelists. Nor is this all, but if we would understand the Gospels rightly, we must never lose sight of the object which their writers had principally in view. That object, as has been already noted, was largely homiletic. The Evangelists were not mere scribes, painfully copying out a story that seemed to them of first importance, in order to secure its transmission

---

[1] Cf. Salmon, *The Human Element in the Gospels*, London, 1907, p. 5 : 'Can we reasonably expect that any writer of the first century should work exactly in the same way as a historian of the nineteenth ? that he should observe the scrupulous care which we now feel ourselves entitled to demand in not going in the slightest degree beyond what he had good authority for stating, and in not, without warning, mixing up inferences of his own with what he had learnt from other well-informed persons ?'

to future ages. They were rather preachers, writing with a direct eye upon the moral and spiritual growth of their readers, and hence led to tell their story in such a way as best to secure that end. That, notwithstanding all that was against them, their narratives have survived throughout the centuries and are held in higher honour to-day than when they were first written, is in itself convincing proof that the Evangelists have succeeded in their effort.[1]

(4) All this is confirmed, when we pass to consider the three Synoptists separately.

(*a*) To St. Mark belongs the honour of being the earliest of our Evangelists. And though he did not invent the gospel-form—that was rather, as we have

(4) Certain characteristics of the individual Gospels.

(a) St. Mark. Language and style.

---

[1] In a striking passage in which Professor Mahaffy contrasts the Gospel books with the other literature of their time the following sentences occur: 'The simplicity, the natural vigour, the unconscious picturesqueness in these narratives are so remarkable that, even had they never laid any claim to inspiration, sound judges must have condoned their faulty grammar and poor vocabulary, and acknowledged in them at least the voice of honest men speaking from the heart, and thus endowed with one of the highest literary qualities.... What was more obvious, what more certain, than that such pictures as the opening scenes of St. Luke's Gospel or the Sermon on the Mount would be described by the critics as the work of late-learning and self-taught people, who knew nothing of the art of expression or of the laws of composition? And yet the world has judged differently... the metaphors on the mount, the parables by the way, have outlived the paradoxes of the Stoic, the rhetoric of the schools' (*The Silver Age of the Greek World*, Chicago and London, 1906, p. 442 f.).

seen, the result of the facts of the case—he gave it a certain fixity which led to its adoption and perpetuation by the later Evangelists. His Greek is that of a man who had learned it as a foreigner, and from intercourse with men of the people rather than with literary circles, while his style, though as a rule of the simplest, is both graphic and forcible.[1]

There are signs, more particularly in the earlier portion of the Gospel, of a desire to abbreviate and compress,[2] but along with this he does not hesitate on occasions to heap up and elaborate details, when he finds them necessary for the more vivid portrayal of his theme. And—though this has been questioned—he appears on the whole to aim at presenting his facts in the order in which they actually occurred.

Relation to St. Peter

At the same time it should be noted that St. Mark's Gospel is not an ordered biography or history in the strict sense of either term, but rather a collection of notes of what, in accordance with the well-known Papias-tradition, the Evangelist had learned when he had once acted as a teacher or catechist

[1] In the first edition of his *Einleitung in die drei ersten Evangelien*, Berlin, 1905, p. 9, Wellhausen says: 'In the Gospels spoken Greek, and such Greek as was spoken by the people, makes its entry into literature.'

[2] Keim (*Jesus of Nazara*, Eng. Tr. i. p. 117 n[2]) thinks that the epithet applied to St. Mark in the third century, ὁ κολοβοδάκτυλος (Hippolytus, *Philos.* vii. 30), 'the stump-fingered,' was due to a desire on the part of the philosophers to ridicule the shortness of his Gospel, but it arose much more probably from some natural defect of St. Mark himself.

under the Apostle Peter.¹ In that case the Gospel was in all probability written at Rome, and we have a natural explanation of the relatively large number of Latin words and forms of speech which it contains.

In addition, moreover, to these Petrine reminis- *and to Q.* cences, there can be no doubt that St. Mark had access to various other sources of information both oral and written, amongst which many modern critics include Q. The point may be said to be still *sub judice*, but in any case the use of Q would seem to have been slight, and rather in the way of occasional reminiscence than of deliberate dependence.²

Reference will be made later to the lost ending of *The apocalypse of* St. Mark's Gospel (see p. 182), but it may be well to *c. xiii.* notice here the question of structure raised by the apocalyptic discourse in c. xiii. In this long discourse—it runs to thirty-seven verses—it has often

---

[1] Cf. Euseb. *Hist. Eccles.* iii. 39. 15: Μᾶρκος μὲν ἑρμηνευτὴς Πέτρου γενόμενος, ὅσα ἐμνημόνευσεν, ἀκριβῶς ἔγραψεν, οὐ μέντοι τάξει τὰ ὑπὸ τοῦ κυρίου ἢ λεχθέντα ἢ πραχθέντα, and *ibid.* vi. 14. 6 f. According to the tradition preserved in the latter passage, when Peter heard of Mark's attempt, ' he neither directly forbade nor encouraged it'—a significant sign of the comparatively little importance then attaching to written documents as compared with the living voice for the purposes of Christian instruction.

[2] Cf. Streeter, *Synoptic Studies*, p. 166 ff., and Sanday, *ibid.* p. xvi f. Both Moffatt, *Introduction to the Literature of the New Testament*, p. 204 ff., and Buckley, *Introduction to the Synoptic Problem*, London, 1912, p. 140 f., decide against the Marcan use of Q, if by Q we understand the source from which St. Matthew and St. Luke drew their common non-Marcan material.

been noted that certain verses which refer more particularly to the circumstances immediately preceding the Fall of Jerusalem (vv. 7-9ª, 14-20, 24-27, 30, 31) can be detached from the intervening exhortations which are of a more general character. And in these circumstances it is a not unreasonable conjecture that the discourse as we have it now is composite and that the writer incorporated with the teaching proper of the Lord a 'little Apocalypse' of Jewish or Jewish-Christian origin, which seemed to him to embody a true tradition. In doing so, he would only be following (what we have already seen to be) a common practice in connexion with all apocalyptic writing.[1] At the same time it must be distinctly recognized that all this is only a hypothesis, and a hypothesis which can never be proved. Because the verses spoken of are detachable, it does not therefore follow that they ought to be detached. They may from the beginning have formed part of the Lord's discourse, and, if so, are the clearest evidence we possess of the extent to which He availed himself of current Jewish imagery in His eschatological teaching.[2]

(*b*) St. Matthew. Hebraic tone and form.

(*b*) As regards St. Matthew's Gospel, we have already seen (cf. p. 137 f.) that it is probably so named, not because in its present form it is the direct work of the Apostle Matthew, but because it embodies in a Greek dress certain Aramaic *logia* or discourses

---

[1] Cf. p. 122, and for the history of the 'little Apocalypse' theory, see Moffatt, *Introduction*, p. 207 ff.

[2] Cf. Sanday, in the *Hibbert Journal*, x. p. 94.

LITERARY CHARACTER OF GOSPELS 147

of the Lord which he had collected. In any case, there can be no doubt as to the Gospel's generally Hebraic character. And no description suits its editor better than that of the householder who 'brings forth out of his treasure things new and old' (c. xiii. 52), so eager is he to connect the new with the old, and to show how in the new old truths have reached their complete and final fulfilment.[1] Hence we are not surprised to find that the Gospel, which is so Hebraic in tone, is also Hebraic in form, and is largely constructed on lines with which Jewish literature makes us familiar.

Very noticeable in this connexion is the manner in which the First Evangelist arranges and systematizes matter that was originally separate. Familiar examples are afforded by the different discourses which he brings together in the Sermon on the Mount (cc. v.-vii.), by the survey of Christ's ministry based on a series of His sayings in c. xi., and by the combination of the parables of the Kingdom in c. xiii. But the principle may be traced still further. An analysis of the Gospel as a whole brings out that just as there are five books of Moses, and five books of the Psalms, so here the editor has divided his material into five great blocks or sections, marked off from each other by the five times repeated

Grouping of materials.

---

[1] This is illustrated by the facts that St. Matthew has more direct quotations from the Old Testament than the other Synoptists combined (Mt. 40, Mk. 19, Lk. 17), and that eighteen of his quotations are peculiar to his Gospel: see Swete, *Introduction to the Old Testament in Greek* (Cambridge, 1900), p. 391.

formula about Jesus 'ending' His sayings (cc. vii. 28, xi. 1, xiii. 53, xix. 1, xxvi. 1). Nor does his love of methodical arrangement stop here, but the contents of these blocks frequently fall into numerical groups of three, seven, and ten, as in the case of the three external duties of alms, prayer, and fasting in c. vi. 1-18, the seven woes of c. xxiii., and the ten miracles of cc. viii., ix.

At first sight to us there may seem something very artificial in all this, but it is in thorough accord with the Hebraic mode of thought, which delighted in such conventional and parallelistic arrangements, and may well, as Sir John Hawkins has suggested, have been especially designed to assist the memories of Jewish-Christian catechists and catechumens.[1]

General character.

The general result, no doubt, is a more calm and balanced, if more prosaic and colourless style than we find in St. Mark. The subsidiary but often picturesque details, which lend so much of its living interest to the earlier Marcan narrative, are frequently omitted or curtailed. And not a few of the roughnesses of St. Mark's Greek are toned down or done away. On the other hand, in the case of the discourses of the Lord, the Hebraic cast of St. Matthew's mind would help him to preserve the style and feeling of the original better than the Hellenistic Luke, so that while the latter's Gospel, owing to its character and contents, has been fittingly described as 'the most beautiful book we possess,' there is good reason for seeing with the

[1] *Horae Synopticae*², p. 163.

LITERARY CHARACTER OF GOSPELS 149

same authority in the Gospel of St. Matthew, 'the most important book of Christianity, the most important book that has ever been written.'[1]

(c) Renan's description of St. Luke's Gospel just cited prepares us for the literary and artistic skill of the Third Evangelist. The only Greek by birth amongst the New Testament writers, St. Luke exhibits constant proof of his Greek origin in the substitution of more cultured terms for the colloquialisms of the other Synoptists,[2] while his treatment of Q is marked by various stylistic alterations.[3] And though the Lucan style as a whole is marked by a general uniformity, which in itself affords convincing proof of the unity of authorship of the Third Gospel and Acts, it is interesting to notice that in a number of passages the phraseology seems to be purposely varied for no other reason than that of imparting a certain literary elegance to the narrative.[4]

(c) St. Luke. Language and style.

---

[1] Renan, *Les Évangiles*, Paris, 1877, pp. 283, 212 f. In keeping with this is the fact that in the varying orders in which the Gospels are arranged by early authorities, St. Matthew's Gospel is almost invariably placed first: cf. p. 294 f.

[2] On such a point a classical scholar like Norden is a particularly good witness: see the instructive discussion in his *Antike Kunstprosa*[2], ii. p. 485 ff.

[3] Cf. Harnack, *The Sayings of Jesus*, Eng. Tr. by Wilkinson, London, 1908, p. 1 ff.; and see Moulton in *The Expositor*, VII. vii. p. 411 ff., on the danger of pressing the evidence in this direction too far.

[4] Cf. J. H. Ropes, *Harvard Studies in Classical Philology*, xii. (1901), p. 301, where examples are quoted from the same context

A like adherence to literary convention leads St. Luke to introduce his Gospel with a Preface, which has the further interest that it exhibits certain parallels with similar passages in medical treatises, and so helps to confirm the tradition that in early life he was a physician, and as such may in the first instance have attached himself to St. Paul (cf. Col. iv. 14).[1]

Selection of materials.

More important in connexion with the general character of the Lucan narrative is the skill with which its writer has selected and arranged his varied materials, and while preserving their several characteristics has still succeeded in imparting a sense of unity to the whole. The Preface which is St. Luke's own composition may be modelled on more classical lines than the rest of the Gospel; the first two chapters resting as they do on early Palestinian sources may exhibit a more Aramaic colouring than the passages derived from the Greek Gospel of St. Mark; and the dialogues may preserve their original popular features even in the

as c. xx. 29, ἀπέθανεν ἄτεκνος, and 31, οὐ κατέλιπον τέκνα καὶ ἀπέθανον, and from different contexts as cc. i. 8, κατὰ τὸ ἔθος, ii. 27, κατὰ τὸ εἰθισμένον τοῦ νόμου, and iv. 16, κατὰ τὸ εἰωθός (c. dat.).

[1] Hippocrates (B.C. 460-357) begins his treatise Περὶ ἀρχαίης ἰατρικῆς, ὁκόσοι ἐπεχείρησαν περὶ ἰητρικῆς λέγειν ἢ γράφειν, while at a later date Galen (A.D. 130-200) dedicates one of his works to Piso in the terms, καὶ τοῦτον σοι τὸν περὶ τῆς θηριακῆς λόγον, ἀκριβῶς ἐξετάσας ἅπαντα, ἄριστε Πίσων σπουδαίως ἐποίησα. On the whole subject of St. Luke's medical knowledge, see further Hobart's Essay already referred to, p. 56 n[1].

editor's Hellenistic setting: but the whole forms an harmonious picture, in which the Evangelist, whom early tradition associates not only with science but with art,[1] has depicted for all time that particular aspect of the Lord which appealed most to himself, and seemed most likely to attract the allegiance of others.

For beyond either of the other Synoptists, St. Luke writes with a definite aim in view. To him Jesus is above all else the Saviour, the Healer of soul and body, not for the Jews only, but for the world. And the form which his Gospel takes down to the minutest particulars is determined by the effort to keep this conception of the Lord constantly before the minds of his readers. Let me take two illustrations, one from the Gospel's opening, the other from its close. *[Object of the Gospel as reflected in the]*

Thus, while generally faithful to the historical sequence of events in accordance with his own expressed resolve to write 'in order' ($\kappa\alpha\theta\epsilon\xi\hat{\eta}s$, c. i. 3), St. Luke does not hesitate to place in the very forefront of his Gospel a scene belonging to a later date, the appearance of Jesus in the Synagogue at Nazareth, apparently because, with its announcement of a Gospel to the poor and a present Deliverer to the oppressed, it seems to him to strike the keynote of the whole of Christ's ministry (c. iv. 16-30). *frontispiece*

---

[1] Plummer, *The Gospel according to St. Luke* (in the *International Critical Commentary*), Edinburgh, 1896, p. xxi f., carries the legend that St. Luke was originally a painter as far back as the sixth century.

and narrative of the Passion.

While, at the other end of the story, in his narrative of the Passion, St. Luke shows so many variations from St. Mark's order of events, as compared with St. Matthew who adheres to it closely, that recourse has been had to the theory that he here follows a different non-Marcan source. Professor Burkitt has suggested that this source may have been a fragment of Q; and if so we are met with the interesting fact that the original Q contained not only discourses but also an account of the Passion.[1] But there is not a little to be said for another view that has recently found favour in various quarters, namely, that in this all-important section of his work St. Luke was largely influenced by memories of the public teaching of St. Paul.[2] As St. Paul's friend and fellow-worker in his later years, St. Luke must have become thoroughly familiar with the Pauline method of depicting 'Christ crucified.' What more natural than that when he came to narrate in his Gospel the same stupendous fact, he should do so in the manner of his great 'illuminator'![3]

General unity of the Synoptists.

It is impossible to carry our discussion of the Synoptic writers further, but before leaving them, let me say that from whatever point of view we regard them, whether we think of their sameness in diversity, or of their diversity in sameness, the

---

[1] *The Gospel History and its Transmission*, p. 134 f.

[2] Cf. Hawkins, *Synoptic Studies*, p. 76 ff.; Moulton, *The Expositor*, VIII. ii. p. 16 ff.

[3] Tertullian, *adv. Marc.* iv. 2.

general impression which their Gospels leave upon our minds is that of an harmonious whole, especially in so far as relates to their Central Figure. 'Verse after verse, Saying after saying,' and here I gladly avail myself of the words of so independent a critic as Professor Burkitt, 'might be quoted to you from the three Synoptic Gospels, and, unless you happened to have special knowledge or had given special attention to such matters, you would be unable to say to which Gospel they really belonged. Morally, ethically, spiritually, they are all on the same plane. We cannot doubt that the common impression which they present of the way in which our Lord spoke, the style of His utterance, the manner of His discourse to rich and poor, to learned and unlearned, is based on true historical reminiscence.'[1]

II. In passing to the Fourth Gospel, we are met with a problem which has been truly described as 'still the most unsettled, the most living, the most sensitive in all the field of Introduction.'[2] And in the present divided attitude of critics, he would be a bold man who would venture to offer a decided opinion upon many of the questions that have been raised.[3] No such attempt at anyrate will be made

II. The Fourth Gospel.

[1] *The Gospel History and its Transmission*, p. 216 f.

[2] B. W. Bacon, *An Introduction to the New Testament*, New York and London, 1900, p. 252.

[3] Useful statements regarding many of these will be found in H. L. Jackson, *The Fourth Gospel and some recent German Criticism*, Cambridge, 1906, and A. V. Green, *The Ephesian Canonical Writings*, London, 1910.

here, and I shall content myself with drawing your attention to one or two points regarding the Fourth Gospel as a whole, which must be reckoned with in all discussions on its origin and composition.

Its style. Before however passing to those, it is right to notice the new light which recent research claims to throw on the style of the Fourth Evangelist. That style, as is well known, is marked by an extreme simplicity as regards both the vocabulary and the form and combination of the sentences. The same words are used again and again, and the different clauses are co-ordinated, instead of being sub-ordinated, by means of the most direct of all connecting particles καί, 'and.' This has usually been put down to Semitism: and it cannot be denied that it does remind us very forcibly of the methods of Hebraic construction. At the same time it is interesting to notice that Deissmann has been able to produce examples of similar paratactic sentences from sources where no Semitic influence can be predicated.[1] The most striking of these, perhaps, is a curious parallel to the account of the healing of the blind man in John ix. 11, inscribed on a marble tablet some time after A.D. 138, probably at the temple of Asclepius in Rome. After recounting the making of the eye-salve, and the anointing of the eyes of the sufferer, the inscription concludes: 'And he received his sight, and came and gave thanks publicly to the god.'[2]

---

[1] Deissmann, *Light from the Ancient East*, p. 129 ff.
[2] Cited from Dittenberger, *Sylloge Inscriptionum Graecarum*[2],

LITERARY CHARACTER OF GOSPELS

And in the same connexion the Berlin Professor draws attention to the resemblance between St. John's solemn use of the first personal pronoun in our Lord's discourses, where as a rule it draws emphatic attention to the nature and personality of the Speaker, and the sacral use of the same pronoun in certain statements of non-Christian deities regarding themselves: as when Isis is represented as saying: 'I am Isis, the mistress of every land. . . . I divided the earth from the heaven. I showed the paths of the stars. I ordered the course of the sun and moon. I devised business in the sea. I made strong the right. . . .'[1]

Many will doubtless feel that even in the matter of style—and it is with it alone that we are at present concerned—these comparisons do not carry us very far; but they at least show how easy it must have been 'for Hellenistic Judaism and Christianity to adopt the remarkable and simple style of expression in the first person singular.'[2]

But not to dwell on this, let us turn to the more general considerations to which I have referred.

Certain general considerations.

(1) The first of these is concerned with its author's attitude towards the Synoptic Evangelists.

(1) Its relation to the Synoptic Gospels.

It is customary to represent this simply as a relation of contrast, and it is certain that he differs

Leipzig, 1900, No. 807[17 f.]: καὶ ἀνέβλεψεν καὶ ἐλήλυθεν καὶ ηὐχαρίστησεν δημοσίᾳ τῷ θεῷ.

[1] From an inscription at Ios written in the second or third century of the Christian era, but with pre-Christian contents.

[2] Deissmann, *ut supra*, p. 138.

widely from them in the impression which he conveys as to the scene and the form of the Lord's ministry. On the other hand, it must be kept in view that his general aim and intention are the same as theirs. His too is a 'gospel,' a message of glad tidings for a sinful world in the revelation of the Word made flesh. And if the earliest of the Evangelists heads his work : 'The beginning of the gospel of Jesus Christ [the Son of God]' (Mark i. 1), the last is careful to announce as his story draws to a close : 'These things are written, that you may believe that Jesus is the Christ, the Son of God; and that believing you may have life in His name' (John xx. 31).

Its own intrinsic character.

This is of course very far from denying that what we may call the interpretative element, to which these last words bear witness, has not a prominence in the Fourth Gospel, to which the Synoptists offer little or no analogy. While they are content for the most part with a bare chronicle of events, leaving them to work their own effect, the Fourth Evangelist deliberately sets himself to indicate the meaning and bearing of his facts, with the result that his Gospel is a study, rather than in the strict sense of the word a history, of the life of Christ.[1]

---

[1] The same distinction underlies Clement of Alexandria's well-known contrast between the 'spiritual' and the 'bodily' Gospels (*apud* Euseb. *Hist. Eccles.* vi. 14. 7). Cf. most recently Streeter, *Foundations*, London, 1912, p. 83, where the Gospel is regarded as primarily 'an *inspired meditation* on the life of Christ,' with due emphasis on the word 'inspired as well as on the word 'meditation.'

LITERARY CHARACTER OF GOSPELS

So prominent indeed is this feature, that it has led in certain quarters to the view that the Gospel is nothing but a thorough-going allegory, in which its writer deliberately invented situations and composed speeches in order to bring home to men's minds more fully the ideal conception of the Christ that had taken possession of him. But what then are we to make of his constant appeals to 'witness,' which is sometimes described as eye-witness (i. 15, 32, iii. 11, xix. 35, xxi. 24, cf. v. 36, x. 25), to say nothing of the impossibility of finding any one able to conceive and carry through successfully a portraiture so harmonious, so self-revealing down to its minutest particulars, so raised above the ordinary conceptions and ideals of the day?

Only as springing from and growing out of the soil of historic fact, does the Johannine conception of the Christ become for a moment possible, judged even from a human standpoint. While, as further evidence of its writer's historicity, it is of interest to notice that in certain particulars where he differs from the Synoptists, as in the case of the date of the Last Supper and the Crucifixion, it is apparently they who require to be corrected by him, and not he by them.

(2) This alone should prepare us for the further fact that the Fourth Gospel as a whole is stamped with a sense of unity, that we do not find in its predecessors. The Synoptic Gospels, as we have just been seeing, were largely compilations from existing materials, and their writers appear accordingly

(2) Its unity.

as skilful editors rather than as original authors. But the Fourth Gospel is dominated throughout by a great personality, who has so meditated on the facts and truths he announces that they have, as it were, been recast in his own experience, and bear traces everywhere of his genius.

Attempts indeed have been made in increasing numbers in recent years to break up the homogeneity of the Fourth Gospel by means of elaborate theories of partition and revision. But without entering into a detailed examination of these,[1] it may fairly be asked whether, even if the evidence were stronger than it is, it would warrant the conclusions that are based upon it. There are few, if any books, however certainly the work of one man, which could bear the test of such microscopic scrutiny as has been applied to the Fourth Gospel. And the 'solid and compact unity' which, as a whole, its contents exhibit, may well lead us to exhaust all other means of explaining its so-called tautologies and incoherences before consenting to rend 'the seamless coat' in which its author has clothed it.[2]

(3) Its authorship.

(3) It is a wholly different question, who this author really was. And it would be altogether

---

[1] Cf. the full statement in Moffatt, *Introduction to the Literature of the New Testament*, p. 551 ff., and for the value and defects of such criticism see A. E. Brooke, *Cambridge Biblical Essays*, p. 322 ff.

[2] Cf. Strauss, *Gesammelte Schriften*, 1877, vii. p. 556: 'This Gospel is itself the seamless coat of which it tells, and though men may cast lots for it, they cannot rend it.'

LITERARY CHARACTER OF GOSPELS 159

beyond our present scope to discuss the arguments, strong and weighty, that can be brought forward in support of the traditional view that he is to be identified with John, the son of Zebedee, or the arguments, not lightly to be set aside, that have led many modern scholars to think of some other John altogether.[1]

This only let me say, as bearing upon the literary character of the book, that many of the difficulties that have been raised against ascribing it to the Palestinian John, in view of the purity of its Greek, and the general form in which it is cast, may be lightened, if we can think of St. John as receiving assistance in the work of transcription and composition.

Nor are we left here wholly to conjecture. In the oldest account we possess of the collection of our New Testament writings into their present form—the Canon Muratori (*c.* A.D. 200)—after mention of the Gospel of St. Luke, we have the following interesting account of the origin of St. John's Gospel:

'The fourth of the Gospels [was written by] John, one of the disciples. When exhorted by

---

[1] The latter arguments have in recent years been reinforced by the stress laid on the statement attributed to Papias that John, the son of Zebedee, instead of dying peacefully at Ephesus at an advanced age, as the tradition of his authorship of the Fourth Gospel requires, in reality suffered martyrdom at the hands of the Jews along with his brother James; but see Dean Armitage Robinson, *The Historical Character of St. John's Gospel*, London, 1908, p. 64 ff., on the insufficiency of the evidence for this statement.

his fellow-disciples and bishops, he said, "Fast with me this day for three days; and what may be revealed to any of us, let us relate it to one another." The same night it was revealed to Andrew, one of the apostles, that John was to write all things in his own name, and they were all to certify (*recogniscentibus cuntis*).'[1]

And recently Professor Burkitt has drawn attention to a somewhat similar statement in the curious Prologue of the Codex Toletanus, a tenth-century manuscript of the Vulgate, now at Madrid. After stating that St. John wrote last of all and at the request of the bishops of Asia Minor, the Prologue goes on to say:

'This Gospel therefore it is manifest was written after the Apocalypse, and was given to the churches in Asia by John while he was yet in the body, as one Papias by name, bishop of Hierapolis, a disciple of John and dear to him, in his *Exoterica*, *i.e.* in the end of the Five Books, related, he who wrote his Gospel at John's dictation (*Iohanne subdictante*).'[2]

Too much stress must not of course be attached to statements such as these, or to the legend that finds expression in so many of the mediaeval manuscripts

---

[1] The passage is reproduced in the facsimile page of the Codex Muratori, Plate XI. Cf. also p. 286 ff.

[2] *Two Lectures on the Gospels*, London, 1901, p. 68 ff. The Latin text will be found, *ibid.*, p. 90 f., or in Wordsworth and White, *Nouum Testamentum Latine*, i. p. 490.

PLATE V.

ST. JOHN DICTATING TO PROCHORUS.

Brit. Mus. Add. MS. 22739.   Fourteenth Century.   By permission of the Museum Authorities.

To face p. 161.

LITERARY CHARACTER OF GOSPELS

of the Gospels that one Prochorus acted as a scribe to St. John (see Plate V.). At the same time it is difficult to understand how they could have arisen at all, unless they had a certain foundation in fact. And though I am quite ready to admit that this dictation-theory may seem a somewhat lame and unsatisfactory conclusion at which to arrive on a question which naturally arouses such keenness of feeling, it has at least the merit of offering a natural explanation of the more Hellenic or Hellenistic side of the Fourth Gospel, while leaving practically undisturbed the real authorship of a book which in its delineation of 'the heart of Jesus' comes so naturally from the disciple 'whom Jesus loved' (John xxi. 7).

III. The only book of the New Testament which remains unnoticed is the Acts of the Apostles. And our consideration of it is much simplified by the growing consensus on the part of critics that, like the Third Gospel, it is the genuine work of St. Luke. Of that Gospel, according to the writer's own statement, it is the direct sequel, in which, starting from the close of the earthly ministry, he traces the history of the Glorified Redeemer still at work in His Church, and through His Spirit leading it ever onward on its triumphal and world-wide progress.[1]

III. The Acts of the Apostles. Relation to the Third Gospel.

---

[1] From this general point of view the Book of Acts had no successor till the great *Historia Ecclesiastica* of Eusebius in the fourth century, though, as the 'Acts' of individual Apostles, it quickly found many imitators. These last can be conveniently

The writer's sources.

From the somewhat abrupt way in which the narrative breaks off with the account of St. Paul's imprisonment, it has been thought that the writer contemplated a third book or volume, in which the remaining events of St. Paul's life and his final martyrdom would be recounted.[1] But, whether this was so or not, the plan of St. Paul's narrative—in the form in which we have it—is so comprehensive that it must have taxed his utmost skill as a writer. Dealing as he does with the history of the Apostolic Church during the most critical period of its history, and referring constantly to events of which he himself cannot possibly have had any personal knowledge, St. Luke would find himself obliged to depend on many and varying sources of information. That he would learn much from oral testimony may be taken for granted, but there can be no doubt that he would also be thrown back, as in the case of his Gospel, upon written documents. And without attempting to limit the number of these, or to define the numerous theories of construction to which they have given rise, we may take it that there were two

---

read in Bernard Pick's volume, *The Apocryphal Acts of Paul, Peter, John, Andrew and Thomas*, Chicago, 1909. For fragments of the original Greek text of the Acts of Peter and of John that have been discovered in Egypt, see *The Oxyrhynchus Papyri*, edd. Grenfell-Hunt, vi. p. 6 ff. Nos. 849 and 850.

[1] W. M. Ramsay, *St. Paul the Traveller and the Roman Citizen*[3], London, 1897, pp. 23, 309. On the little stress that can be laid on πρῶτον (not πρότερον) λόγον in this connexion, see Moulton, *Prolegomena*[3], p. 79.

LITERARY CHARACTER OF ACTS

which largely affected the general character of his work.[1]

Thus in the earlier, the more Jewish, section of his narrative, St. Luke would seem to have drawn from an Aramaic source, more particularly with reference to certain episodes in which St. Peter played the leading part. And in these circumstances there is not a little to be said for Blass's idea that this source may be ascribed to John Mark who wrote it as a sequel to his Gospel, in order to describe the first actions of the Risen Christ, and what the same Christ did afterwards by means of His Apostles.[2] But at best this is a conjecture, and we are safer to content ourselves with thinking generally of a Jewish-Christian document, dealing with the growth of the Church at Jerusalem. *A Jewish-Christian source.*

With regard to the second, the more Hellenic, half of the Acts, we can go further. Imbedded in it are certain paragraphs which, from the fact that the writer changes suddenly in them to the use of the first person plural, have come to be known as the 'We Sections.' All are occupied with the journeyings of St. Paul (cc. xvi. 10-17, xx. 5-15, xxi. 1-18, xxvii. 1–xxviii. 16) and are most readily explained *The Travel-Diary.*

---

[1] On the source-criticism of Acts, see again Moffatt, *Introduction to the Literature of the New Testament*, p. 286 ff.

[2] *Philology of the Gospels*, London, 1898, pp. 141 f., 193. Harnack, while opposed generally to the idea of written sources underlying the first half of Acts, is willing to admit the use of an Aramaic source in the Petrine episodes, translated by St. Luke himself (*Luke the Physician*, p. 116 ff.).

as extracts from a travel-diary kept by one of his companions. Timothy, Silas, and Titus have all been proposed as possible authors of this diary. But much greater probability attaches to the belief that we have here notes made by St. Luke himself in the course of his wanderings with St. Paul, which he was able afterwards to utilize when he came to write the connected narrative of Acts.[1] In this way not only are the remarkable similarities of vocabulary and style between these sections and the rest of the book fully accounted for,[2] but we can also understand how the use of the first person was allowed to remain in them unchanged. Had St. Luke borrowed the sections from another, it is almost inconceivable that a writer of his care should not have changed the first person into the third in order to lend smoothness and unity to his narrative. Whereas, if he were only using his own words over again, he might very well retain the first person in order to make perfectly clear that he was actually present in person at the scenes described.[3]

[1] As a partial parallel, we may compare the manner in which Philostratus utilized the travel-notes of Apollonius's companion Damis in his book *In Honour of Apollonius of Tyana* (Eng. Tr. by Phillimore, i. p. 6).

[2] Cf. Hawkins, *Horae Synopticae*[2], p. 182 ff.; Harnack, *Luke the Physician*, pp. 67 ff., 81 ff.

[3] Cf. Peake, *A Critical Introduction to the New Testament*, p. 126. For an ancient travel-narrative, told in the first person plural, Deissmann (*St. Paul*, p. 25 n[2]) compares the account by King Ptolemy Euergetes I. of his voyage to Cilicia and Syria in the *Flinders Petrie Papyri*, edd. Mahaffy-Smyly, II. No. 45 and III. No. 144.

LITERARY CHARACTER OF ACTS

From these then, and doubtless other sources, St. Luke drew in the composition of his book. And the skill with which he has blended his varied materials into an harmonious whole is again a striking proof of his literary powers. But this is not all. These powers are still more convincingly displayed in the manner in which he varies his style 'in obedience to the feeling of the moment and the changes of scene.' No one has brought this out more clearly than Sir W. M. Ramsay, as he contrasts 'the intensity of the Hebraistic tinge' that marks St. Luke's style in dealing with the history of the Church in its Jerusalem days with 'the sweep and rush' of the later narrative, as it follows Paul's fortunes from point to point, from country to country.[1]

St. Luke's literary skil

The same qualities may be seen in St. Luke's treatment of the speeches which he records. The materials for these would probably be drawn principally from oral tradition, and they would necessarily require to be recast to a considerable extent by their editor. And here again we are struck with the artistic way in which, in each case, 'the special aim and character of the original speech' is retained. The narrator's fine dramatic sense enables him to throw himself, as it were, into the position of the

[1] *Luke the Physician*, pp. 50, 48: cf. Harnack, *The Acts of the Apostles*, p. xxxvii: 'Very gradually he [Luke] passes over to a freer and at the same time more classical type of narrative. The style becomes, so to say, more profane, and even thereby more cosmopolitan, yet without detracting from the dignity of the narrative.'

successive speakers in such a way that he is able to reproduce not only the substance of what they said, but their manner of saying it.[1]

and historical accuracy.

From other points of view the Book of Acts has been subjected to the closest scrutiny, and the general result of recent archaeological discovery has been to confirm its historical accuracy to a remarkable extent.[2] That occasional flaws and inconsistencies should be discovered in it is only what we should expect when we remember the circumstances under which it was written: the real wonder is that they should be few. And even they might have disappeared if we could accept the suggestion that the work never received the final revision which St. Luke intended to give it.[3]

The double-texts of Acts.

In any case, it is a curious fact that the Book of Acts should have come down to us in two distinct

---

[1] Professor Percy Gardner, while attributing to St. Luke very considerable freedom in his reports of the Pauline speeches, adds that 'by being what he is, and working according to the dictates of his own genius, Luke has probably succeeded better in portraying for us the manner of Paul's speech than if he had striven for a realism which is unknown in ancient art, whether plastic or literary' (*Cambridge Biblical Essays*, p. 416).

[2] The importance of Sir W. M. Ramsay's work in this direction is familiar to all. Reference may also be made to an article by Bishop Lightfoot published so far back as May, 1878, in *The Contemporary Review*, entitled, 'Discoveries illustrating the Acts of the Apostles.' It has since been reprinted in *Essays on Supernatural Religion*, p. 291 ff. See also Vigoroux, *Le Nouveau Testament et les Decouvertes Archéologiques modernes*[2] (Paris, 1896), p. 195 ff.

[3] Ramsay, *Luke the Physician*, p. 24.

forms of text, one, the ordinarily received text, the other, a so-called 'Western' recension. The exact relation of these two forms of text is still a matter of eager discussion amongst critics. Blass would have it that the 'Western' text follows more closely the first draft of St. Luke's work, which he afterwards re-issued in the form known to us, while others reverse this order, and maintain that it is the 'Western' which is really secondary.[1] But the very fact that such divergent recensions were current within a short period of the book's composition may be taken as but one proof out of many of the uncertainties which from the first attended the publication of our New Testament documents, and of the difficulties we still encounter in the attempt to get back to the *ipsissima verba* of their original writers.

So far, however, from these difficulties in connexion either with this, or any New Testament book, being a source of discouragement to us, they are rather the divinely appointed means for urging us on to ever-increased efforts that we may 'learn the certainty' of the things wherein we have been instructed.[2]

General conclusion.

---

[1] See the full discussion in Knowling's Introduction to his Commentary on the Acts of the Apostles in the *Expositor's Greek Testament*, ii. p. 41 ff., where attention is drawn to the fact that Bishop Lightfoot had already conjectured that St. Luke himself might have issued two separate editions of both Gospel and Acts (*On a Fresh Revision of the New Testament*[3], London, 1891, p. 32).

[2] See Lake, *The Earlier Epistles of St. Paul*, p. 48 ff., for the removal of the difficulties attending the Apostolic Decree of Acts xv. 28, by the adoption of the 'Western' reading, in so far as it omits all reference to 'things strangled,' and independently to the

While, as regards 'the power of the Spirit of Jesus in the Apostles manifested in history,' which it is the aim of the whole book to illustrate,[1] it is enough to recall the triumphant passage in which Clement of Alexandria re-echoes its closing word: 'As for our teaching, from its first proclamation kings and despots and rulers in divers countries, and governors with all their armies—yea, with men innumerable, forbid it, making war against us, and endeavouring themselves with all their might to cut us off. Howbeit it blossoms the more; it dies not, as though it were a human teaching, nor, as though it were a gift without strength, does it fade away; for no gift of God is without strength: nay, though prophecy saith of it that it shall be persecuted even unto the end, it abideth as that which cannot be forbidden—μένει ἀκώλυτος.'[2]

same effect, Wilson, *The Origin and Aim of the Acts of the Apostles*, London, 1912, p. 46 ff.

[1] Harnack, *The Acts of the Apostles*, London, 1909, p. xviii.

[2] *Stromata*, vi. 18: cf. Acts xxviii. 31: διδάσκων τὰ περὶ τοῦ κυρίου Ἰησοῦ Χριστοῦ μετὰ πάσης παρρησίας ἀκωλύτως. I owe the reference to Chase, *The Credibility of the Acts of the Apostles*, London, 1902, p. 101.

LECTURE V.

THE CIRCULATION OF THE NEW TESTAMENT
WRITINGS.

Εἶτα δὲ ἀποδημίας στελλόμενοι, ἔργον ἐπετέλουν εὐαγγελιστῶν, τοῖς ἔτι πάμπαν ἀνηκόοις τοῦ τῆς πίστεως λόγου κηρύττειν φιλοτιμούμενοι καὶ τὴν τῶν θείων εὐαγγελίων παραδιδόναι γραφήν.   EUSEBIUS, *Hist. Eccles.* iii. 37. 2.

V.

THE CIRCULATION OF THE NEW TESTAMENT WRITINGS.

ἵνα ὁ λόγος τοῦ κυρίου τρέχῃ καὶ δοξάζηται.
2 Thess. iii. 1.

εὐαγγέλιον αἰώνιον εὐαγγελίσαι ἐπὶ τοὺς καθημένους ἐπὶ τῆς γῆς καὶ ἐπὶ πᾶν ἔθνος καὶ φυλὴν καὶ γλῶσσαν καὶ λαόν.
Rev. xiv. 6.

IN previous lectures we have been engaged in tracing the rise of the New Testament writings, and in trying to form some idea of their general literary characteristics. We have seen that for the most part they were occasional writings, intended to meet certain immediate practical needs, and sent forth with little or no idea of the great future that awaited them. *Summary of previous Lectures.*

And we have seen, further, that if St. Paul and other of the Apostolic writers in their correspondence with the Churches adopted the ordinary letter-form of the day, with such adaptations as were necessary for their special purposes, the Evangelists had recourse to a form of composition which was practically new, and which owed its origin to the nature of the facts it embodied and the purpose it was intended to serve.

The dates of the New Testament autographs.

Nothing has been said as to the dates of the New Testament writings, nor is it necessary here to enter into any lengthened examination of them from that point of view. It is enough that in this respect there has been a marked return in recent years on the part even of advanced critics towards the older, traditional position, and that, with the probable exception of 2 Peter, all our New Testament writings may now be placed within the first century.

The most striking evidence perhaps in this connexion is the result reached by Professor Harnack in his investigations into *The Date of the Acts and of the Synoptic Gospels*.[1] Starting from the identity of the author of the 'We' sections of the Acts of the Apostles with the author of the rest of the book, Harnack has shown that this author is the Evangelist Luke, and that it is 'in the highest degree probable that the work was written at a time when St. Paul's trial in Rome had not yet come to an end' (p. 99). If this be so, Acts must have been written about A.D. 62, and the Third Gospel, which preceded it, about A.D. 60; St. Mark's Gospel, on which St. Luke was dependent, cannot then have been later than A.D. 50-60; while St. Matthew's Gospel, in its present shape, probably belongs to the years immediately after the Fall of Jerusalem in A.D. 70, though it is conceivable that it may have been composed before the catastrophe. It is true, of course, that these dates are not universally accepted by critics, but the very fact that they should have been

[1] Eng. Tr. by Wilkinson, London, 1911.

suggested by a scholar of Harnack's repute, and as the result of a free and independent investigation of the documents themselves, shows how far we have receded from the second century dates, to which for so long the Tübingen school lent the whole weight of their authority.

I. But not to dwell further upon this, the point with which at present we are specially concerned is the circulation of the different New Testament writings during the three hundred years that were still to elapse before they were finally gathered together into *the* New Testament. For, from the first, the books of which we have been thinking, notwithstanding their often limited address and occasional character, possessed an undoubted vitality and power of growth. And long before the original documents had disappeared, the demand for copies must have arisen.

<small>I. The circulation of the New Testament writings in roll-form.</small>

1. Nor is it difficult to understand how this came about. We have seen already that in the case of the Pauline Epistles, the autographs, after being publicly read, would be carefully preserved in the archives of the communities to which they were addressed (cf. p. 20), and, though there is no direct evidence to this effect in the New Testament itself,[1]

<small>1. The multiplication of copies due to practical needs,</small>

---

[1] When in 1 Tim. iv. 13 St. Paul exhorted Timothy to give heed to 'the reading' (τῇ ἀναγνώσει), he was referring to the public reading of the law and prophets, which had been continued from the Synagogue in the Christian Church. Cf. Acts xiii. 15, 2 Cor. iii. 14, and see p. 210.

it is impossible to doubt that they would be produced from time to time, and re-read at meetings of the congregation. Nor would their use stop there. The encyclical character of so many of the Epistles in itself rendered necessary a multiplication of copies, in order that each of the Churches in the address might possess a copy of its own.[1] And may we not also be sure that those Churches, which had become the possessors of Epistles or Gospels, would not fail in readiness to share their treasures with other Churches less happily situated? Even private persons might be permitted to make copies or extracts for their own use of those parts that specially interested them.[2]

This is of course very far from saying that anything like a general circulation of the New Testament writings took place at this early period. The difficulty and expense of multiplying copies would alone render this impossible,[3] to say nothing of the

---

[1] See especially Eph. i. 1, where the blank space after τοῖς ἁγίοις τοῖς οὖσιν caused by the omission of the words ἐν Ἐφέσῳ from the true text would be filled up in each case by the name of the particular congregation for which a copy was made. Cf. also Gal. i. 2, 2 Cor. i. 1, 1 Pet. i. 1.

[2] On the private use of Holy Scripture during the period with which we are dealing, see especially Harnack, *Bible Reading in the Early Church*, Eng. Tr. by Wilkinson, London, 1912.

[3] Comparisons with the cost of production of the literary works of the time do not carry us very far, the circumstances were too different, but it may be mentioned that the poet Martial complains that a little book of his was charged at four *sestertii* (about eightpence in the money value of that time, or between two and three

CIRCULATION OF THE N.T. WRITINGS

fact that the early Christians had not come to regard these books in such a light as would make the reading of them an incumbent religious duty. Nevertheless, as time passed, and the prestige of the Apostles grew, copies of the new writings could not fail to be more and more widely sought, until before the middle of the second century the four Gospels at any rate appear to have been known in a very large number of the Churches throughout the Empire.[1]

The ease with which this result was brought about —let me say in passing—was largely due to the facilities for travel and intercourse that then existed within the Roman Empire. 'It is the simple truth,' writes Sir William M. Ramsay, 'that travelling, whether for business or for pleasure, was contemplated and performed under the Empire with an indifference, confidence, and, above all, certainty, which were unknown in after centuries until the introduction of steamers and the consequent increase in ease and sureness of communication.'[2] And as a

[sidenote: and the facilities for intercourse amongst the first Christian communities.]

---

shillings in the money value of to-day), when it might have been produced at the half, and still left a profit to the bookseller (*Epigr.* xiii. 3). See further Birt, *Die Buchrolle in der Kunst*, Leipzig, 1907, p. 29 f.

[1] Cf. Harnack, *The Mission and Expansion of Christianity in the First Three Centuries*[2], Eng. Tr. by Moffatt (London, 1908), i. p. 374.

[2] Art. 'Roads and Travel (in N.T.)' in Hastings' *Dictionary of the Bible*, Extra Volume, p. 396. Cf. also Harnack's *Mission and Expansion of Christianity*[2], i. p. 369 ff., and Miss Skeel's interesting Essay, *Travel in the First Century after Christ*, Cambridge, 1901.

concrete example of this, the case of a merchant may be recalled, who boasts in an inscription on a tomb at Hierapolis in Phrygia that he voyaged from Asia to Rome seventy-two times (*C.I.G.* 3920).

There would be nothing therefore to prevent the first Christian teachers and missionaries passing freely from one place to another in the interests of their work, and in so doing they would naturally carry with them copies of the principal Apostolic writings.[1]

<small>2. The danger of textual corruption arising from</small>

2. These copies would in the main be faithful transcripts of the originals. At the same time there were not a few causes which would lead to textual corruption at an early date.

<small>(1) the material on which the autographs were written,</small>

One such cause arose very readily from the nature of the material on which the originals were written, and on which the copies themselves were made. That material, as we have seen, was papyrus, and papyrus, while in itself very durable when not exposed to damp, is, on the other hand, very brittle in its composition.[2] And we can therefore understand how readily through constant handling *lacunae* or breaks would occur in the New Testament texts.[3]

---

[1] For the later interchange of letters of a non-Apostolic character, cf. Polycarp, *ad Philipp.* c. xiii., also Eusebius, *Hist. Eccles.* iii. 36, v. 25.

[2] It was obviously to guard against this danger that the papyrus, on the back of which our new text of the Epistle to the Hebrews was written (see p. 61), was first patched and strengthened by strips from other papyrus documents.

[3] Cf. the *lacunae* in the texts reproduced in Plates I.-IV., VIII. of the present volume.

Letters, words, sometimes even lines and sentences would be dropped out, and in the restoration of these a door would at once be opened for numerous, though often, insignificant textual changes at the hands of transcribers.

Instances of these are probably to be found in several difficult passages in St. Mark's Gospel. If, as we shall see directly, all our copies of St. Mark are derived from a single manuscript mutilated at the end, this mutilation may well have taken place at other points in the body of the document, and led to readings other than those which the original author intended.[1] And in the same way Dr. Hort has suggested that some of the harshnesses which mark our present text of the Epistle to the Colossians may be due to primitive corruption, arising from the Epistle's having been badly preserved in ancient times.[2]

The danger of textual corruption would be still further increased by the manner in which many of these copies were made. In the case of copies,

(2) the employment of non-professional scribes,

---

[1] Burkitt finds instances of such corruption in c. iii. 17, viii. 10, and xii. 4, where the difficult reading ἐκεφαλίωσαν may be nothing more than a palaeographical blunder for ἐκολάφισαν (*American Journal of Theology*, April, 1911, p. 173 ff.).

[2] *Notes*[2], p. 127. These harshnesses centre in the two difficult phrases of c. ii. 18, θέλων ἐν ταπεινοφροσύνῃ and ἃ ἑόρακεν ἐμβατεύων, where Hort suggests ἐν ἐθελοταπεινοφροσύνῃ, and approves the emendation of Dr. C. Taylor (*Journal of Philology*, vii. p. 130 ff.) ἀέρα κενεμβατεύων 'treading the void of air.' But see now Ramsay, *Athenaeum*, Jan. 25, 1913, p. 107, for ἐμβατεύω as a *t.t.* from the Mysteries = 'enter on the new life of the initiated.'

expressly designed for Church use, care would doubtless be taken to ensure as great accuracy as possible, though the employment of private individuals, instead of professional scribes, in the work of transcription would be a source of constant mistakes.[1] But when, in addition to these more or less official copies, we think of the large number of private copies that soon came into existence, often made hurriedly and without any thorough-going revision, errors in transcription became almost a matter of necessity.

(3) the literary ideas of the time.

And all the more so, because the very thought of the need of absolute verbal reproduction would be strange to the early scribes. We have seen the habit of free quotation already at work amongst the Synoptic writers in the use of their sources (cf. p. 142). And if they permitted themselves this liberty, it is obvious how readily their own narrative would come to be treated in a similar way by subsequent copyists.

In so acting, these last were very far from imagining that they were showing any disrespect to the original writings. On the contrary, the very esteem in which they held them made them anxious to

---

[1] As showing the dangers attending copying, even in the case of those who made it their business, Strabo, writing shortly before the birth of Christ, tells us that as the making of books became common, there were constant complaints as to the deficiencies and inaccuracies of the copies offered for sale (xiii. i. 54): cf. G. H. Putnam, *Authors and their Public in Ancient Times*[3] (New York and London, 1896), pp. 120 f., 182 f.

remove any apparent blemishes of language or of meaning. Hence the constant tendency to which our early manuscripts bear witness of improving on so-called vulgarisms of spelling or grammar. And hence too the insertion of explanatory words to make the meaning clearer, and even of deliberate changes in the supposed interests of historic or dogmatic truth.[1]

To us with our keen sense of the duty of faithfully reproducing an author's exact words, this freedom may well seem very surprising. But we must remember that at the time of which we are speaking literary ideas were very different. A book once published was regarded as practically public property, and any man who had become possessed of a copy would not hesitate to annotate or edit its contents in any way that seemed to him to add to their interest and value.[2]

---

[1] How readily this tendency would extend to heretical writers is proved by Marcion's mutilated edition of St. Luke's Gospel (cf. p. 217). And in this same connexion it is interesting to find Dionysius of Corinth, in view of the circulation of his epistles in a falsified form, naïvely comforting himself with the thought that the same fate had befallen the Scriptures (Eusebius, *Hist. Eccles.* iv. 23. 12).

[2] 'After the most painstaking researches through the records left us by the Greeks, we are compelled to conclude that in none of the Greek states was any recognition ever given under provision of law, to the right of authors to any control over their own productions' (Clement, *Étude sur la Propriété Littéraire chez les Grecs et chez les Romains*, Grenoble, 1867, cited by Putnam, *Authors and their Public*[3], p. 54 f.). See also Dziatzko, art. 'Buch' in Pauly-Wissowa, iii. p. 966 f.

In some such way alone can we explain the striking variations of the Greek and Hebrew text of our Old Testament writings. 'The evidence of the Septuagint,' writes Dr. W. Robertson Smith, 'proves that early copyists had a very different view of their responsibility from that which we might be apt to ascribe to them. They were not reckless or indifferent to the truth. They copied the Old Testament books knowing them to be sacred books, and they were zealous to preserve them as writings of Divine authority. But their sense of responsibility to the Divine word regarded the meaning rather than the form, and they had not that highly-developed sense of the importance of preserving every word and every letter of the original hand of the author which seems natural to us.'[1]

If this were so even in the case of the admittedly sacred writings of the Old Testament, the same tendency could hardly fail to assert itself in connexion with the new Christian writings, which were still far from enjoying their present authoritative and canonical position. And the general result is, that instead of assigning textual corruption to a comparatively late date, as was at one time believed to be the case, everything rather points to the conclusion that, the nearer we get to the original manuscripts, the greater were the dangers to which their text was exposed.

3. But it is not only with regard to questions of text

[1] *The Old Testament in the Jewish Church*[2] (London, 1902), p. 91.

that the outward conditions under which the New Testament books were written may help us. Their original roll-form must also be taken into account in considering various points of structure that have for long engaged the attention of students.

3. Bearing of the roll-form on questions of structure connected with

Thus, when we remember that the tear and wear of a papyrus roll would naturally show itself most at the beginning and at the end (cf. p. 11), we are prepared for the conjecture of the possible disappearance of an opening leaf to the Epistle to the Hebrews, which, had it been preserved, would have shown the true epistolary character of the writing, and perhaps set at rest the vexed questions of authorship and destination.[1] But it must be at once admitted that there is absolutely no direct evidence for the existence of any such introduction. The Epistle opens, if somewhat abruptly, at least quite naturally, with words which point forward clearly to its main theme, the finality of the revelation that has been given us in Christ: 'God, having of old time spoken unto the fathers in the prophets by divers portions and in divers manners, hath at the end of these days spoken unto us in a Son' (c. i. 1). And we may turn, therefore, at once to another case of supposed loss, for which a better case can be made out.

(1) the Epistle to the Hebrews,

---

[1] *E.g.* Barth, *Einleitung in das Neue Testament*² (Gütersloh, 1911), p. 114. On Overbeck's theory (*Zur Geschichte des Kanons*, Chemnitz, 1880, p. 12 ff.) of the *deliberate* amputation of the opening paragraph of Hebrews, see Sanday's *Inspiration*, p. 24, n¹.

182 THE NEW TESTAMENT DOCUMENTS

(2) the end of St. Mark's Gospel,

The closing verses of St. Mark's Gospel from c. xvi. 9 onwards are, as is well known, wanting in our two most important manuscripts, the Vatican and Sinaitic codices, both of which end the Gospel with the unfinished Greek sentence ΕΦΟΒΟΥΝΤΟ ΓΑΡ, 'for they were afraid' (see Plate VII.). And their evidence is now confirmed by the very important Old Syriac Gospels, in which the Gospel of St. Mark is again ended at c. xvi. 8, and this time in a manner which clearly suggests that its scribe cannot have been aware of any further passage that was wanting.

In view, then, of this documentary evidence, combined with the internal evidence of difference of authorship which the extant endings exhibit, we may not unreasonably conjecture that the last leaf of the original manuscript was lost at a very early date, and that the additional twelve verses with which we are familiar in our ordinary version, and the shorter ending which other authorities offer as an alternative, as well as the expanded account of the newly discovered Freer manuscript, were all added later at different times and by different hands to round off the mutilated Marcan account of the Resurrection.[1]

(3) the closing chapters of Romans,

In the Epistle to the Romans, on the other hand, a possible addition to the original writing meets us. Both on the ground of textual phenomena and on internal evidence, the authenticity of the last two

[1] See further Additional Note I, 'Alternative Endings of St. Mark's Gospel.'

PLATE VI.

ST. MARK xvi. 12-17, ἐξ αὐτῶν . . . ὀνόματί μου.

From the Freer (Washington) Manuscript. Fourth to Fifth Century.
By permission of the J. C. Hinrichs'sche Buchhandlung, Leipzig.

chapters has been attacked. And though in c. xv. this attack seems to be more than met by the positive arguments in favour of genuineness, there is much in c. xvi. which makes it difficult to accept it as an integral part of the original Epistle. For one thing, the personal greetings in c. xvi., with their detailed references, are suspiciously numerous in the case of a Church which St. Paul had never visited, and for another, great confusion exists in our authorities regarding the position of the various benedictions and doxologies towards the close of the Epistle. A full discussion of the bearing of these points must be left to the critics, but confining ourselves to what we may learn from external form, there is nothing impossible, to say the least, in the idea, which has found wide favour, that in c. xvi. 1-20, or according to another view, 1-23, we have an independent miniature Epistle of St. Paul, addressed perhaps to the Ephesian Church, with which the Apostle stood in such close relation,[1] which at some early date was attached to the larger roll of the Roman Epistle, perhaps for convenience of preservation,

[1] The positive evidence in favour of Ephesus is contained in the mention of Epaenetus (ver. 5), and especially of Prisca and Aquila (ver. 3), who, according to other testimony (Acts xviii. 18, 1 Cor. xvi. 19, 2 Tim. iv. 19), would seem to have taken up their abode at Ephesus. Recent evidence from the inscriptions has also shown conclusively that other names mentioned in the greetings are by no means so characteristic of Rome as was at one time imagined: see especially, J. Rouffiac, *Recherches sur les charactères du Grec dans le Nouveau Testament d'après les inscriptions de Priène* (Paris, 1911), p. 87 ff.

and so in time came to be regarded as an integral part of it.¹

(4) the composition of 2nd Corinthians.

A more complicated problem is suggested by the Second Epistle to the Corinthians, which modern criticism represents not as one Epistle, but as a combination of several Epistles or parts of Epistles. Hausrath,² for example, has found many supporters for the suggestion that the last four chapters were in reality written before the first nine, and contain the substance of the severe letter to which St. Paul refers in 2 Cor. vii. 8: 'For though I made you sorry with my Epistle, I do not regret it, though I did regret; for I see that that Epistle made you sorry, though but for a season.' It is certain, at least, that these chapters with their troubled and anxious language, contrast very strangely with the overflowing joy of the earlier portion of the Epistle, and that the historical circumstances, so far as we can now reconstruct them, would be well met if we

¹ On Bishop Lightfoot's theory, according to which St. Paul himself deliberately omitted the last two chapters of the original Epistle, along with the words ἐν ‘Ρώμῃ in i. 7, 15, in order to give it a more general character, and added the doxology at the end to round it off: see his *Biblical Essays* (London, 1893), p. 285 ff. Dr. Hort's criticism of the theory is reprinted in the same volume, p. 321 ff. For a different, and in many ways attractive, theory that the short recension was the original form of the Epistle, and was afterwards added to by St. Paul to adapt it to the needs of the Roman Church, see Kirsopp Lake, *The Earlier Epistles of St. Paul* (London, 1911), p. 325 ff.

² *Der Vier-Capitel Brief des Paulus an die Corinther*, Heidelberg, 1870.

could imagine the sequence of St. Paul's relations with the Corinthian Church to be:—the Epistle which we describe as First Corinthians, preceded, however, as we learn from that Epistle itself (1 Cor. v. 9), by one still earlier; then the severe letter, 2 Cor. x.-xiii., which the Apostle was led to write on hearing that his previous communications had failed in their effect; and finally, yet another Epistle, practically identical with 2 Cor. i.-ix., in which he gave expression to his satisfaction that at length his Corinthian brethren had listened to his appeals, and harmony had once more been restored between him and them.

Nor is this all, but it is possible that even this last letter may itself be composite. It has often been remarked that c. vi. 14–vii. 1 interrupts the progress of thought, while c. vii. 2 connects itself very readily with c. vi. 13. May it be, that in this paragraph we have yet another fragment of St. Paul's correspondence with Corinth—a portion, perhaps, of that earliest letter of all to which reference has just been made, which either by accident or by editorial handling, came afterwards to be inserted in the later Epistle?

As to how far all this can be substantiated, I am not prepared at present to offer any definite opinion. Whatever may be said for an apparent disarrangement of the contents on internal grounds, we cannot lose sight of the fact that this is not corroborated by any trace of unsettlement of text in the external evidence, as was the case with Rom. xvi. And, on the whole, it is probably wise to content ourselves with pointing out that, should other circumstances demand it, there is nothing in the methods of book-production at the time to prevent separate Epistles, or fragments of Epistles, addressed by St. Paul to the same community, being combined and handed down as if they had formed a single Epistle from the first.[1]

(5) the arrangement of the Fourth Gospel. An even greater caution must be observed in dealing with the displacements that have been alleged in the case of the Fourth Gospel. In an Essay published in 1893 Friedrich Spitta held that in certain sections of the Gospel, notably in cc. xiii-xvii, a serious disarrangement of the text had taken place.[2] And now we find Mr. Warburton Lewis, in a recent Essay,[3] following the German scholar and arguing that not a few of the chronological and other difficulties which the Gospel presents are best met on the supposition that its contents are no longer arranged in the order which their author intended. And the most likely explanation he can offer is, that through some mischance the separate papyrus leaves on which the Gospel was written were put together in a wrong order when they were fastened together in a roll. But if this happened to the original manuscript, we

[1] Cf. Kirsopp Lake, *The Earlier Epistles of St. Paul* (London, 1911), p. 144 ff., where an interesting parallel is cited from Cicero's letters in the combination of two drafts of *Ad Fam.* v. 8, in a single letter.

It is right, however, to note that the most recent commentators on 2 Corinthians, Lietzmann, Bachmann, and Menzies, all agree in upholding its integrity.

[2] *Zur Geschichte und Litteratur des Urchristentums*, i. p. 155 ff., 'Unordnungen im Texte des 4. Evangeliums.'

[3] *Disarrangements in the Fourth Gospel*, Cambridge, 1910.

CIRCULATION OF THE N.T. WRITINGS

are at once led to ask how a writer who shows such anxious and loving care in the composition of his book could have allowed it to go forth to others in this confused form. Or, if it was a later copy that was at fault, we are met with the curious state of things that all the correct copies of the Gospel have wholly disappeared, and that it is from an exemplar thus carelessly constructed that the subsequent copies in use in the Church have been made.[1]

The difficulties, in fact, surrounding any such theory are in themselves greater than any peculiarities of construction which the Gospel in its present form is supposed to exhibit, and surely do not warrant the arbitrary rearrangement of its contents that is here suggested.[2]

4. The marginal additions which in other instances have been thought to have found their way into our present New Testament texts stand on a somewhat different footing. I have pointed out already that the general structure of a papyrus roll with its narrow columns following closely on each other does not, as a rule, leave much space for these additions (see p. 14). At the same time, it is impossible to ignore the possibility that many additional facts and comments which came to the knowledge of the New Testament scribes, and were

4. Marginal additions.

---

[1] Cf. Zahn, *Introduction to the New Testament*, iii. p. 348.

[2] It may be noted that, according to Mr. Lewis, the re-arranged Gospel stands thus: c. i.-ii. 12; iii. 22-30; ii. 13–iii. 21 + 31-36; iv.; vi.; v. + vii. 15-24 + viii. 12-20; vii. 1-14 + 25-52 + viii. 21-59; ix.-xii.; xiii. 1-32; xv.-xvi.; xiii. 33–xiv.; xvii.; xviii.-xx.; xxi.

at first treated by them as *marginalia*, would afterwards be incorporated in the body of the text.

A familiar example is afforded by the well-known pericope John vii. 53–viii. 11, the incident of the woman taken in adultery, which is now generally admitted not to belong to the original text of the Fourth Gospel. And the probability is that it represents a genuine tradition, derived perhaps from the Gospel according to the Hebrews or from Papias's *Exposition of the Lord's Oracles*, which, on account of the intrinsic beauty of the story, had been noted by some scribe at the end of his copy of the Gospel, and was transferred by a later copyist to what seemed to him a suitable place for it at the end of c. vii. 52.

<small>II. Change from the papyrus roll to the papyrus codex.</small>

II. We have been thinking hitherto of the circulation of our New Testament writings in the papyrus roll-form, but it must not be lost sight of that from a very early date they also took the form of papyrus codices. The original meaning of the word codex was the trunk of a tree (*caudex*), and hence it came to be applied to the pile of wooden tablets (*pugillares*) smeared over with wax, which were commonly used both by the Greeks and Romans for ordinary writing purposes, as when a ledger was called *codex accepti et expensi*. And from this again the word was extended to denote any collection of papyrus or parchment sheets, in which the sheets were not rolled within one another, but laid over one another, as in a modern book.

1. The use of papyrus in this manner has not always been recognized. The older authorities sometimes speak as if the introduction of the codex marked the close of the papyrus period. But more recently evidence has been accumulating to show that the papyrus codex was in such use in Egypt for theological purposes in the third century, that by that time it must already have had a considerable history behind it.[1]

1. Early use of papyrus codices.

Thus it is interesting to notice that the oldest New Testament text recovered from the sands of Egypt, and, indeed the oldest original manuscript of any part of the New Testament at present known, is the sheet of a papyrus codex, containing most of the first chapter of St. Matthew (Plate II.), which cannot be later than the beginning of the fourth century, and is assigned by its discoverers, Dr. Grenfell and Dr. Hunt, with 'greater probability' to the third.[2] And from the same period we have another sheet with fragments of the first and twentieth chapters of St. John's Gospel. As this must have formed very nearly the outermost sheet of a large quire, the same authorities calculate that the codex, when complete, consisted of a single quire of twenty-five sheets, of which the first was probably blank, or contained only the title.[3]

(1) Fragmentary New Testament texts.

---

[1] Cf. Grenfell and Hunt, *The Oxyrhynchus Papyri*, ii. p. 2 f.

[2] *The Oxyrhynchus Papyri*, edd. Grenfell-Hunt, i. p. 4 ff., No. 2.

[3] *The Oxyrhynchus Papyri*, edd. Grenfell-Hunt, ii. p. 1 ff., No. 208.

Yet another fragment belonging to the third century has recently been published by Dr. Hunt amongst the Rylands Papyri, consisting of part of a leaf out of a papyrus book, the *recto* of which originally contained Titus i. 11-15, and the *verso* c. ii. 3-8 from the same Epistle.[1] Unfortunately the leaf is now so mutilated as to be of little value textually, but it preserves, as its editor points out, one interesting reading ἀφθονίαν for ἀφθορίαν in c. ii. 7 'which is recorded as a variant in two ninth century manuscripts, but has apparently not previously been found in any actual text.'

(2) The 'Sayings of Jesus.'

To return, however, to our immediate subject, when to these New Testament texts we add the third century leaf discovered at Oxyrhynchus in 1897, containing the so-called Λόγια Ἰησοῦ, or 'Sayings of Jesus,' to which reference has already been made (see p. 131), we have another direct proof of the early prevalence of the papyrus codex-, as compared with the papyrus roll-, form.

2. Handwriting of the papyrus codices.

2. Nor is this all, but these fragments have for us this further interest, that in their script we can see what has been called 'the prototype' of the handwriting of our great Biblical codices.[2] That handwriting, with its thick and heavy strokes, has usually been regarded as possible only in the case of a strong substance such as parchment, but its beginnings are clearly traceable in these papyrus codices.

[1] *Catalogue of the Greek Papyri in the John Rylands Library, Manchester*, Manchester, 1911, i. p. 10 f., No. 5.
[2] Grenfell and Hunt, *The Oxyrhynchus Papyri*, ii. p. 3.

And further, if, as appears likely from their general character and size, these fragments of which we have been speaking formed parts of books intended originally for private rather than for general use, they offer an emphatic and independent testimony to the growing reverence that was being paid to the written word, as well as to the increasing hold it was gaining upon all classes of the population. As the earliest specimens we possess of 'Poor Men's Bibles,' they have in their own way as deep a significance for the student of our New Testament writings, as the splendid parchment codices which mark the next stage of their history.

<small>'Poor Men's Bibles.'</small>

III. Anything like a detailed description of these parchment codices would carry us far beyond the limits of our present inquiry.[1] But it may be well to note a few points of a general character, more particularly in view of the significance of the parchment codex for the final collection of our scattered writings into a single volume.

<small>III. Parchment codices.</small>

1. In doing so, we have to guard at the outset against the common error that, because parchment is now first heard of in connexion with our Biblical manuscripts, it was previously unknown as a writing-

<small>1. Manufacture of parchment.</small>

---

[1] Full particulars will be found in such well-known works as Nestle's *Introduction to the Textual Criticism of the Greek New Testament*, London, 1901 (a third and enlarged German edition appeared in 1909); Gregory's *Canon and Text of the New Testament*, Edinburgh, 1907; and Kenyon's *Handbook to the Textual Criticism of the New Testament*, of which a new and revised edition appeared in 1912.

material. So far was this from being the case that in a rough form it would seem to have been in common use even before papyrus, while its improvement and consequent adoption for literary purposes may be dated from the reign of Eumenes II. at Pergamum, B.C. 197-158. According to the story related by Varro,[1] Eumenes, desiring to found a library of his own which should rival the library at Alexandria, found his efforts frustrated by the refusal of Ptolemy Epiphanes to permit the exportation of papyrus from Egypt, and accordingly he had to fall back on the use of skins, after submitting them to a special preparation. From the place where this was done, the new material came to be known as περγαμηνή, *pergamena*, parchment.[2] The name of vellum (*vitulinum*), which is now used as practically synonymous, was at first confined to a fine variety manufactured from the skins of very young calves.

2. Use of parchment in connexion with Christian literature.

2. The story has been called in question, but without sufficient cause,[3] though it is undoubtedly remarkable that, during the succeeding three centuries, there should be so little evidence of any general use of parchment for literary purposes.[4] But with the

[1] *Apud* Pliny, *Nat. Hist.* xiii. 11.

[2] The actual name *pergamena charta* does not occur before an edict of Diocletian, A.D. 301.

[3] See Birt, *Das antike Buchwesen*, p. 50 ff., and, on the other side, Gardthausen, *Das Buchwesen*, p. 93.

[4] Amongst the most notable remains of classical writings preserved on parchment during this period are a leaf of the other-

beginning of the fourth century, and the ever-increasing demand for copies of the new Christian writings, the advantages of parchment or vellum over papyrus began to assert themselves. For one thing, parchment could be manufactured in any country, and not merely in a limited area like papyrus, and for another, owing to its greater strength and flexibility, it lent itself more readily to the convenient codex-form, which we have already found coming into use during the papyrus period. We are not astonished, therefore, to learn that when in A.D. 331 Constantine ordered fifty copies of the Scriptures for his new capital, he gave special instructions that they should be written in a legible manner, 'on prepared skins,'[1] or that about twenty years later the two priests, Acacius and Euzoius, when rewriting the damaged volumes of Pamphilus' library at Caesarea, substituted parchment codices for the original papyrus rolls.[2]

wise unknown *Cretans* of Euripides, and some small fragments of Demosthenes. For the more ordinary use of parchment for notebooks, or for the rough drafts of literary works, cf. Cicero, *ad Attic.* xiii. 24; Horace, *Serm.* ii. 3. 1 f.; Quintilian, *Inst. Orat.* x. 3. 31.

[1] Eusebius, *De vita Constantini*, iv. 36, ed. Heikel: πεντήκοντα σωμάτια ἐν διφθέραις ἐγκατασκεύοις. The Codex Sinaiticus, which Tischendorf believed to have been one of these fifty Bibles, is written on fairly thin parchment, made, according to the same authority, from antelope skins.

[2] Hieronymus, *Epist.* cxli.: 'Quam [bibliothecam Caesareae urbis] ex parte corruptam Acacius dehinc et Euzoius, eiusdem ecclesiae sacerdotes, in membranis instaurare conati sunt.'

The practice quickly spread, and mainly through the influence of the Christian Church, parchment came to supersede papyrus as the medium for conveying to the world the contents not only of its own sacred books but of literature generally.[1]

3. Construction of a parchment codex.

3. A few words are still required as to the construction of a parchment codex, and the character of the handwriting employed upon it.

The two sides of parchment naturally varied, according as they represented the hair or the flesh side of the skin. And in making up a codex, great care was taken that hair-side should always face hair-side, and flesh-side flesh-side. This was secured by folding the quire in sheets, and as the ordinary quire consisted of four sheets (τετράδιον, *quaternus*), a single folding made eight leaves or sixteen pages.

As a rule, both sides of the parchment were used for writing purposes, and while, in the case of papyrus, no ruling was necessary, the fibres of the plant affording sufficient guidance to the scribe (cf. p. 13), parchment offered no such natural aid, and lines were ruled by a μόλιβδος or disc of lead, kept straight by a κανών or ruler.[2] The ruling was, however, generally confined to the hair-side of the skin,

---

[1] It is noteworthy that in an inventory of Church property of the fifth or sixth century, twenty-one parchment books are mentioned as compared with only three on papyrus—βιβλία δερμάτι(να) κα', ὁμοί(ως) χαρτία γ' (*Greek Papyri*, second series, edd. Grenfell-Hunt, p. 160 ff., No. 111[27 f.]).

[2] For the later history of this interesting word, see Westcott, *On the Canon*[5], p. 504 ff., or Souter, *Text and Canon*, p. 154 ff.

PLATE VII.

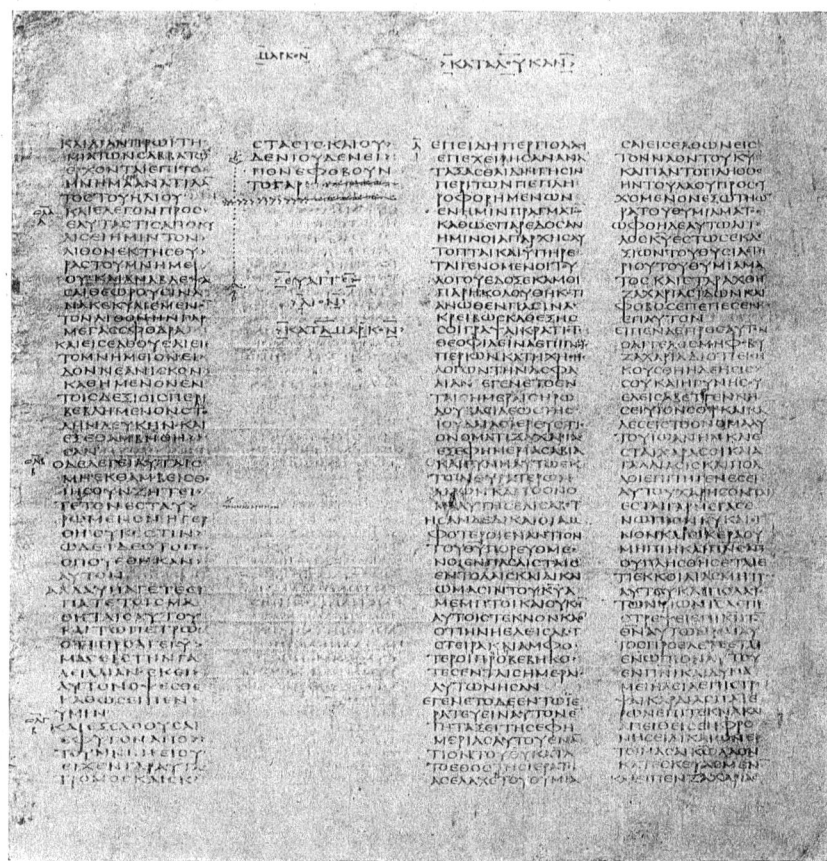

CODEX SINAITICUS. FOURTH CENTURY.

The page shown contains Mark xvi. 2—Luke i. 18, the last twelve verses of St. Mark being omitted.

the pressure of the disc causing the lines to show also on the reverse side.

The handwriting employed, with its square, upright uncials, was, as has been previously noted, a development of the best hands of the papyrus codices of the second and third centuries (see p. 190), and in the principal exemplars, such as the Codex Vaticanus and the Codex Sinaiticus, was marked by great distinction and beauty. While, too, as a rule, in Greek manuscripts where the lines are of uniform length there are only two columns to the page, these codices show three and four columns respectively, possibly a reminiscence of the narrow columns of the papyri from which they were copied. In the remarkable Graeco-Latin manuscript, Codex Bezae, on the other hand, where the lines are divided in κῶλα or short clauses according to the sense, there is only a single column to each page. *Character of the handwriting.*

4. The fact that both sides of the parchment were written upon naturally secured a great saving of space, and rendered possible the combining of a larger number of documents in a single codex than was convenient in the case of a papyrus roll without extending it to an altogether undue length. We shall see afterwards the importance of this consideration in the determination of the New Testament canon, but meanwhile it must be kept in view that for long it was only in exceptional instances, such as the magnificent Vatican and Sinaitic codices, that anything like a general collection of the scattered writings took place. As a rule they continued to be *Suitability of the codex-form for collection of writings.*

circulated either singly or in small groups of Gospels and Epistles, and that, too, even after the general employment of a more running hand of script had still further diminished the size of the codices in which they could be included.[1]

Pocket Bibles. How great indeed must have been the desire from early times to have copies of the new writings in modest dimensions has been recently illustrated in an interesting manner by the recovery at Oxyrhynchus of a leaf from a fourth century codex of the Apocalypse. Though written in fair-sized uncials, the book, when complete, must have been of such miniature proportions as virtually to form a pocket edition (see Plate VIII.),[2] while the leaf of an uncanonical gospel, found in same place, is so small that 'the written surface only slightly exceeds two inches square.'[3]

---

[1] The employment in literary documents of this smaller or minuscule hand for uncial or majuscule writing is usually assigned to the eighth or ninth century. But in view of constant misapprehension it is perhaps not superfluous to recall that alongside of the literary uncial hand a non-literary cursive hand had been in regular use for ordinary purposes as far back as we have any specimens of Greek writing extant, and that it was from this non-literary cursive hand that the literary minuscule hand was afterwards developed.

[2] *The Oxyrhynchus Papyri*, ed. Hunt, viii. p. 14 ff., No. 1080. Textual students will recall Dr. Hort's ingenious reconstruction of a 'small portable' manuscript of this same book from the text of the Apocalypse preserved in Codex Ephraemi (*Introduction to the New Testament in the Original Greek*[2], p. 268).

[3] *The Oxyrhynchus Papyri*, ed. Grenfell-Hunt, v. p. 1, No. 840.

PLATE VIII.

APOCALYPSE iii. 19—iv. 1.

A leaf from a pocket edition in vellum, belonging to the Fourth Century. From Oxyrhynchus. By permission of the Egypt Exploration Fund.

To face p. 196.

CIRCULATION OF THE N.T. WRITINGS 197

In dealing with the circulation of the New Testament writings in the first Christian centuries, I have had occasion to refer somewhat pointedly to the dangers to which the transmission of the true text was exposed. And it is possible that the impression has been left upon some minds that the state of our New Testament text is one of great uncertainty and confusion. This is very far, however, from being the case. Without seeking to minimise the possible sources of corruption, which, indeed, are placed beyond dispute by the enormous mass of variant readings that have arisen,[1] we must not forget that as regards both the number and antiquity of our manuscripts, we are in a far better position for getting back to the original words of a New Testament writing than in the case of any other ancient book. Thus it is by no means generally realized how few in number are the manuscripts on which we are dependent for our knowledge of the great classical writings of Greece and Rome, and by what a long period of time they are generally separated from the original writers. For our knowledge of Sophocles, for example, we are mainly dependent on a single manuscript written about fourteen hundred years after the poet's death, and though in the case of Vergil we are fortunate in possessing one nearly

General trustworthiness of the New Testament text.

---

[1] When Mill issued his edition of the Greek New Testament in 1707, he included a critical apparatus of about 30,000 various readings. The number now must be four or five times as many —'almost more variants than words' (Nestle, *Textual Criticism of the Greek Testament*, p. 15).

complete manuscript belonging to the fourth century, the total number of Vergilian manuscripts can be numbered only by hundreds, as compared with thousands in the case of the New Testament writers.[1] And yet if neither in the case of Sophocles or Vergil we have any serious doubt as to our being in possession of what is substantially a true text, why should we refuse to show a proportionately higher confidence in our New Testament text, when our principal direct witnesses to it are not separated by more than two hundred and fifty or three hundred years from the autographs, and in certain portions are confirmed by evidence that carries us nearly a century further back? I am thinking here not of the early versions, which in themselves supply most important aid for the determination of the true New Testament text, but of those third century Greek texts, to which reference has already been made more than once, which, however fragmentary, confirm, so far as they go, the general type of text found in the Vatican and Sinaitic codices.

While, then, there are still many grave textual problems awaiting solution, before we can be sure that we have 'the New Testament in the Original Greek' in our hands, we may take it that in all substantial particulars the words of the autographs

---

[1] See further Kenyon, *Handbook to the Textual Criticism of the New Testament*, p. 3. Reference may also be made to two articles by Bishop Welldon, 'The Authenticity of Ancient Literature, Secular and Sacred,' in *The Nineteenth Century and After*, vol. 62 (1907), pp. 560 ff., 830 ff.

have been recovered. The great English scholars, Dr. Westcott and Dr. Hort, to whom so much of this result is due, were accustomed to weigh their words, and this is what they say: 'The books of the New Testament as preserved in extant documents assuredly speak to us in every important respect in language identical with that in which they spoke to those for whom they were originally written.'[1]

[1] *Introduction to the New Testament in the Original Greek*², p. 284. Cf. Souter, *The Text and Canon of the New Testament*, London, 1913, p. 138: 'It appears to the present writer that a great advance upon the text of Westcott and Hort in the direction of the original autographs is highly improbable, at least in our generation. If they have not said the last word, they have at least laid foundations which make it comparatively simple to fit later discoveries into their scheme.'

LECTURE VI.

THE COLLECTION OF THE NEW TESTAMENT
WRITINGS.

Εἶτα φόβος νόμου ᾄδεται καὶ προφητῶν χάρις γινώσκεται καὶ εὐαγγελίων πίστις ἵδρυται καὶ ἀποστόλων παράδοσις φυλάσσεται καὶ ἐκκλησίας χαρὰ σκιρτᾷ. *Ep. ad Diognetum*, xi. 6.

'Uerum scriptura omnis in duo testamenta diuisa est... sed tamen diuersa non sunt quia nouum ueteris adimpletio est et in utroque idem testator est Christus.'

LACTANTIUS, *Instit.* iv. 20, ed. Brandt.

VI.

THE COLLECTION OF THE NEW TESTAMENT WRITINGS.

Εἰ δὲ ἡ διακονία τοῦ θανάτου ἐν γράμμασιν ἐντετυπωμένη λίθοις ἐγενήθη ἐν δόξῃ, ὥστε μὴ δύνασθαι ἀτενίσαι τοὺς υἱοὺς Ἰσραὴλ εἰς τὸ πρόσωπον Μωυσέως διὰ τὴν δόξαν τοῦ προσώπου αὐτοῦ τὴν καταργουμένην, πῶς οὐχὶ μᾶλλον ἡ διακονία τοῦ πνεύματος ἔσται ἐν δόξῃ;   2 Cor. iii. 7.

WE have seen how, by the substitution of the codex-form for the roll, the collection of the different New Testament writings into one volume was rendered possible. This, however, is very far from saying that any such collection on a complete or final scale took place at once. For long, even after their joint-authority was recognized, the books of the New Testament still continued to be circulated separately or in small groups.[1] At the same time, the very fact that they could, when necessity arose, be thus brought together, formed a distinct step in that process of collection, and eventually of canonization, which we have now to trace.

At present it is possible to do so only in the

The circulation of the New Testament writings.

---

[1] At least four-fifths of our uncial manuscripts of the Gospels contain the Gospels only.

barest outline. To tell the story at any length would lead us into many questions with which we are not immediately concerned. But any inquiry into the rise and growth of the New Testament writings would be very incomplete, unless I at least tried to indicate how, as the result of a long and largely informal process, the scattered writings of which we have been thinking were united to form the New Testament, which henceforth took its place along with the Old Testament, as the Holy Scriptures of the Christian Church.

Light in which these writings were at first regarded. Of such a future for their writings the original writers do not seem to have had any idea. They wrote for the most part, as we have had frequent occasion to notice, in order to meet immediate and pressing needs, and no ulterior purpose of laying the foundations of a new sacred book appears on the surface of their writings. In the canonical books of the Old Testament both they and their readers possessed a Bible already. Jesus Himself had used no other. It was to the Old Testament that, both before and after His Resurrection, He appealed as pointing forward to the 'all things' which had at length been fulfilled in Himself.[1] And in this attitude He was followed by the first Christian teachers. 'Beginning from this Scripture'—the great prophecy of Isaiah regarding the Suffering Servant—Philip 'preached Jesus' to the Ethiopian eunuch: 'by the Scriptures' Apollos 'powerfully confuted the Jews' at Ephesus, and showed 'that Jesus was the Christ.'[2]

[1] Luke xxiv. 44 f., 25.   [2] Acts viii. 35, xviii. 28.

COLLECTION OF THE N.T. WRITINGS 205

How unique was the position which the Old Testament occupied in the mind of the early Church is sufficiently proved by the simple fact that the words γραφή, γραφαί, and the introduction of citations by the formula γέγραπται, wherever they occur in the New Testament writings, invariably refer to passages from the Hebrew Canon, and never to any of the Christian writings that were already in circulation at the time. The only apparent exception is 2 Peter iii. 16, where the writer seems to equate the Epistles of St. Paul with the Scriptures of the Old Testament. But not only is the interpretation of the words 'the rest of the Scriptures' somewhat doubtful, but we have already seen good reason to believe that this Epistle is not really Apostolic, but a pseudonymous work of the second century.[1]

We may take it, then, that during the Apostolic age the only *documents* invested by the Church with a definitely sacred character were the books of the Old Testament. And yet, before a century had elapsed, we are met with the fact that alongside of this older collection, a new collection had begun to assert itself, which not only had made the idea of Christian sacred writings familiar, but actually

Supremacy of the Old Testament.

---

[1] Cf. p. 113 f. The first undoubted application of the term 'Scripture' to any part of our present New Testament Canon occurs in the so-called Second Epistle of Clement, when, after quoting from Isaiah liv. 1, the author introduces the citation of Matt. ix. 13 with the words, 'and again another Scripture saith' (καὶ ἑτέρα δὲ γραφὴ λέγει, ii. 4).

embraced the larger part of those which now make up our New Testament.

I. Influences leading to the collection of the New Testament writings.

I. Of the evidence on which this statement rests, I shall have something to say later. Meanwhile it may be well to notice certain influences at work in the Apostolic and sub-Apostolic Church which helped to bring about this result.

1. The existence of the Old Testament Canon.

1. Amongst these may be mentioned, in the first place, the existence of the Old Testament Canon.

The formation of that Canon was itself the result of a long and gradual process, which was only completed at the beginning of the Christian era.[1] And though, as we have just seen, in one way its existence rendered unnecessary at first the thought of further sacred writings, in another, it supplied a model which, in process of time, the Christian Church could hardly fail to follow.

The Greek Old Testament.

And this was rendered easier by the fact that the Old Testament then in general use was in Greek, and not in Hebrew. The Septuagint, the Greek translation of the Old Testament Scriptures, had been adopted not only by the Jews of the Dispersion, but by large numbers of Jews within the confines of

---

[1] Cf. Ryle, *The Canon of the Old Testament* (London, 1892), p. ix f.: 'The measure of the completeness of the Canon had scarcely been reached, when "the fulness of the time came." The close of the Hebrew Canon brings us to the threshold of the Christian Church. The history of the Canon, like the teaching of its inspired contents, leads us into the very presence of Him in Whom alone we have the fulfilment and the interpretation of the Old Testament, and the one perfect sanction of its use.'

COLLECTION OF THE N.T. WRITINGS 207

Palestine. And, to judge from the language of their citations, as well as from innumerable unconscious reminiscences of phraseology, it was upon it that the New Testament writers themselves had been principally nurtured. We are not perhaps going too far when we say, that, with the exception of the peculiar parts of St. Matthew's Gospel, there is nothing in their writings which actually necessitates a knowledge of the original Hebrew.[1]

No considerations of language, therefore, interposed any barrier to the addition of a Greek New Testament to the Greek Old Testament already in use. And the way would be still further prepared for such a result by the collections of excerpts from the Old Testament which were used from an early period for the purposes of Christian teaching and propaganda.[2] Occasionally, no doubt, these *Testimonia*, to adopt the name given to similar collections later, such as Cyprian's *Testimonia*, may have been written in Hebrew or Aramaic, but as a rule they were in Greek, and so familiarized the minds of their

<small>Collections of *Testimonia*.</small>

---

[1] That the early Church regarded the Septuagint as not merely the translation of an inspired original, but as in itself inspired, is shown by the stories of the miraculous circumstances accompanying its production, as that the translators all finished their work at the same moment, and that the seventy-two copies were found to be in complete agreement. See the collection of *Testimonia* appended to Wendland's edition of *Aristeae ad Philocratem Epistula* (Leipzig, 1900), p. 85 ff.

[2] *E.g.* the *Eclogae* of Melito (*c.* A.D. 180), to which Eusebius refers, *Hist. Eccles.* iv. 26. 12.

readers with the thought of an authoritative Christian tradition in that tongue.[1]

2. The contents and character of the New Testament writings. The words of Jesus.

2. An even stronger influence leading to the collection of the New Testament writings lay in the contents and character of the writings themselves.

No mention has as yet been made of the fact that, in the oldest Christian communities, there was another authority which had taken its place alongside of the Hebrew Scriptures, and that was the words of Jesus, as they were handed down in the current oral tradition of the time. It is to such words, for example, that St. Paul appeals so confidently on various occasions to enforce some lesson (Acts xx. 35), or to settle some difficulty (1 Thess. iv. 15, 1 Cor. vii. 10), or to confirm some rite (1 Cor. xi. 23), and whose remembrance, as St. John recalls, the Lord Himself assured by His promised gift of the Holy Spirit: 'But the Advocate, the Holy Spirit, whom the Father will send in My name, He shall teach you all things, and bring to your remembrance all that I said unto you' (John xiv. 26).

The significance attached to these words lay at first, it will be noted, in the fact that they were

---

[1] On the general character of these Testimonies, see Hatch, *Essays in Biblical Greek* (Oxford, 1889), p. 203 ff., and Rendel Harris, 'The Use of Testimonies in the Early Christian Church,' in the *Expositor*, VII. ii. p. 385 ff. Cf. Burkitt, *The Gospel History and its Transmission* (Edinburgh, 1906), p. 127: 'To collect and apply the Oracles of the Old Testament in the light of the New Dispensation was the first literary task of the Christian Church.'

directly attributed to Jesus Himself, and not in their inclusion in any sacred book. And even towards the middle of the second century Papias, Bishop of Hierapolis, is found declaring in the Preface to the five books which he devoted to the interpretation of similar λόγια κυριακά, that for his knowledge of these he preferred to rely on oral reports of what Andrew, or Peter, or other disciples of the Lord had said, 'for,' as he significantly adds, 'I did not think that what I could derive from the books would profit me as much as what came from the living and abiding voice.'[1] At the same time, as these living witnesses died out, and men had perforce to content themselves with the written documents in which the most important of the Lord's words had come to be recorded, it is obvious that the words would inevitably impart some of their own sacred character to these documents, and consequently that the germs of their future Scriptural authority were in our Gospels from the first.

The same thing applies, though in a lesser degree, to the writings of the Apostles. As the personal followers of Jesus, and consequently the immediate

The Apostolic teaching.

---

[1] Eusebius, *Hist. Eccles.* iii. 39. 4: οὐ γὰρ τὰ ἐκ τῶν βιβλίων τοσοῦτόν με ὠφελεῖν ὑπελάμβανον ὅσον τὰ παρὰ ζώσης φωνῆς καὶ μενούσης.

The title of Papias's work, now unfortunately lost, was Λογίων κυριακῶν ἐξηγήσεις. For our knowledge of its contents we are dependent on a few fragmentary notices preserved by Irenaeus and Eusebius. See further Lightfoot, *Essays on the Work entitled Supernatural Religion* (London, 1889), p. 142 ff.

witnesses to His life and teaching, the Apostles were regarded with a prestige which was bound to communicate itself in turn to their writings. And though it necessarily took time before the Apostolic Epistles were put on an equality with the Gospels, the early use of them in connexion with Christian worship gradually led to their being regarded as an inspired court of appeal in all that concerned the doctrine or rule of the Church.

<small>3. The use of the new documents in public worship.</small>

3. This public use of the new Christian documents had indeed such an important influence upon their future history that it requires to be separately emphasized.

The reading aloud of the Law had always formed a part of the Jewish synagogue services, and already in New Testament times had come to be followed by a lesson from the Prophets, as when in the synagogue at Nazareth Jesus read a passage from Isaiah on which He afterwards founded His 'words of grace,' or as when in the synagogue of Pisidian Antioch, St. Paul addressed the assembled brethren 'after the reading of the Law and the Prophets.'[1]

It is easy, therefore, to understand how readily there would come to be conjoined with these Old Testament lessons the public reading of the new writings. No more fitting opportunity could be found for making those to whom they were addressed acquainted with their contents, than when they were thus assembled for the purpose of worship. And the same use would be made of other writings of a

[1] Luke iv. 17 ff., Acts xiii. 15.

similar character, as copies came to be multiplied amongst the different Christian communities.

It is sometimes thought that St. Paul's emphatic adjuration to the Thessalonian Church to see that his Epistle to them be 'read aloud to all the brethren' (1 Thess. v. 27) was due to the fact that the reading of such a letter had not yet been officially established, but it is sufficiently explained by the importance the Apostle himself attached to its contents in view of the dangers surrounding his converts, or, it may be in this instance, by a presentiment that a wrong use might be made of his name and authority (as is indicated in 2 Thess. ii. 2, iii. 17). And, similarly, when in writing to the Colossians the same Apostle bade them pass on their Epistle, when they had read it, to the Church of the Laodiceans, and receive back in return the Epistle he had addressed to that Church (Col. iv. 16), it was obviously in order that messages which concerned both Churches might be directly brought under the notice of the members of both. *The Epistles.*

No thought, let me again repeat, of putting the new writings on the same footing as the Old Testament Scriptures to which he had just been listening would occur to any one. And yet their very juxtaposition with these Scriptures in the public services of the Church would inevitably give them an increasing importance and authority.

'What manner of things lie in your case?' demanded the Proconsul of a North African Christian, Speratus, about the year A.D. 180. 'Books,' was the answer, 'and Epistles of Paul a just man.'[1] And whatever is to be understood by 'books,' whether they are to be confined to the books of the Divine Law, or may include also the Gospels, in any case the passage proves that along with them certain Pauline writings were treasured in the archives of the Church, obviously for the purposes of public reading and edification.

The Gospels. As regards the Gospels, we have still earlier evidence to the same effect in the well-known passage in Justin Martyr, in which he describes as the first act in the worship of God on Sundays the reading aloud before the whole congregation of a portion of Scripture from 'the Memoirs of the Apostles, or the writings of the Prophets.'[2] And as by 'the Memoirs of the Apostles' Justin means 'gospels,'[3] and more particularly, to judge from the nature of his references to them, our four canonical Gospels,[4] we may accept

---

[1] *Passio Sanctorum Scilitanorum*, ed. Robinson in *Texts and Studies*, I. ii. p. 114: 'Libri [uenerandi (-da B) libri legis divinae BC] et epistolae Pauli uiri iusti.' The answer of Speratus is given at greater length in the Greek version, Αἱ καθ' ἡμᾶς βίβλοι καὶ αἱ προσεπιτούτοις ἐπιστολαὶ Παύλου τοῦ ὁσίου ἀνδρός.

[2] *Apol.* i. 67, ed. Otto: τὰ ἀπομνημονεύματα τῶν ἀποστόλων ἢ τὰ συγγράμματα τῶν προφητῶν.

[3] *Ibid.* 66: ἐν ἀπομνημονεύμασιν, ἃ καλεῖται εὐαγγέλια.

[4] Cf. *e.g. Dial.* c. 103, where, with reference to the incident recorded in the received text of Luke xxii. 44, Justin refers to the Memoirs, 'which I say were composed by the Apostles and those who followed them' (ἅ φημι ὑπὸ τῶν ἀποστόλων αὐτοῦ καὶ τῶν ἐκείνοις παρακολουθησάντων συντετάχθαι)—a description which covers exactly the traditional authorship of St. Matthew and St. John, and of St. Mark and St. Luke.

THE GOSPEL ACCORDING TO PETER X.-XI. καὶ ἐνφανίσαι ... ἐφλέγοντο.

From the Fayûm.   Second Century.   By permission of M. Ernest Leroux of Paris.

To face the preceding.

PLATE IX.

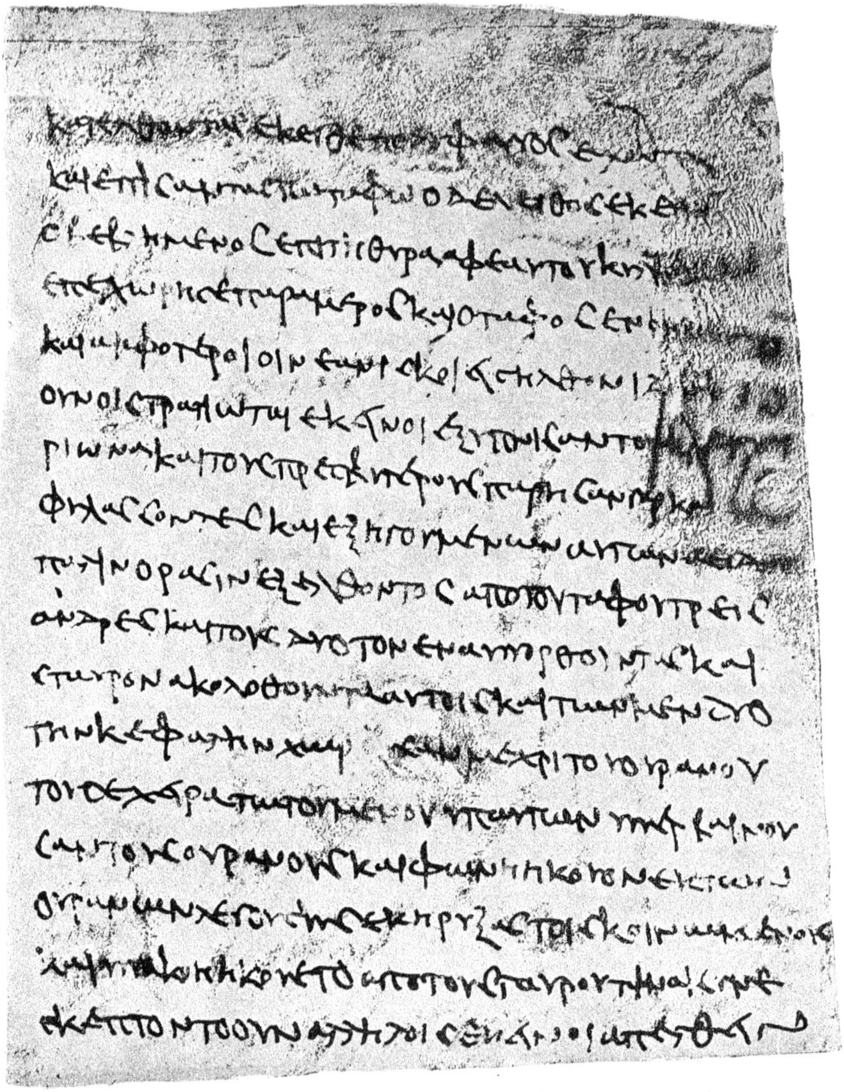

THE GOSPEL ACCORDING TO PETER IX.–X. κατελθόντας . . . ἀπελθεῖν.

From the Fayûm. Second Century. By permission of M. Ernest Leroux of Paris.

To face p. 213.

COLLECTION OF THE N.T. WRITINGS 213

him as a witness that in the first half of the second century at latest, and the practice may well have been in existence for a considerable time previously, the Gospels and the prophetical writings could be used interchangeably in connexion with Christian worship.

We must not, however, imagine that at this early period our four Gospels had gained the exclusive place which they now occupy in the use of the Church. On the contrary, there is good reason for believing that, along with the canonical Gospels, Justin also made use of the apocryphal Gospel of Peter, of which a considerable fragment was discovered in a tomb at Akhmîm in Upper Egypt during the winter of 1886-87 (see Plates IX., X.). And so late as the close of the second century, as we learn from an incidental notice in Eusebius, this same Gospel was still read in the Church at Rhossus. It was only when Serapion, Bishop of Antioch, came to realize its departure in certain respects from the true faith, that he warned the brethren against its continued use.[1]

Apocryphal books.

Nor was this freedom extended only to writings bearing Apostolic names, but, as we learn from Eusebius again, it was the custom from the beginning to read the Epistle of Clement regularly in the Church at Corinth;[2] while the inclusion of this Epistle along with the so-called Second Epistle

---

[1] Eusebius, *Hist. Eccles.* vi. 12. See further Additional Note J, 'The Gospel according to Peter.'

[2] *Ibid.* iv. 23. 11.

of Clement in the fifth century Codex Alexandrinus, and of the Epistle of Barnabas and the Shepherd of Hermas in the earlier Codex Sinaiticus, in itself constitutes sufficient evidence of the almost 'canonical' light in which these and other early Christian writings must have been for long regarded.

4. The part they played in controversy. 4. The growing authority of the New Testament writings may be illustrated still further by the part they played in controversy.

It is an interesting fact, as showing how widespread was the estimation in which the various books of the New Testament were held, that some of the earliest references to them as Scripture come to us not from within, but from without, the Church. Basilides of Alexandria, for example, the founder of a Gnostic sect in the beginning of the second century, is credited with being the first to introduce quotations from New Testament writers with such formulas as 'The Scripture saith' and 'As it is written,' which had hitherto been confined to quotations from the Old Testament. To another heretic, Marcion (*c.* A.D. 140), we owe the first definite attempt to define a New Testament Canon;[1] while in Heracleon (*c.* A.D. 170), the most prominent follower of the school of Valentinus, we have the author of the first commentary on a book of the New Testament of which we have any knowledge, a commentary, namely, on the Fourth Gospel, to which Origen in the extant portions of his own commentary on the same book repeatedly refers.

[1] See further, p. 217.

COLLECTION OF THE N.T. WRITINGS

It was indeed the constant claim of the sects that they represented the true tradition of the Apostles. And consequently in its conflict with them the Church was led to appeal more and more to that tradition as it understood and accepted it, and to collect the writings in which it was embodied into a class by themselves, marked off in ever-increasing degree from the rest of the Christian literature of the day.

II. For a detailed history of the process by which this was brought out, as reflected in the testimonies that can be gathered from early Christian writers, reference must be made to works on the Canon of the New Testament.[1] But, speaking very generally, it falls into two periods, the first extending from the time of the autographs to the year A.D. 200, and the second embracing the two following centuries until the completion of the canon about A.D. 400.

II. History of the collection and authorization of the New Testament writings.

1. The earlier of these periods saw the rise of two well-defined collections of Christian writings, a *Corpus Evangelicum* and a *Corpus Paulinum*, of which the latter was probably formed first, notwithstanding the greater honour attaching to the Gospel narratives, simply because the Pauline Epistles were earlier in circulation and lent themselves readily to collection. The Church that had the honour of having received a letter from the Apostle addressed to itself would naturally desire to share its contents with some neighbouring Church, receiving back, it

1. From the time of writing to A.D. 200.

(1) The Corpus Paulinum.

---

[1] See Additional Note N, 'Recent Literature on the Canon of the New Testament.'

might well be, some similar communication in return. And in this way little bundles of Pauline letters came to be formed, whose preservation in the same chest in itself imparted a unity to them, which was still further increased when they came to be copied out together in codices designed for the purpose.

<small>Traces of the knowledge of Pauline Epistles in Christian literature.</small>

In the letter addressed by Clement of Rome to the Corinthians before the close of the first century, there are various expressions which show that he must have been acquainted with several of the Pauline Epistles. And by the second decade of the second century, we have clear evidence in the writings of Ignatius and Polycarp that collections of these Epistles must have existed in the Churches of Antioch and Smyrna. Thus, in his letter to the Ephesians (xii. 2), Ignatius says that St. Paul makes mention of them 'in every Epistle' (ἐν πάσῃ ἐπιστολῇ), an hyberbole which may be taken as implying, on Ignatius' part, the knowledge at least of Romans (xvi. 5), 1 Corinthians (xv. 32, xvi. 8, 19), 2 Cor. (i. 8 f.), and the two Epistles to Timothy, in addition to the Epistle to the Ephesians itself.[1] And reminiscences of the language of no fewer than eight of the Pauline Epistles (Romans, 1, 2 Corinthians, Galatians, Ephesians, Philippians, 1, 2 Timothy) have been found in Polycarp's letter to the Philippians.[2]

[1] See Lightfoot's note on Ignatius, *Ephes.* xii. in *The Apostolic Fathers*, Part II. ii. p. 65.

[2] For the evidence see *The New Testament in the Apostolic Fathers* (Oxford, 1905), p. 84 ff.

COLLECTION OF THE N.T. WRITINGS 217

A generation later, the heretic Marcion, for purposes of his own, published, along with a mutilated edition of St. Luke's Gospel, a collection of the Pauline Epistles in the order—Galatians, 1 and 2 Corinthians, Romans, 1 and 2 Thessalonians, Laodiceans (= Ephesians), Colossians, Philippians, and Philemon. The omission of the Pastorals was probably due to Marcion's dislike of their contents. But, in any case, the important point is, that before the middle of the second century, a definite collection of Pauline writings had been made, doubtless, in the first instance, for practical and controversial reasons, but also out of a strong sense of the all-important character of their contents, and the respect that was due to their author.[1] {Canon of Marcion.}

The evidence regarding the use of the Gospels during this early period is, unfortunately, not free from doubt. The author, for example, of the *Didache*, or the *Teaching of the Twelve Apostles*, who probably wrote about A.D. 100,[2] makes use of {(2) The *Corpus Evangelicum*.} {Witness of the *Didache*,}

---

[1] For a restoration of the text of Marcion's Gospel and Apostolicon, see Zahn, *Geschichte des Neutestamentlichen Kanons*, ii. p. 449 ff.

[2] This document, so significant for the early history of Christianity, was discovered by Bryennius in the library of the Jerusalem Monastery of the Holy Sepulchre at Constantinople about 1875. A full account of the questions it raises, with an account of the literature to which it has given rise, will be found in Bartlet, art. 'Didache' in the Extra Volume of Hastings' *Dictionary of the Bible*, p. 438 ff. See also more recently Dean Armitage Robinson, 'The Problem of the Didache' in the *Journal of Theological Studies*, xiii. p. 239 ff.

218   THE NEW TESTAMENT DOCUMENTS

of Clement of Rome,

and others.

the Synoptic tradition, but not in such a way as to convince us that he was acquainted with the individual Gospels.¹ And while Sayings of the Lord are cited by Clement of Rome and others, there is nothing to prove that they, too, may not have been derived from the common tradition of the time, or from some written or unwritten form of Catechesis.² On the other hand, when we find Ignatius writing to the Philadelphians (viii. 2): 'Unless I find it [the point at issue] in the archives (ἐν τοῖς ἀρχείοις), that is in the Gospel (ἐν τῷ εὐαγγελίῳ), I do not believe it,' we seem to have an instance of 'Gospel,' used collectively for a body of documents. Papias again, as we have seen, shows undoubted acquaintance with the documents lying at the base of our First and Second Gospels;³ and when we come to Justin Martyr the knowledge of all our four Gospels in their present form is clearly established.

The Diatessaron.

I need not repeat the evidence that has already been adduced to this effect, but rather pass on to point out how Justin's evidence is confirmed by the *Diatessaron* of his pupil Tatian. The manner in which the true character of this work has been discovered forms one of the most striking stories in recent Biblical research;⁴ but the only point

---

¹ *The New Testament in the Apostolic Fathers* (Oxford, 1905), p. 24 ff. The most likely reference is in c. viii. 2, where the Lord's Prayer may be quoted from Math. vi. 9 ff.

² *Ibid.* p. 61.   ³ See p. 137 f. Cf. also p. 269 ff.

⁴ Cf. Hemphill, *The Diatessaron of Tatian*, Dublin and London, 1888; J. Hamlyn Hill, *The Earliest Life of Christ, being the*

COLLECTION OF THE N.T. WRITINGS 219

that we need recall at present is, that the *Diatessaron*, as its name denotes, was a Harmony of the Four Gospels, introduced by Tatian into the Syriac Church, and used by it in preference to the *Evangelion Da-Mepharreshê*, that is 'the Gospel according to the Separated (Evangelists),' until the beginning of the fifth century.[1]

It is thus a witness to the fact that by the beginning of the third quarter of the second century there were already four records of Gospel history, which stood on such a different footing from all similar documents, that from them, and apparently from them alone, this one harmonized Gospel-narrative was formed.[2]

The same testimony underlies the traditions of Asia Minor, Egypt, and North Africa during the next few decades.

Irenaeus.

To Irenaeus (*c.* A.D. 180-190), who had been trained in Asia Minor under Polycarp, and from him had learned what St. John and other eye-witnesses had to tell 'concerning the Lord, and concerning His

---

Diatessaron of Tatian, Edinburgh, 1894, new edit. 1910. The work has been translated with an Introduction in the Additional Volume of the *Ante-Nicene Christian Library* (Edinburgh, 1897), p. 35 ff.

[1] See Burkitt, *S. Ephraim's Quotations from the Gospel* in *Texts and Studies*, vii. 2 (Cambridge, 1901), and *Evangelion Da-Mepharreshê* (Cambridge, 1904), ii. pp. 101 ff., 180 ff.

[2] For an ingenious attempt to reconstruct the *Diatessaron*, see Zahn, *Forschungen zur Geschichte des neutestamentlichen Kanons*, i. p. 112 ff., and cf. *Geschichte d. Neut. Kanons*, ii. p. 530 ff.

miracles and His teaching,'[1] it seemed that the Gospel could only be given 'under a four-fold form, but held together by one Spirit.'[2] And though the reasoning by which he reached this conclusion may well seem to us now very fanciful, with its appeal to the four regions of the world, and the four several winds, it is at least decisive as to the supreme place of the four Gospels in Irenaeus' thoughts.

Clement of Alexandria.

The evidence of Clement of Alexandria is less clear, and is marked by the general tendency of his school to extend the limits of the new sacred writings, as when he quotes from the apocryphal *Gospel according to the Hebrews*.[3] At the same time, from the manner in which he elsewhere refers to the four canonical gospels, Clement evidently regarded them as occupying a place by themselves.[4]

Tertullian.

In this he was followed with still greater emphasis by the North African Tertullian. After defending the Gospel of St. Luke against Marcion on the

---

[1] Eusebius, *Hist. Eccles.* v. 20. 6.

[2] *Adv. Haer.* iii. 11. 8, ed. Harvey: ὁ τῶν ἁπάντων τεχνίτης Λόγος, ... φανερωθεὶς τοῖς ἀνθρώποις, ἔδωκεν ἡμῖν τετράμορφον τὸ εὐαγγέλιον, ἑνὶ δὲ πνεύματι συνεχόμενον. For the whole passage, see Additional Note H.

[3] *Strom.* ii. 9. 45, ed. Stählin: ᾗ κἂν τῷ καθ' Ἑβραίους εὐαγγελίῳ 'Ὁ θαυμάσας βασιλεύσει, γέγραπται, καὶ ὁ βασιλεύσας ἀναπαήσεται.

[4] *Ibid.* vii. 16. 94-7: αἱ κυριακαὶ γραφαί. According to Professor Nicol, *The Four Gospels in the Earliest Church History* (Edinburgh, 1908), p. 47: 'We may confidently assume from the clear and explicit references which we find in his [Clement's] works that his Gospel canon was exactly that which we ourselves acknowledge.'

authority of the Churches of the Apostles, Tertullian goes on to show that the same authority 'will uphold the other Gospels which we have in due succession through them and according to their usage, I mean those of [the Apostles] Matthew and John: although that which was published by Mark may also be maintained to be Peter's, whose interpreter Mark was: for the narrative of Luke also is generally ascribed to Paul: [since] it is allowable that that which scholars publish should be regarded as their master's work.' And then he concludes: 'These are for the most part the summary arguments which we employ when we argue about the Gospels against heretics, maintaining both the order of time which sets aside the later works of forgers (*posteritati falsariorum praescribenti*), and the authority of Churches which upholds the tradition of the Apostles; because truth necessarily precedes forgery, and proceeds from them to whom it has been delivered.'[1]

These last words of Tertullian show that the ultimate ground for admitting any Gospel to a place in the primary rank of accepted writings was the fact that it was written or vouched for by an Apostle. And the same consideration determined the judgment of the Church with reference to various other writings which by this time had come to be associated with the Epistles of St. Paul as parts of the rapidly forming New Testament Canon.

[1] *Adv. Marc.* iv. 5. The translation is taken from Westcott, *On the Canon*, p. 345 f.

222 THE NEW TESTAMENT DOCUMENTS

The Muratorian Canon.

Thus according to the so-called Muratorian Fragment, a Latin catalogue of the books of the New Testament, discovered by Muratori in the Ambrosian Library in Milan (see Plate XI.),[1] the Roman Church possessed about A.D. 200, rather a decade earlier than later, a collection which included St. Matthew (though the section relating to this gospel is now wanting), St. Mark, St. Luke, and St. John, the Acts of the Apostles, thirteen Epistles of St. Paul, the Epistle of St. Jude, two Epistles of St. John, and the Apocalypse of St. John. The only books therefore omitted which now belong to our New Testament Canon are the Epistle to the Hebrews, the Epistle of St. James, an Epistle of St. John, and the two Epistles of St. Peter, the omission of 1 Peter being possibly accidental; while the book known as the Apocalypse of Peter is added, 'though some of our brethren will not have it read in their churches.' Such a book again as the Shepherd of Hermas may be used privately, but is not admitted to the public reading of the Church either among the Prophets or among the Apostles, while various heretical works are rejected, 'for it is not fitting that gall should be mingled with honey.'

2. From A.D. 200-400. Determination of the limits of the new collection.

2. The principle of a New Testament collection being thus by this time definitely established, all that now remained was to determine its precise limits, both with regard to books that had already been included and with regard to others whose claims had not yet been fully recognized.

[1] For the full text, see Additional Note K.

quibus tamen interfuit et ita posuit
Tertio euangelii librum secundo Lucan
Lucas iste medicus post ascensum xpi
Cum eo paulus quasi ut iuris studiosum
secundum adsumsisset numeni suo
ex opinione concriset dnm tamen nec ipse
uiuit in carne et ideo pro asequi potuit
Ita et ad natiuitate Iohannis incipet dicere
Quarti euangeliorum Iohannis ex decipolis
cohortantibus condescipulis et eps suis
dixit conieiunate mihi odie triduo et quid
cuique fuerit reuelatum alterutrum
nobis enarremus eadem nocte reue
latum andreae ex apostolis ut recognis
centibus cunctis Iohannis suo nomine
cuncta discriberet et ideo licet uaria sin
culis euangeliorum libris principia
doceantur nihil tamen differt creden
tium fidei cum uno ac principali spu de
clarata sint in omnibus omnia de natiui
tate de passione de resurrectione
de conuersatione cum decipulis suis
ac de gemino eius aduentu
primo in humilitate dispectus quod fo
secundum potestate regali pre
clarum quod foturum est. quid ergo
mirum si Iohannes tam constanter
singula etiam in epistulis suis proferat
dicens in semet ipsu que uidimus oculis
nostris et auribus audiuimus et manus
nostrae palpauerunt haec scripsimus

THE CANON OF MURATORI, SHOWING THE PASSAGE RELATING TO THE ORIGIN OF ST. JOHN'S GOSPEL.

End of Second Century.

COLLECTION OF THE N.T. WRITINGS 223

The great name that meets us here is that of Origen, who, while giving a list of books 'uncontroverted' in the Church like the four Gospels, or 'generally acknowledged' like the First Epistle of St. Peter,[1] elsewhere quotes from others, such as the Epistles of St. James and St. Jude, in a way that shows that doubts had been raised regarding them.[2] And in this attitude he was followed by the historian Eusebius (A.D. 270-340), with his well-known division into (1) the acknowledged, (2) the disputed, and (3) the heretical books, the two former classes being regarded as canonical and the last as uncanonical.[3] *[side: Origen. Eusebius.]*

It would take too long to examine in detail the lists either of Origen or of Eusebius, but it may illustrate the general attitude of the Church during this period if we notice briefly the varying fortunes that for a time attended two books which eventually gained an assured place in our New Testament Canon. *[side: General attitude of the Church illustrated in the case of]*

In view of its close relation to Jewish prophecy and the authoritative claims made by its author with reference to it,[4] it is not surprising that the Apocalypse should from early times have been regarded with special honour, and should at first *[side: the Apocalypse,]*

---

[1] *Apud* Eusebium, *Hist. Eccles.* vi. 25.

[2] *Comm. in Joann.* T. xix. 6 : ὡς ἐν τῇ φερομένῃ Ἰακώβου ἐπιστολῇ ἀνέγνωμεν. *Comm. in Matt.* T. xvii. 30: εἰ δὲ καὶ τὴν Ἰούδα πρόσοιτό τις ἐπιστόλην.

[3] *Hist. Eccles.* iii. 25.

[4] Rev. i. 3, xxii. 7 ; cf. Deut. iv. 10.

have received nearly unanimous recognition both in the West and in Egypt.[1]

But in the course of the third century a strong reaction took place, largely owing to the difficulty on linguistic grounds of ascribing it to the same author as the Fourth Gospel. And though Dionysius of Alexandria, who was the first, as we have seen (see p. 123), to raise these difficulties in a truly critical manner, was willing to accept the book as canonical while denying its Apostolic authority, others in the East took varying attitudes. Cyril of Jerusalem (A.D. 315-386) rejected it; Athanasius († A.D. 373) regarded it, along with the other writings of our New Testament, as one of 'the springs of salvation'; Chrysostom († A.D. 407) was evidently acquainted with it, but never, so far as we can gather from his voluminous writings, appealed to it as Scripture. Nor did it find any place in the *Peshitta* of the Syriac Church.

In the West, on the other hand, the Apocalypse was generally received as one of the twenty-seven books which went finally to form the collected Canon.[2]

---

[1] Leipoldt, *Geschichte des neutestamentlichen Kanons* (Leipzig, 1907), i. 33 ff., claims for the Apocalypses a foremost place in the early history of the New Testament Canon. And as showing how long this state of things continued, in certain quarters at any rate, it may be noted that the list of canonical books appended to the sixth century Graeco-Latin Codex Claromontanus of St. Paul (D_2) includes the Apocalypse of John, the Apocalypse of Peter, and the Shepherd of Hermas.

[2] It is perhaps significant of the difficulty which the Apocalypse had later in maintaining its place in the Canon that amidst the

In the case of the Epistle to the Hebrews, the attitude of the Churches ran a different course. The Western Church as a whole, both in Rome and Africa, by declaring itself against the Pauline authorship, refused the Epistle the place generally assigned by this time to a genuine Apostolic writing.[1] The Eastern Church, on the other hand, began by accepting the Epistle as the work of St. Paul. And though later it was sometimes understood to be his only in a secondary sense, in the main it continued to be assigned to the Apostle, without any serious attempt to determine the exact nature of his connexion with it. Gradually this view spread to the West until, largely through the influence of Augustine and Jerome, its place in the Canon alongside of the thirteen Epistles of St. Paul was assured. The desire for uniformity, which had led the East to accept the Apocalypse in accordance with the general tradition of the West, was now rewarded by the West in its turn accepting the Epistle to the Hebrews in accordance with the general tradition of the East.

and the Epistle to the Hebrews.

---

variations in the order of the other parts of the New Testament, it practically always occupies the last place, though we cannot ignore that it was peculiarly suited for this place in view of the character of its contents. See further Additional Note L, 'The Order of the New Testament Writings.'

[1] That, however, the Epistle was well-known at Rome from a very early date is proved by the traces of its use in the letter written by Clement of Rome to the Corinthians between A.D. 93 and 97.

226 THE NEW TESTAMENT DOCUMENTS

Other Christian writings.

The want of a trustworthy Apostolic title, on the other hand, served to rule out many Christian writings which had hitherto been regarded with great favour, such as the Epistle of Clement. And the general result was the collection of the twenty-seven attested works of Apostles and Apostolic men, which we know as the New Testament.[1]

Its different parts might not all be regarded as equally inspired. Doubts might continue to be expressed regarding the authorship or the authority of this or that book. But, from this time onwards, there was no longer any serious attempt to add to the collection. The New Testament, in the extent in which we now know it, formed an inseparable whole, ready to take its place along with the Old Testament as the Divine Scriptures of the Christian Church.[2]

III. General remarks.

III. Looking back on this somewhat complicated historical résumé, four remarks of a general character suggest themselves.

1. The collection of the New Testament writings was a gradual process.

1. This collection of the New Testament writings was a gradual process.

There is a widely prevalent popular idea that the New Testament sprang into existence all at once

---

[1] See Additional Note M, 'Extracts from Festal Letter xxxix of Athanasius, A.D. 367.'

[2] Cf. Harnack, *History of Dogma*, Eng. Tr. by Buchanan, London, 1896, ii. p. 62 n[1]: 'No greater creative act can be mentioned in the whole history of the Church than the formation of the apostolic collection and the assigning to it of a position of equal rank with the Old Testament.'

and as a completed whole, and that all its different parts were forthwith accepted by the Christian Church as the divinely inspired record of God's new revelation of Himself to man. But, as we have just seen, this was far from being the case. The writings of which the New Testament is now made up were in the first instance independent, occasional writings, called forth at different times and under different circumstances to meet immediate and practical needs. And though from the nature of the case—from the character of their writers and of the truths with which they dealt—they were quickly invested with an ever-increasing sacredness and authority, it was not until something like three hundred years had elapsed that these scattered writings were definitely and finally combined into the New Testament as we have it now.

2. This, again, was not due in the first instance to any authoritative pronouncement on the part of the Christian Church.

<small>2. It was largely informal and unofficial.</small>

It was not until the year A.D. 397 that the Third Council of Carthage, in dealing with the subject of the Scriptures, formally enumerated the contents of the New Testament, as at present received, while it was three hundred years later, A.D. 691, before this Canon was synodically determined for the Church of East and West by the Quini-sextine Council. And consequently for the earlier stages in the history of the canon we are led to look to the divinely guided instinct of the whole Christian community. Not by the judgments of Church rulers and theologians, but by the appeal they made to the heart and conscience of the early believers, were the New Testament writings separated from the other Christian writings of the day. And the supreme religious value that was then ascribed to them has been fully endorsed and justified by the whole course of their later history.

3. It included, on the whole, all that was best worth preserving.

3. For no one will deny that the New Testament has preserved for us all that was best worth preserving in early Christian literature.

It is no doubt true that all its contents do not stand on the same level of certainty and authority. The Gospels come to us more fully attested than some of the Epistles: the teaching of 2 Peter cannot be put on the same footing as the teaching of the Epistle to the Romans, to say nothing of the teaching of the Sermon on the Mount. But we have only to compare our New Testament books as a whole with other literature of the kind to realize how wide is the gulf which separates them from it. The uncanonical gospels, it is often said, are in reality the best evidence for the canonical. And whatever the final decision regarding the weight to be attached to the newly discovered 'Sayings of Jesus,' no one can pretend that, intensely interesting as some of them are, they add anything of importance to the sayings of the Gospels.

The very fact that no serious effort has been ever made to reinstate the books which were once read in the Church, but were afterwards classed as uncanonical, is in itself a proof that the Church acted rightly in drawing the line where it did.

4. With the utmost confidence and thankfulness, then, we may acknowledge the unique position of our completed New Testament. <small>4. The unique character of the completed New Testament.</small>

The writings which it embodies are the title-deeds of our Christian faith and life. The truth which they teach is the truth as it is in Jesus. 'For me,' says Ignatius in a famous passage (*ad Philad.* viii.), 'the archives are Jesus Christ: the inviolable archives are His Cross and death, and His Resurrection and the faith that is through Him.' And it is just because of the manner in which in their turn both Gospels and Epistles bear witness to these same great saving truths, that they continue to exercise an authority over the mind and heart of the Church to which no other writings, however venerable, can lay claim.

> *MERCIFUL LORD, we beseech Thee to cast Thy bright beams of light upon Thy Church, that it being enlightened by the doctrine of Thy blessed Apostles and Evangelists may so walk in the light of Thy truth, that it may at length attain to the light of everlasting life; through Jesus Christ our Lord.* AMEN.

[λέγει Ἰη(σοῦ)ς·
μὴ παυσάσθω ὁ ζη[τῶν . . . . ἕως ἂν
εὕρῃ καὶ ὅταν εὕρῃ [θαμβηθήσεται καὶ θαμ-
βηθεὶς βασιλεύσει κα[ὶ βασιλεύσας ἀναπαήσεται.   New 'Saying of Jesus.'

APPENDIX
OF
ADDITIONAL NOTES

NOTE A.

SOME BOOKS FOR THE STUDY OF THE GREEK PAPYRI.

In view of the number of references in this volume to the Greek Papyri, and to the increasing sense of their value for New Testament study generally, the following note of certain books dealing with them may prove of use.

The original texts can probably be most conveniently Texts. studied in the annual volumes edited for the Graeco-Roman Branch of the Egypt Exploration Fund by Dr. Grenfell and Dr. Hunt. Vol. I. was published in 1898, and of *The Oxyrhynchus Papyri* alone nine volumes have already appeared. An annual subscription of one guinea to the Branch (payable at the Offices of the Fund, 37 Great Russell Street, London, W.C.) entitles subscribers to the annual volume, and also to the annual Archaeological Report.

Amongst other papyrus texts published in this country, mention may be made of *The Flinders Petrie Papyri*, edited by Dr. Mahaffy and Professor Smyly (in the Proceedings of the Royal Irish Academy—'Cunningham Memoirs,' Nos. viii., ix., xi., Dublin, 1891, 1893); of the *Greek Papyri in the British Museum*, edited by Sir F. G. Kenyon and Dr. H. I. Bell, 3 vols. (London, 1893, 1898, 1907); and of the *Catalogue of the Greek Papyri in the John Rylands Library, Manchester*, edited by Dr. A. S.

Hunt, of which Vol. I. appeared in 1911 (Manchester: at the University Press).

Many collections of texts are also in course of publication on the continent, of which the principal is *Aegyptische Urkunden aus den Koeniglichen Museen zu Berlin: Griechische Urkunden*. Of these, four volumes, comprising 1209 texts, have now been published (Berlin, 1895, 1898, 1903, 1912).

Selected texts. A large selection of leading documents from the above and other sources, accompanied by valuable historical and legal introductions, will be found in *Grundzüge und Chrestomathie der Papyruskunde* by L. Mitteis and U. Wilcken (4 half-volumes, Leipzig, 1912, 40s.).

Smaller collections are provided by H. Lietzmann, *Greek Papyri* (eleven texts with brief notes, Deighton, Bell & Co., Cambridge, 6d.), A. Laudien, *Griechische Papyri aus Oxyrhynchos* (Texts with brief notes in German for school use, Berlin, 1912, 1s. 6d.), S. Witkowski, *Epistulae Privatae Graecae*[2] (a collection of private letters of the Ptolemaic period with a Latin commentary, Leipzig, 1911, 3s. 3d.), and G. Milligan, *Selections from the Greek Papyri* (fifty-five representative Greek texts with English translations and notes, Cambridge University Press, new edition, 1912, 5s. net).

Christian texts. In *Les plus anciens Monuments du Christianisme* (being *Patrologia Orientalis*, iv. 2, Paris, 1907, about 6s.), C. Wessely has edited the most important early Christian documents written on papyrus, with French translations and commentaries, and in *Aus den Papyrus der Königlichen Museen* (Berlin, 1899, about 4s.), A. Erman and F. Krebs have issued German translations of a number of the papyri in the Berlin Museum.

General discussions. Discussions on many points raised by the new discoveries, which have proved epoch-making by the interest they have awakened in the subject, will be found in Deissmann's *Bible Studies* (1901, 9s.), *New Light on the*

NOTE A 235

New Testament (1907, 3s.), *The Philology of the Greek Bible* (1908, 3s. net), and *Light from the Ancient East* (1910, 16s. net).

At present Professor Deissmann is engaged on a new Lexicon of the Greek New Testament, in which the evidence of the papyri and inscriptions will be fully utilized. Meanwhile reference may be made to H. van Herwerden, *Lexicon Graecum suppletorium et dialecticum* (new edition, Leyden, 1910, 48s.), and to the *Lexical Notes from the Papyri* contributed by Professor J. H. Moulton and the present writer to the *Expositor* from 1908 onwards. The authors hope to republish these last with much additional material as a first attempt at the systematic lexical illustration of the New Testament vocabulary from contemporary sources.

Language.

The history of the Greek language at this period has been traced by A. Thumb, *Die Griechische Sprache in Zeitalter des Hellenismus* (Strassburg, 1901). See also the article 'Hellenistic and Biblical Greek' by the same writer in the *Standard Bible Dictionary* (London and New York, 1909), Deissmann's article on 'Hellenistisches Griechisch (mit besonderer Berücksichtigung der griechischen Bibel)' in the *Realencyklopädie für protestantische Theologie und Kirche*[3], ed. Hauck, and J. H. Moulton, 'New Testament Greek in the light of modern discovery' (in *Cambridge Biblical Essays*, London, 1909, 12s.).

On the grammar of later Greek, see A. Jannaris, *An Historical Greek Grammar* (London, 1897), and with special reference to Biblical Greek, J. H. Moulton, *A Grammar of New Testament Greek*, Vol. i. *Prolegomena* (3rd edit., 1908, 8s. net), and H. St. John Thackeray, *A Grammar of the Old Testament in Greek according to the Septuagint*, Vol. i. *Introduction, Orthography, and Accidence* (Cambridge, 1909, 8s. net). Reference may also be made to L. Radermacher, *Neutestamentliche Grammatik*, being *Handbuch zum Neuen Testament*, I. i. (Tübingen,

Grammar.

1911), and to R. Helbing, *Grammatik der Septuaginta: Laut- und Wortlehre* (Göttingen, 1907, 6s.).

Palaeography. For the palaeographical importance of the papyri in relation to the autographs of the New Testament writings, see F. G. Kenyon, *The Palaeography of Greek Papyri* (Oxford, 1899, 10s. 6d.) and *Handbook to the Textual Criticism of the New Testament*, Chap. II. (new edition, London, 1912, 5s. net). See also Sir E. M. Thompson's *Introduction to Greek and Latin Palaeography*, Oxford, 1912, with its splendid collection of facsimiles, of which forty-two are taken from the papyri.

Value for N.T. Exegesis. The value of the papyri in elucidating the orthography and meaning of our New Testament texts is fully recognized in most of the recent commentaries, as in the volumes on *Ephesians* by J. Armitage Robinson and *Thessalonians* by G. Milligan in Macmillan's Standard Series, on *Matthew* by W. C. Allen, *1 Corinthians* by A. Robertson and A. Plummer, *Thessalonians* by J. E. Frame, and *The Johannine Epistles* by A. E. Brooke in the International Critical Commentary, and in the commentaries by various leading German scholars in the useful *Handbuch zum Neuen Testament* (Tübingen, various dates).

Other books and dissertations dealing with special points are noted by Milligan, *Selections from the Greek Papyri*, p. xv ff., while full bibliographies and many articles indispensable to the serious student of papyrology appear from time to time in the *Archiv für Papyrusforschung*, edited by U. Wilcken, Leipzig, 1901 and subsequent years.

NOTE B.

THE TITLES AND SUBSCRIPTIONS OF THE NEW TESTAMENT WRITINGS.

IT has been pointed out (p. 19) that the titles or addresses of the New Testament autographs would in all probability be of the shortest. And it is certain at any rate that the full designations to which we have become accustomed in our English Bibles were added at a so much later date, as to lie altogether outside the period with which at present we are specially concerned. At the same time it may be convenient to indicate generally the character of the evidence afforded by the Greek manuscripts in this direction, more especially in view of the light which it throws upon the manner in which the New Testament writings had been collected into different classes or groups, as described in Lecture VI. _{Titles.}

Full particulars will be found in von Soden, *Die Schriften des Neuen Testaments*, I. i. (Berlin, 1902), p. 294 ff., on whose lists the following account is based. The exact dates of the manuscripts are not given, but it must be kept in view throughout that many of those referred to do not by any means belong to an early period.

As regards the Gospels, the oldest separate designations we meet with are simply κατὰ Ματθαῖον, κατὰ Μᾶρκον etc., the four books being included under the general title τὸ εὐαγγέλιον. _{Gospels.}

Afterwards the general title comes to be applied to each of the four parts, εὐαγγέλιον κατὰ Ματθαῖον etc., or more precisely τὸ εὐαγγέλιον κ. Ματθ., while the character of the books is frequently emphasized by the addition of ἅγιον—τὸ ἅγιον εὐαγγέλιον κτλ.

Acts. The book of the Acts is generally headed by the familiar title, πράξεις τῶν (ἁγίων) ἀποστόλων, but in some cases its author is directly mentioned by name, as Λουκᾶ εὐαγγελιστοῦ πράξεις τῶν ἀποστόλων.

Catholic Epistles. The Catholic Epistles appear to have been rarely introduced by a general title, such as αἱ ἑπτὰ ἐπιστολαί, but the designation καθολική is applied to individual members of the group, e.g. ἐπιστολὴ (τοῦ ἁγίου) Πέτρου καθολικὴ αʹ, 'The First Epistle General of (the holy) Peter.'

As interesting peculiarities in this class von Soden mentions the following:

ἐπιστολὴ καθολικὴ τοῦ ἁγίου ἀποστόλου Ἰακώβου τοῦ ἀδελφοῦ θεοῦ [α 457].
γράμμα πρὸς Ἑβραίους Ἰακώβου ἀδελφοῦ θεοῦ [α 555].
τοῦ ἁγίου Ἰωάννου τοῦ θεολόγου ἐπιστολὴ καθολικὴ πρώτη [α 457].

Pauline Epistles. As in the case of the Gospels, the Pauline Epistles form a definite class, introduced by some such general title as ἐπιστολαὶ (τοῦ ἁγίου) Παύλου (τοῦ ἀποστόλου), while the individual Epistles are known simply as πρὸς Ῥωμαίους, πρὸς Κορινθίους αʹ etc.

Gradually, however, these individual titles are enlarged to ἐπιστολὴ Παύλου πρὸς κτλ., such further designations as τοῦ (ἁγίου or ἁγίου καὶ πανευφήμου) ἀποστόλου being of frequent occurrence.

Sometimes the Epistles are numbered throughout: hence such a title as Παύλου ἐπιστολὴ δευτέρα, αʹ δὲ πρὸς Κορινθίους, 'The Second Epistle of S. Paul, but the First to the Corinthians.'

Apocalypse. For the Apocalypse, von Soden mentions three titles, all of which are interesting in connexion with the traditional Johannine authorship :

ἀποκάλυψις (τοῦ ἁγίου) Ἰωάννου τοῦ θεολόγου.
ἀποκάλυψις τοῦ εὐαγγελιστοῦ παρθένου καὶ θεολόγου Ἰωάννου.
ἀποκάλυψις Ι. τ. θ., ἣν ἐν Πάτμῳ τῇ νήσῳ ἐθεάσατο.

The subscriptions to the Gospels are often wanting altogether, or consist simply in the repetition of the title, (τὸ) κατὰ Ματθαῖον (εὐαγγέλιον). Sometimes we find, τέλος τοῦ κατὰ ... εὐαγγελίου, or τέλος εἴληφεν τὸ κατὰ ... εὐαγγέλιον. *Subscriptions. Gospels.*

On the other hand, the subscriptions not infrequently give the scribes an opportunity of adding various particulars regarding the supposed date, place of origin, or language of the originals. Thus, such an inscription as ἐξεδόθη τὸ κατὰ ... εὐαγγέλιον μετὰ ἔτη ... τῆς τοῦ Χριστοῦ ἀναλήψεως may be further enlarged in the case of Matthew by the notes ἐν Ἱεροσολύμοις and ἑβραϊστί, or of Mark, ἐν Ῥώμῃ and ῥωμαϊστί.

One or two examples of a more special character may also be noted :

τὸ κατὰ Ματθαῖον εὐαγγέλιον τῇ ἑβραΐδι διαλέκτῳ γραφὲν ἐξεδόθη ὑπ' αὐτοῦ ἐν Ἱερουσαλὴμ μετὰ χρόνους ὀκτὼ τῆς Χριστοῦ ἀναλήψεως· ἑρμηνεύεται δὲ ὑπὸ Ἰακώβου τοῦ ἀποστόλου τοῦ ἀδελφοῦ τοῦ κυρίου τοῦ κατὰ σάρκα ἐπισκόπου ὄντος καὶ ὑπὸ τῶν ἁγίων ἀποστόλων χειροτονηθέντος.

τὸ κατὰ Μᾶρκον ἅγιον εὐαγγέλιον ὑπηγορεύθη ὑπὸ Πέτρου τοῦ ἀποστόλου ἐν Ῥώμῃ μετὰ χρόνους δέκα τῆς τοῦ Χριστοῦ ἀναλήψεως καὶ ἐπεδόθη Μάρκῳ τῷ εὐαγγελιστῇ καὶ ἐκηρύχθη ἐν Ἀλεξανδρείᾳ καὶ πάσῃ τῇ περιχώρῳ αὐτῆς.

τέλος τοῦ κατὰ Ἰω. εὐαγγελίου ἐγράφη διὰ Προχόρου μαθητοῦ αὐτοῦ ἐν Πάτμῳ τῇ νήσῳ μετὰ χρόνους λβ' τῆς Χριστοῦ ἀναλήψεως.

Other subscriptions refer to the fact that the copies have been collated with ancient transcripts, *e.g.* εὐαγγέλιον ... ἀντεβλήθη ἐκ τῶν ἐν Ἱεροσολύμοις παλαιῶν ἀντιγράφων τῶν ἐν τῷ ἁγίῳ ὄρει ἀποκειμένων.

Acts and Catholic Epistles.
The subscriptions to the Acts and Catholic Epistles contain as a rule little of interest.

Pauline Epistles.
But the Pauline Epistles leave scope for many notes. Two must suffice by way of illustration:

(Romans) ἐγράφη ἀπὸ Κορίνθου διὰ Φοίβης (τῆς) διακονίσσης (διακόνου τῆς ἐν Κεγχρέαις ἐκκλησίας).

(Titus) πρὸς Τίτον τῆς Κρήτων ἐκκλησίας πρῶτον ἐπίσκοπον, ἐγράφη ἀπὸ Νικοπόλεως τῆς Μακεδονίας.

The Epistle to the Hebrews, again, ἐγράφη ἀπὸ (τῆς) Ἰταλίας διὰ Τιμοθέου.

Apocalypse.
The subscriptions to the Apocalypse call for no remark, unless the following may be taken as intended to confirm its canonical character in the face of opposition:

Ἰωάννου τοῦ θεολόγου ἡ κανονικὴ ἀποκάλυψις.

The early versions contain much interesting evidence bearing on the subject of this Note, but as we are here concerned primarily with the existing Greek manuscripts, I have thought it better not to attempt to refer to it at length.

It may, however, be noted that as the Latins kept CATA in the titles of the Gospels down to about the middle of the fourth century A.D., it is probable that titles were exactly reproduced by the early translators. Compare also the subscription to Mark in the early Sahidic (ed. Horner, 1911). The further fact that in the title of Acts some at least of the Syriacs took πραξεισ (written πραξισ) as if it were πραξισ (singular), is of interest as showing that they understood the word in the abstract, the 'method' of the Apostles.

NOTE C.

DICTATION AND SHORTHAND.

In his *Canon and Text of the New Testament*, p. 300, Professor C. R. Gregory writes in connexion with the composition of the Pauline Epistles: [Dictation in the N.T.]

'Here we must observe how strangely history repeats itself in varying forms. The older men of to-day grew up at a time at which most men wrote for themselves what they wished to entrust to paper. To-day, however, everyone is eager to have a stenographer with a writing-machine, or to tell his thoughts to a gramophone, and hand that over to his type-writing clerk. At Paul's day, much as is the case to-day in the East and in the South, even men who could write were in the habit of having scribes to do the drudgery of writing for them. If a man were not rich, he might have a young friend or a pupil who was ready to wield the pen for him. It comports less with the dignity of age in the East to write. The old man strokes his beard and dictates his words to the scribe. That is what Paul did, although I do not know whether or not he had the beard which Christian art gives him. . . . Let us turn to the Epistle to the Romans. For our purpose one Epistle is as good as another, and which one could be better than this chief Epistle? It was Tertius who wrote it if the sixteenth chapter belongs to it. Timothy and Lucius, Jason, and Sosipater were probably all sitting around Paul and Tertius at

Corinth or at Cenchrea when Tertius wrote their greetings in 16[21], and he added his own before he went on to name Gaius.'

The details of the foregoing picture may be somewhat elaborated, and a too great air of modernity imparted to the ancient practice; but the passage at least serves to draw pointed attention to an aspect of the composition of the New Testament writings which is apt to be overlooked. We have, as we have just heard, the testimony of the Pauline Epistles themselves, that the Apostle made use of the assistance of scribes or friends in the transcription of certain of them. Nor can there be any doubt that other New Testament writers would do the same. And though we have no direct evidence that these amanuenses fell back upon any system of shorthand to assist them in their work, it is a by no means unreasonable conjecture that they would do so in accordance with what seems to have been an established custom in similar circumstances.

Shorthand.

It is true, indeed, that references to this practice are not so numerous as we might have expected, and also that there is considerable dubiety as to the nature of the shorthand employed. But there is at least sufficient evidence to show that certain forms of shortened or contracted writing were in vogue, tending to greater ease and rapidity in the recording of a spoken or dictated message. And as the subject is rarely even referred to in books on New Testament Introduction, it may be of interest to illustrate it briefly.

Greek tachygraphy.

For the first example of Greek tachygraphy, or shorthand, we are usually referred to an inscription discovered at Athens in 1884, belonging to the fourth century before Christ, which describes how certain vowels and consonants could be expressed by strokes placed in various positions. If this can be accepted as a true instance of tachygraphic writing, in which signs or symbols take the place of words, it carries us back to a very early date for the practice.

But it is possible that nothing more than a contracted form of writing is intended.¹

Unfortunately too the passage from Diogenes Laertius, which was formerly relied upon in the same connexion, does not help us much. For when Xenophon is described as ὑποσημειωσάμενος the lectures of Socrates, the usage of the word elsewhere leads us to think of 'making notes or memoranda' of them, rather than of actually 'taking them down in shorthand.'²

Nor does even the mention in Galen (περὶ τῶν ἰδίων βιβλίων γραφή) of a copy made by one who was able to write swiftly in signs (διὰ σημείων εἰς τάχος γράφειν) necessarily imply shorthand in the modern sense of the word, though something of the sort is evidently implied.³

It is fortunate, therefore, that we can supplement this scanty evidence both directly and indirectly from the Greek papyri.

Evidence of the papyri.

We have had occasion more than once to notice that both official documents and private letters are constantly written in one hand and signed in another, pointing to a widespread use of dictation (see p. 23 ff.). And now amongst the Oxyrhynchus papyri Dr. Grenfell and Dr. Hunt have published a very interesting contract which

---

¹ It may be noted that in the LXX version of Ps. xlv. 1, 'the pen of the ready writer' is rendered by κάλαμος γραμματέως ὀξυγράφου.

² ii. 48: cf. ii. 122.

³ The same phrase is found in Philostratus' account of Apollonius of Tyana, who is described as journeying accompanied by two secretaries —ὁ μὲν ἐς τάχος γράφων, ὁ δὲ ἐς κάλλος, 'the one a shorthand writer, and the other a calligrapher (i. 18; Engl. Tr. by Phillimore, i. p. 24).

In an elaborate note on ὑπογραφεύς in his *Animadversiones in Charitonem Aphrodisiensem* (Amsterdam, 1750), i. 1. p. 5, D'Orville cites *Eunap.* p. 138: ἀξιῶ δοθῆναί μοι τοὺς ταχέως γράφοντας οἳ καθ' ἡμέραν μὲν τὴν τῆς Θέμιδος γλῶσσαν ἀποσημαίνονται. I owe my acquaintance with this note to my colleague, Professor Phillimore.

shows that scribes or clerks were often prepared for this work by a regular training in shorthand.[1]

The contract belongs to A.D. 155, and in it a citizen of Oxyrhynchus apprentices his slave to a shorthand writer (σημιογράφῳ) for two years, in order that he may be taught the art. 'I have placed,' so he begins after the customary greeting, 'with you my slave Chaerammon to be taught the signs (πρὸς μάθησιν σημείων) which your son Dionysius knows.' And then, after a reference to the salary already agreed upon between them, he proceeds: 'You will receive the second instalment consisting of forty drachmae when the boy has learnt the whole system (τὸ κομεντάρ[ι]ον), and the third you will receive at the end of the period when the boy writes fluently in every respect and reads faultlessly (τοῦ παιδὸς ἐκ παντὸς λόγου πεζοῦ γράφοντος καὶ ἀναγεῖνώσ[κον]τος ἀμέμπτως).'[2]

Nor have we only this reference to the art as a whole, but a few scattered examples of symbols employed in this way have been recovered. The earliest of these consists in a line in a papyrus now preserved in Leyden, belonging to the year 104 B.C.[3] And with this may be compared another line in the long magical papyrus in the British Museum, which is dated in the third century after Christ.[4] Of about the same date are four fragments at Leipzig with

---

[1] *Oxyrhynchus Papyri*, iv. p. 204 f. No. 724.

[2] A clause in a papyrus letter of A.D. 27 (*Oxyrhynchus Papyri*, ii. p. 293, No. 293 [3 ff.]) to the effect οὐδεμίαν μοι φάσιν ἀπέστειλας περὶ τῶν ἱματίων οὔτε διὰ γραπτοῦ οὔτε διὰ σημε⟨ί⟩ου has been quoted as an earlier reference to tachygraphic writing, but the contrast with γραπτοῦ leads us to understand rather by σημείου, something *not* written, perhaps a 'message,' as the Editors translate: see Wilcken, *Archiv für Papyrusforschung*, iv. p. 259 f.

[3] *Papyri graeci Musei antiquarii publici Lugduni-Batavi*, ed. Leemans, i. Pap. N.

[4] *Greek Papyri in the British Museum*, ed. Kenyon, i. p. 114 (= B.M. Pap. 121, l. 904).

PLATE XII.

WAXEN TABLET (BRIT. MUS. ADD. MS. 33270) INSCRIBED WITH TACHYGRAPHIC SYMBOLS.

Probably Third Century A.D. By permission of the Council of the Hellenic Society.
(Slightly reduced in size.)

To face p. 245.

tachygraphic signs,[1] and a few papyri in the Rainer Collection at Vienna.[2]

Our principal witness, however, is a third century waxed book in the British Museum, consisting of seven wooden tablets, covered over with symbols (see Plate XII.). The key to their interpretation has not yet been discovered, but from the manner in which the same symbols are repeated, it evidently formed the exercise-book of a shorthand scribe or pupil.[3] *Waxed book.*

What we have thus learned from Greek sources is strongly confirmed by the corresponding practice among the Latins. *Latin tachygraphy.*

It is well known that wealthy Romans were in the habit of keeping slaves or freedmen, for the purpose of writing their letters, or of making extracts, who were known as *ab epistulis*, or *ad manum*, and later by the familiar title *amanuenses*. And we have also evidence of a class who from their proficiency in some sort of shorthand were known as *notarii*.[4] Thus the younger Pliny tells us that when his uncle, the elder Pliny, went on a journey he had always a shorthand writer by his side with note-books and tablets, ready to take down any thoughts that occurred to him.[5] And a more detailed account of the art is given by Plutarch in his description of the speech of Cato on the punishment of the Catilinarian conspirators: 'This only of all Cato's speeches, it

---

[1] Cf. Gardthausen, *Griechische Palaeographie*, Leipzig, 1879, p. 219.

[2] Wessely, *Ein System altgriechischer Tachygraphie* (in *Denkschriften d. Kaiserl. Akademie d. Wissenschaften*, xliv.), Vienna, 1896.

[3] For a description of this book, see Foat, 'On Old Greek Tachygraphy,' in *Journal of Hellenic Studies*, xxi. (1901), p. 252 ff.

[4] Marquardt, *Das Privatleben der Römer*, Leipzig, 1879, p. 802 f. *Notarii* were known later as *Exceptores* (*Dig.* xix. 2. 19 *in fine*).

[5] *Ep.* iii. 5. 14: 'In itinere... ad latus notarius cum libro et pugillaribus': cf. *ib.* ix. 36. 2: 'Notarium voco, et die admisso, quae formaveram dicto.'

is said, was preserved; for Cicero, the consul, had disposed, in various parts of the senate-house, several of the most expert and rapid writers (τοὺς διαφέροντας ὀξύτητι τῶν γραφέων), whom he had taught to make figures (σημεῖα) comprising numerous words in a few short strokes (ἐν μικροῖς καὶ βράχεσι τύποις πολλῶν γραμμάτων ἔχοντα δύναμιν); as up to that time they had not used those we call shorthand writers (σημειογράφους), who then, as it is said, established the first example of the art.'[1]

It is to Cicero, it will be noticed, that the introduction of shorthand among the Romans is here ascribed; and we know that he himself was in the habit at times of employing some form of cipher for the purpose of secrecy in his letters.[2] But a clearer indication of actual tachygraphic art is rather to be found in the well-known *notae Tironianae*, invented by Cicero's freedman, M. Tullius Tiro, in which each word was represented by a character.[3] And to such perfection was this or some similar system carried that in one of his epigrams (xiv. 208) Martial writes:

'Currant verba licet, manus est velocior illis:
 nondum lingua suum, dextra peregit opus.'[4]

---

[1] *Cato min.* xxiii.; Eng. Tr. by A. H. Clough, iv. p. 393.

[2] *ad Attic.* xiii. 32. 3: 'Quod ad te de decem legatis scripsi, parum intellixisti, credo, quia διὰ σημείων scripseram.' Similarly, Aulus Gellius (*Noctes Atticae* xvii. 9) says that Julius Caesar used to correspond in cipher with Balbus and Oppius: his phrase ('litterae singulariae sine coagmentis syllabarum') shows that the cipher was partly in shorthand.

[3] With these may be compared the *notae vulgares*, or shorthand symbols in common use, which, according to Isidore (*Orig.* i. 22), were the invention of Ennius, though it is by no means clear whether he was thinking of the grammarian of the Augustan period, or of the poet.

[4] Cf. Seneca, *Ep.* 90. 25: 'Quid verborum notas, quibus quamvis citata excipitur oratio, et celeritatem linguae manus sequitur,' and *ib. Ludus de morte Claudii*, ix. 2: 'Quae notarius persequi non potuit.'

NOTE C

Amongst others who practised the art was the Emperor Titus, who is said to have been so proficient that he engaged in friendly contests with his scribes.[1]

It is unnecessary to carry the evidence further down. And to some it may well appear that, even as it is, we have wandered a long way from the immediate subject of these Lectures, the more especially as the extent to which the New Testament writers may have availed themselves of the literary devices of their time must always remain a matter of conjecture. *General conclusion.*

We can only repeat that in the practice of dictation, especially if it were accompanied by the use of shorthand on the part of the reporting scribes, we should have a ready explanation of some of the peculiarities in language and style amongst the New Testament writings which have often caused difficulty (cf. pp. 21 ff., 103, 159 ff.).

It is further obvious that some connexion is to be traced between the signs and symbols of which we have been speaking, and the abbreviations and contractions of our ordinary manuscripts. *Abbreviations and contractions.*

Reference may be made in this connexion to Mr. T. W. Allen's *Notes on Abbreviations in Greek Manuscripts* (Oxford, 1889), while the early history of the contraction of the Divine names is fully treated in Traube, *Nomina Sacra*, Munich, 1907.

Some interesting examples of the development of shorthand at a later period for the purpose of taking down sermons, episcopal addresses, etc., will be found in Smith's *Dictionary of Greek and Roman Antiquities*[3], London, 1891, ii. p. 243 ff., Art. 'Notae.'

---

[1] Suetonius, *Titus*, 3: 'E pluribus comperi notis quoque excipere velocissime solitum, cum amanuensibus suis per ludum jocumque certantem.' Cf. also Quintilian, *Inst. Orat.* xi. 2. 25.

NOTE D.

NEW TESTAMENT TEXTS ON PAPYRUS.

THE following list of New Testament texts on papyrus is based on the list in Professor C. R. Gregory's *Die Griechischen Handschriften des Neuen Testaments* (Leipzig, 1908), pp. 45-47, and *Textkritik des Neuen Testaments* (Leipzig, 1900-1909), iii. pp. 1084-1092. By the kindness of Professor Gregory I have been able to add his numbers for a few papyrus fragments that have been published since his list appeared. Von Soden's method of enumeration is appended in brackets. A corresponding list is given by Kenyon, *Handbook to the Textual Criticism of the New Testament*^{2}, London, 1912, pp. 41-44, and for a few of the papyri mentioned here (in particular $\mathfrak{p}^1$, $\mathfrak{p}^5$, $\mathfrak{p}^{10}$), cf. Wessely, *Les plus anciens Monumens du Christianisme écrits sur papyrus* (= *Patrologia Orientalis*, iv. 2), Paris [1907].

$\mathfrak{p}^1$. [Soden, ε 01]: Part of a sheet from a papyrus book discovered at Oxyrhynchus in 1896, and published by Grenfell and Hunt, *Oxyrhynchus Papyri*, i. p. 4 ff., No. 2, with a facsimile: cf. Facsimile II. in the present volume, and see p. 61. Original now in the Museum of the University of Pennsylvania, Philadelphia. Third century. 'It may thus claim to be a fragment of the oldest known manuscript of any part of the New Testament' (Edd.).

Contains Matt. i. 1-9, 12, 14-20, in a text which closely resembles the text of the Vatican and Sinaitic codices where they agree, and, on the whole, is nearer the former where they differ. In ver. 18, however, the new text reads τοῦ δὲ Ἰησοῦ Χριστοῦ with the Sinaitic as against the Vatican codex.

𝔭². Edited by E. Pistelli, 'Papiri Evangelici' in *Studi religiosi*, vi., Florence, 1906, p. 129 ff. Original in the Archaeological Museum, Florence. Fifth or sixth century.

Contains John xii. 12-15 in Greek on the *verso*, and Luke vii. 18 ff. in Sahidic on the *recto*.

𝔭³. A leaf out of a Gospel-book brought by Th. Graf from the Fayûm to Vienna, and now in the Rainer Collection there: cf. *Führer durch die Ausstellung*, Vienna, 1894, p. 129, No. 539, and see Wessely, *Wiener Studien*, 1882, Heft 2, pp. 198-214, and 1885, Heft 7, pp. 69-70. Sixth century.

Contains an excellent text of Luke vii. 36-45, x. 38-42, written in a cursive hand.

𝔭⁴. [Soden, ε 34]: A fragment from a small book, now in the Bibliothèque Nationale at Paris: see F. V. Scheil, *Revue Biblique*, i., Paris, 1892, p. 113 ff. Fourth century.

Contains, in a very fragmentary form, Luke i. 74-80, v. 3-8, v. 30–vi. 4.

𝔭⁵. [Soden, ε 02]: A sheet of a papyrus codex discovered at Oxyrhynchus, and published by Grenfell and Hunt, *Oxyrhynchus Papyri*, ii. p. 1 ff. No. 208. Now in the British Museum [Pap. 782]. The Editors ascribe the text to the third century, but

Gregory (*Textkritik*, iii. p. 1085) inclines rather to the fourth.

The left-hand leaf contains John i. 23-31 and 33-41, and the right-hand leaf John xx. 11-17 and 19-25 (much mutilated), in a text which agrees generally with the Codex Sinaiticus, and in several instances supports it with reference to readings not found elsewhere.

On the importance of the form in the early history of book-production, see the Editors' Introduction, and cf. Schmidt, *Archiv für Papyrusforschung*, i. p. 539.

𝔓⁶. A papyrus fragment of three short lines, now in the University Library, Strassburg, and published by Gregory, *Textkritik*, iii. p. 1085 f.

Contains John xi. 45, with the reading ἅ (not ὅ) ἐποίησεν, and the omission of ὁ Ἰησοῦς after ἐποίησεν.

𝔓⁷. [Soden, ε 11]: Two papyri in the Archaeological Museum at Kieff.

The contents, according to Gregory, who saw the papyri in 1903, include Luke iv. 1 f.

𝔓⁸. [Soden, α 8]: Two leaves, now in the Berlin Museum (P. 8683). Fourth century.

The text, which embraces Acts iv. 31-37, v. 2-9, vi. 1-6, 8-15, is given in full by Gregory, *Textkritik*, iii. p. 1087 ff.

𝔓⁹. Fragment of a leaf from a papyrus book discovered at Oxyrhynchus, and published by Grenfell and Hunt, *Oxyrhynchus Papyri*, iii. p. 2 f. No. 402. Now in Harvard University Library, Cambridge, Massachusetts. Fourth or fifth century.

Contains 1 John iv. 11-12, 14-17.

$\mathfrak{p}^{10}$. [Soden, α 1032]: A fragment discovered at Oxyrhynchus, and published by Grenfell and Hunt, *Oxyrhynchus Papyri*, ii. p. 8 f., No. 209, with facsimile. Now in Harvard University Library, Cambridge, Massachusetts. First half of fourth century.

Contains Rom. i. 1-7 (with the exception of part of ver. 6) in a rude uncial hand. The Editors think it may have formed originally a schoolboy's exercise, but Deissmann (*Light from the Ancient East*, p. 232 n¹) prefers to think rather of a Gospel amulet or charm belonging to the Aurelius Paulus who is named in a cursive hand beneath the text.

In ver. 1 the fragment reads Χριστοῦ Ἰησοῦ with B as against Ἰησοῦ Χριστοῦ ℵAD, and in ver. 7 Κυρίου Χριστοῦ Ἰησοῦ as against the ordinarily received Κυρίου Ἰησοῦ Χριστοῦ.

$\mathfrak{p}^{11}$. [Soden, α 1020]: Five fragments brought from the East by Bishop Porphyry Uspensky, and now in the Imperial Library, St. Petersburg, where they were seen by Tischendorf in 1862. Fifth century.

The fragments contain 1 Cor. i. 17-20, vi. 13-18, vii. 3, 4, 10-14, in large letters without breathings or accents.

$\mathfrak{p}^{12}$. [Soden, α 1033]: Part of Heb. i. 1 written in a small uncial hand on the margin of the letter of a Roman citizen, and published by Grenfell and Hunt, *Amherst Papyri*, i. p. 30 f. No. 3 (*b*). Third or fourth century, and therefore amongst the earliest known Biblical fragments.

As regards text, the word ἡμ[ῶ]ν, which is not found in the manuscripts, is inserted after το[ῖς π]ατρά[σιν].

APPENDIX

$\mathfrak{p}^{13}$. Considerable portions of a papyrus roll discovered at Oxyrhynchus, and published by Grenfell and Hunt, *Oxyrhynchus Papyri*, iv. p. 36 ff. No. 657. Now in the British Museum [Pap. 1532]. First half of the fourth century.

Written on the back of the roll, the *recto* of which contains the new epitome of Livy (*Oxyrhynchus Papyri*, No. 668), is about one-third of the Epistle to the Hebrews (ii. 14–v. 5, x. 8–xi. 13, xi. 28–xii. 17). The text agrees closely with the Codex Vaticanus in cc. ii.-v., and this makes the papyrus an important authority for the later chapters, which are wanting in that Codex. In c. iii. 2 and 6, it confirms readings in which B stands alone amongst Greek manuscripts.

On the system of punctuation adopted by means of a double point somewhat freely inserted, cf. p. 109 of the present volume, and see further Blass, *Die Rhythmen der asianischen und römischen Kunstprosa*, Leipzig, 1905, p. 78 ff.

$\mathfrak{p}^{14}$. [Soden, α 1036]: Seven small fragments discovered by Dr. J. Rendel Harris in the monastery of St. Catherine on Mount Sinai, and edited by him in *Biblical Fragments from Mount Sinai*, London, 1890, pp. xiii., 54 ff. Fifth century.

Contains 1 Cor. i. 25-27, ii. 6-8, iii. 8-10, 20, in a very fragmentary condition.

$\mathfrak{p}^{15}$. Two leaves from a papyrus book discovered at Oxyrhynchus, and published by Hunt, *Oxyrhynchus Papyri*, vii. p. 4 ff. Nos. 1008, 1009. Second half of fourth century.

The leaves contain the text of 1 Cor. vii. 18–viii. 4, Phil. iii. 9-17, iv. 2-8, in a form agreeing in the main with the Vatican, Sinaitic, and

NOTE D 253

Alexandrine Codices, though occasionally they exhibit variants peculiar to themselves.

$\mathfrak{p}^{16}$. An extract from Rom. xii., now in the John Rylands Library, Manchester, and published by Hunt, *Catalogue of the Greek Papyri in the John Rylands Library*, Manchester, i. p. 9, No. 4. Late sixth or seventh century.

The Editor thinks that the verses (3-8) may have been copied out for reading in church, though, as the *verso* is blank, they can hardly have formed part of a regular lectionary.

In v. 8 the papyrus shares with Codex Sinaiticus the reading προεις(א ιστ)ανομενος.

$\mathfrak{p}^{17}$. A leaf from a papyrus book belonging to the same collection as the preceding, and published by Hunt as No. 5 in the *Catalogue*, with a facsimile. Third century.

Contains Titus i. 11-15, ii. 3-8, with an interesting variant in c. ii. 7: see p. 190 of this volume.

$\mathfrak{p}^{18}$. Part of a leaf from a papyrus book discovered at Oxyrhynchus, and published by Hunt, *Oxyrhynchus Papyri*, viii. p. 11 ff. No. 1078. Fourth century.

Contains Heb. ix. 12-19. The same system of punctuation found in $\mathfrak{p}^{13}$ again occurs here.

$\mathfrak{p}^{19}$. Fragment of a papyrus roll discovered at Oxyrhynchus, and published by Hunt, *Oxyrhynchus Papyri*, viii. p. 13 f. No. 1079. Late third or fourth century.

On the *verso* of a roll, containing the book of Exodus (*Oxyrhynchus Papyri*, No. 1075), a copy of the Apocalypse has been written. And of this the fragment preserves c. i. 4-7. In v. 5 Ἰησοῦς

APPENDIX

Χριστός is written $\overline{ιη}$ $\overline{Χρ}$, an unusual form of contraction in literary texts (see the Editor's Introduction).

𝔓²⁰. A leaf from a papyrus book discovered at Oxyrhynchus, and published by Hunt, *Oxyrhynchus Papyri*, ix. p. 7 ff. No. 1170. Fifth century.

Contains Matt. x. 32–xi. 5. According to the Editor, this text is probably the oldest authority for reading αὐτόν in c. x. 32. In ver. 34 it stands alone in inserting οὖν before νομίσητε.

𝔓²¹. A strip from a leaf of a papyrus book discovered at Oxyrhynchus, and published by Hunt, *Oxyrhynchus Papyri*, ix. p. 9 ff. No. 1171, with facsimile. Late third century,

Contains James ii. 19–iii. 9, the text being in general agreement with that of the Vatican Codex.

𝔓²². Fragment of a papyrus book of the Gospel of St. Matthew discovered at Oxyrhynchus, and published by Vitelli, *Papyri Greci e Latini*, i. (Florence, 1912) p. 1 f. No. 1. Seventh century.

Contains on the *recto* Matt. xxv. 12-15, and on the *verso* xxv. 20-23.

𝔓²³. Fragments of two leaves of a papyrus book which commenced with St. John's Gospel. Discovered at Oxyrhynchus, and published by Vitelli, *Papyri Greci e Latini*, i. p. 5 f. No. 3.

One leaf contains on the *recto* John iii. 14-17, and on the *verso*, iii. 17-18. The *recto* of the other leaf contains iii. 31-32. In ver. 18 the words εἰς τὸ ὄνομα have been added after ὁ μὴ πιστεύων, perhaps by error, and in ver. 31, after ὁ ὢν ἐκ τῆς γῆς, the ordinarily received words ἐκ τῆς γῆς ἐστι καὶ ἐκ τῆς γῆς λαλεῖ are wanting.

NOTE E.

GREEK PAPYRUS LETTERS.

THE following are the Greek texts of the Papyrus Letters quoted on pp. 88-92, with some additional notes.

The Oxyrhynchus Papyri, edd. Grenfell-Hunt, iv. p. 246, A commendatory letter.
No. 746. A.D. 16.

Θέων Ἡρακλείδηι τῶι ἀδελφῶι
πλεῖστα χαίρειν καὶ ὑγιαίνειν.
Ἑρμόφιλος ⟨ὁ⟩ ἀποδ[ι]δούς σοι τὴν
ἐπιστολήν [ἐ]στ[ι] . [. .] . κ[. .]μ . φ[.]ηρι
5 [.]ερίου, καὶ ἠρώτησέν με γράψαι σοι.
[π]ροφέρεται ἔχειν πραγμάτιον
[ἐν τῆι] Κερκεμούνι. τοῦτο οὖν ἐάν
σοι φα[ί]νηται σπουδάσεις κατὰ τὸ
δίκαιον. τὰ δ' ἄλλα σεαυτοῦ ἐπιμελοῦ
10 ἵν' ὑγιαίνῃς.
ἔρρωσο.
(ἔτους) γ´ Τιβερίου Καίσαρος Σεβαστοῦ Φαῶφι γ´.
(Addressed)
Ἡρακλείδηι βα(σιλικῶι) γρ(αμματεῖ) Ὀξυ(ρυγχίτου)
Κυνοπ(ολίτου).

The Editors conjecture that Theon is perhaps the same as the writer of a similar letter of introduction, published

APPENDIX

in *The Oxyrhynchus Papyri*, ii. p. 292, No. 292 (= *Selections from the Greek Papyri*², No. 14), of date *c.* A.D. 25.

For a Christian example of an ἐπιστολὴ συστατική, see the fourth century letter of the presbyter Leon, commending a brother-Christian to the priests and deacons of a local church, in *The Oxyrhynchus Papyri*, viii. p. 266, No. 1162. The concluding formula of pagan letters ἔρρωσο is there expanded into ἐρρῶσθαι ὑμᾶς [ε]ὔχομε (= αι) ἐν κ(υρί)ῳ [θ](ε)ῷ, 'I pray for your health in the Lord God.' It is also interesting to notice that this signature is witnessed by a certain Emmanuel—'Εμμ(ανουὴ)λ μάρτ(υς?).

An official letter.

The Oxyrhynchus Papyri, edd. Grenfell-Hunt, i. p. 101 ff., No. 45. A.D. 95.

Φανίας καὶ Ἡρακλᾶ[ς] καὶ Διογένης ὁ καὶ Ἑρμ(αῖος)
οἱ ἀσχολούμ(ενοι) τοὺς καταλοχ(ισμοὺς) τοῖς ἀγορανό(μοις)
χαίρειν. Διογένους τοῦ Πτολεμαίου
παρακεχωρημένου παρὰ Ταποτά-
5 μωνος τῆς Πτολεμαίου τοῦ Κολύλιδ(ος),
μετὰ κυρίου τοῦ θυγατριδοῦς Πλουτάρχ(ου)
τοῦ Πλουτάρχου τοῦ Πλουτάρχου, καθ' ὁμο(λογίαν)
γεγονυῖαν τῇ ἐνεστώσῃ ἡμέρᾳ τὴν
ὑπάρχουσαν αὐτῇ περὶ κώμην Κορωβ(ιν?)
10 ἐκ τοῦ Μενοιτίου κλήρου κατοικικῆς
γῆς σειτοφόρου σπορίμου ἐξ ὀρθογω(νίου)
ἄρουραν μίαν ἥμισυ τρίτον δωδέ-
κατον, διὸ γράφομεν ὑμεῖν ἵν' εἰδῆτε.
ἔρρω(σθε).

After the date there follows in a different hand the signature of one of the senders of the letter, the body of the document having been written doubtless by a clerk,

Ἡρακλ(ᾶς) σεση(μείωμαι).

NOTE E 257

With this official letter may be compared a document registering certain cattle, which is reproduced from *The Oxyrhynchus Papyri*, ii. p. 195, No. 246, by Deissmann, *Light from the Ancient East*, p. 159 ff. The facsimile with which it is accompanied shows very clearly the difference in handwriting between the document itself and the signatures of the attesting officials.

Berliner Griechische Urkunden, ii. p. 267, No. 615. Second century A.D.

Family letters.
A daughter to her father.

Ἀμμωνοῦς τῷ γλυκυτάτῳ
πατρὶ χαίρειν.
Κομισάμενός σου τὸ ἐπιστόλιον
καὶ ἐπιγνοῦσα, ὅτι θεῶν θελόν-
5 των διεσώθης, ἐχάρην πολλά·
καὶ αὐτῆς ὥρας ἀφορμὴν εὑρὼν
ἔγραψά σοι ταυοῦτα τὰ γράμματα σπουδάζουσα προσκυνῆ-
σέ σαι· ταχύτερον τὰ ἐπίγοντα
10 ἔργα φροντίζετε· ἐὰν ἡ μικρά
τι ἴπῃ, ἔστε· ἐάν σοι ἐνέκῃ κα-
λάθιν ὁ κομιζόμενός σοι τὸ
ἐπιστόλειον, πέμ[π]ω· ἀσπάζον-
τέ σε οἱ σοὶ πάντ[ε]ς κατ' ὄνομα,
15 ἀσπάζετέ σε Κέλερ καὶ οἱ αὐτοῦ
πάντας.
Ἐρρῶ[σ]θέ σοι ε[ὔ]χομαι.

The surprising concords, which this and so many of the more illiterate documents of the time exhibit, have been appealed to as illustrating the peculiarities of the Greek of the writer of the Apocalypse.

'Apart from places,' says Professor Moulton, 'where he may be definitely translating a Semitic document, there is no reason to believe that his grammar would have been materially different had he been a native of Oxyrhynchus, assuming the extent of Greek education the same' (*Prolegomena*[3], p. 9). And to much the same effect Dean Armitage Robinson writes with reference to the writer's disregard of the primary rules of grammar: 'This is not ignorance in the ordinary sense: it is familiarity with a relaxed standard of speech, such as we find often enough in the professional letter-writers who indited the petitions and private correspondence of the Fayûm' (*Journal of Theological Studies*, x. p. 10).

For κατ' ὄνομα in the closing greetings of the above letter, obviously in the sense of 'individually,' 'one by one,' cf. 3 John 15 : ἀσπάζου τοὺς φίλους κατ' ὄνομα.

A slave to her master.

Griechische Papyri im Museum des Oberhessischen Geschichtsvereins zu Giessen, edd. Kornemann-Meyer, i. No. 17. Time of Hadrian.

Τᾶυς Ἀπ[ολλ]ωνίωι τῶι κυρίωι πλεῖστα
   χαίρειν.
Πρὸ τῶν ὅλων ἀσπάζομαί σε, δέσποτα,
καὶ εὔχομαι πάντοτε περὶ τῆς ὑγιείας σου.
5 Ἠγωνίασα, κύριε, οὐ μετρίως, ἵνα ἀκούσω
ὅτι ἐνωθρεύσας, ἀλλὰ χάρις τοῖς θεοῖς πᾶσι
ὅτι σε διαφυλάσσουσι ἀπρόσκοπον. Παρακαλῶ σε, κύριε, ἐάν σοι δόξῃ, καὶ πέμ-
ψαι ἐφ' ἡμᾶς, εἰ δὲ μή, ἀποθνήσκομεν
10 ὅτι οὐ βλέπομέν σε καθ' ἡμέραν. Ὤφελον
εἰ ἐδυνάμεθα πέτασθαι καὶ ἐλθεῖν καὶ προσ-
κυνῆσαί σε· ἀγωνιῶμεν γὰρ με[..] ἔπου-
σαί σε. Ὥστε διαλλάγηθι ἡμεῖν κα[ὶ π]έμ-
ψον ἐφ' ἡμᾶς. Ἔρρωσο κύριε [
15   καὶ πάντα ἔχομ[εν καλῶς ?].
Ἐφεὶπ κδ'.

(Addressed)
Ἀπολλωνίωι **X** στρατηγῶι.

With the formal use of τῶι κυρίωι in the address cf. 2 John 1, and see p. 116, and with the construction ἠγωνίασα ... ἵνα in l. 5 cf. John viii. 56, ἠγαλλιάσατο ἵνα ἴδῃ ... The ἀποθνήσκομεν of l. 9 recalls the Pauline καθ' ἡμέραν ἀποθνήσκω (1 Cor. xv. 31): while, as the first Editor points out, Tays' longing to 'fly' in l. 11, in order to reach her master as quickly as possible, has a special interest for us to-day. The interchange of the first person singular (ἀσπάζομαι, εὔχομαι, etc.) and the first person plural (ἐφ' ἡμᾶς, ἀποθνήσκομεν) may be noted in connexion with the vexed question as to whether St. Paul ever used an epistolary plural: see further the present writer's commentary on the *Epistles to the Thessalonians*, Note B, p. 131 f.

Berliner Griechische Urkunden, iii. p. 170 f., No. 846; cf. *ibid. Berichtigungen*, p. 6, for various textual emendations by Schubart. Second century A.D.   *A prodigal son to his mother.*

Ἀντῶνις Λόνγος Νειλοῦτι

[τ]ῇ μητρὶ π[λ]ῖστα χαίρειν. Καὶ δι-
ὰ πάντω[ν] εὔχομαί σαι ὑγειαίνειν. Τὸ προσκύνη-
μά σου [ποι]ῶ κατ' αἰκάστην ἡμαίραν παρὰ τῷ
5 κυρίῳ [Σερ]απείδει. Γεινώσκειν σαι θέλω, ὅ-
τι οὐχ [ἤλπ]ιζον, ὅτι ἀναβένις εἰς τὴν μητρό-
πολιν. χ[ά]ρειν τοῦτο οὐδ' ἐγὸ εἰσῆθα εἰς τὴν πό-
λιν. αἰδ[υ]σοπο[ύ]μην δὲ ἐλθεῖν εἰς Καρανίδα·
ὅτι σαπρῶς παιριπατῶ. Αἴγραψά σοι, ὅτι γυμνός
10 εἰμει. Παρακα[λ]ῶ σαι, μήτηρ, δ[ι]αλάγητί μοι. Λοι-
πὸν οἶδα τί [ποτ'] αἰμαυτῷ παρέσχημαι. παιπαίδ-
δευμαι, καθ' ὃν δὶ τρόπον. οἶδα, ὅτι ἡμάρτηκα.
Ἤκουσα παρὰ το[ῦ Ποστ]ούμου τὸν εὑρόντα σαι
ἐν τῷ Ἀρσαινοείτῃ καὶ ἀκαίρως πάντα σοι δι-
15 ήγηται. Οὐκ οἶδες, ὅτι θέλω πηρὸς γενέσται,
εἰ γνοῦναι, ὅπως ἀνθρόπῳ [ἔ]τ[ι] ὀφείλω ὀβολόν;
[......] ο [..........] σὺ αὐτὴ ἐλθέ.

  [............] χανκ[...]ον ἤγουσα, ὅτι..
  [...............].λησαι[..] παρακαλῶ σαι
20 [.....................]...α[.]. αἰγὼ σχεδν
  [...................]ῳ παρακαλῶ σαι
  [...................]ωνου θέλω αἰγὼ
  [...................]σει......οὐκ ἔ.
  [...................].... ἄλλως ποι[.]
25 [σεις...]

The papyrus is broken off here.

(Addressed)

[......]μητρεὶ ἀπ' Ἀντωνίω Λόνγου νεἱοῦ

A commentary on this touching letter will be found in *Selections from the Greek Papyri*[2], p. 93 ff., No. 37. See also Deissmann, *Light from the Ancient East*, p. 176 ff.

It may be added that in his Note 'On some current epistolary phrases' in his commentary on *St. Paul's Epistle to the Ephesians*, p. 275 ff., Dean Armitage Robinson collects a number of illustrations of the more formal parts of our New Testament Epistles from the ordinary epistolary correspondence of the time. Those who wish to pursue the matter further may be referred to G. A. Gerhard, *Untersuchungen zur Geschichte des griechischen Briefes*. Heft i. *Die Anfangsformel* in *Philologus*, lxiv. p. 27 ff.; to P. Wendland, *Die urchristlichen Literaturformen*[2] (in *Handbuch zum Neuen Testament*, i. 3, Tübingen, 1912), p. 411 ff.; and to the elaborate discussion by F. Ziemann, *De epistularum graecarum formulis sollemnibus quaestiones selectae* in *Dissertationes philologicae Halenses* xviii. 4, Halle, 1911.

Much valuable information on the subject of 'the letter' in classical literature will be found in the elaborate monograph, *Der Brief in der Römischen Litteratur*.

NOTE E

Litterargeschichtliche Untersuchungen und Zusammenfassungen, contributed by H. Peter to the *Abhandlungen der philologisch-historischen Klasse der Königl. Sächsischen Gesellschaft der Wissenschaften*, xx. iii., Leipzig, 1901. The monograph was also published separately, but copies are now scarce.

NOTE F.

DIONYSIUS OF ALEXANDRIA ON THE AUTHORSHIP OF THE APOCALYPSE.

Dionysius of Alexandria, †A.D. 265.

EUSEBIUS has preserved in his *Hist. Eccles.* vii. 24 f. certain fragments of a treatise περὶ Ἐπαγγελιῶν by Dionysius, a pupil of Origen and Bishop of Alexandria from A.D. 248 to A.D. 265. Amongst them is the passage dealing with the authorship of the Apocalypse referred to on p. 123, which is so important alike from the position of the author and the critical acumen he displays, that it is reproduced here at greater length.[1]

The complete Greek text will be found in Eusebius *ut supra*, or in Dr. Feltoe's useful edition of *The Letters and other Remains of Dionysius of Alexandria* (in 'Cambridge Patristic Texts'), Cambridge, 1904, p. 114 ff. In the translation I have in the main followed Dr. M'Giffert in his edition of *The Church History of Eusebius* (in the 'Select Library of Nicene and Post-Nicene Fathers of the Christian Church'), Oxford and New York, 1890.

Τινὲς μὲν οὖν τῶν πρὸ ἡμῶν ἠθέτησαν καὶ ἀνεσκεύασαν πάντῃ τὸ βιβλίον, καὶ καθ' ἕκαστον κεφάλαιον διευθύνοντες ἄγνωστόν τε καὶ ἀσυλλόγιστον ἀποφαίνοντες, ψεύδεσθαί τε τὴν ἐπιγραφήν. Ἰωάννου γὰρ οὐκ εἶναι

[1] 'I do not think there is any other piece of pure criticism in the early Fathers to compare with it for style and manner' (Westcott, *On the Canon of the New Testament*[7], p. 367, n[1]).

NOTE F 263

λέγουσιν.... ἐγὼ δὲ ἀθετῆσαι μὲν οὐκ ἂν τολμήσαιμι τὸ βιβλίον, πολλῶν αὐτὸ διὰ σπουδῆς ἐχόντων ἀδελφῶν ... καὶ εἶναι τὴν γραφὴν Ἰωάννου ταύτην, οὐκ ἀντερῶ. ἁγίου μὲν γὰρ εἶναί τινος καὶ θεοπνεύστου συναινῶ, οὐ μὴν ῥᾳδίως ἂν συνθοίμην τοῦτον εἶναι τὸν ἀπόστολον, τὸν υἱὸν Ζεβεδαίου, τὸν ἀδελφὸν Ἰακώβου, οὗ τὸ εὐαγγέλιον τὸ κατὰ Ἰωάννην ἐπιγεγραμμένον καὶ ἡ ἐπιστολὴ ἡ καθολική. τεκμαίρομαι γὰρ ἔκ τε τοῦ ἤθους ἑκατέρων καὶ τοῦ τῶν λόγων εἴδους καὶ τῆς τοῦ βιβλίου διεξαγωγῆς λεγομένης μὴ τὸν αὐτὸν εἶναι...... Καὶ ἀπὸ νοημάτων δὲ καὶ ἀπὸ τῶν ῥημάτων καὶ τῆς συντάξεως αὐτῶν εἰκότως ἕτερος οὗτος παρ' ἐκεῖνον ὑποληφθήσεται. συνᾴδουσι μὲν γὰρ ἀλλήλοις τὸ εὐαγγέλιον καὶ ἡ ἐπιστολή, ὁμοίως τε ἄρχονται. τὸ μέν φησιν Ἐν ἀρχῇ ἦν ὁ λόγος· ἡ δὲ Ὃ ἦν ἀπ' ἀρχῆς.... ἔχεται αὐτοῦ, καὶ τῶν προθέσεων οὐκ ἀφίσταται, διὰ δὲ τῶν αὐτῶν κεφαλαίων καὶ ὀνομάτων πάντα διεξέρχεται· ὧν τινὰ μὲν ἡμεῖς συντόμως ὑπομνήσομεν. ὁ δὲ προσεχῶς ἐντυγχάνων εὑρήσει ἐν ἑκατέρῳ πολλὴν τὴν ζωήν, πολὺ τὸ φῶς, ἀποτροπὴν τοῦ σκότους, συνεχῆ τὴν ἀλήθειαν, τὴν χάριν, τὴν χαράν, τὴν σάρκα καὶ τὸ αἷμα τοῦ κυρίου.... καὶ ὅλως διὰ πάντων χαρακτηρίζοντας ἕνα καὶ τὸν αὐτὸν συνορᾶν τοῦ τε εὐαγγελίου καὶ τῆς ἐπιστολῆς χρῶτα πρόκειται. ἀλλοιοτάτη δὲ καὶ ξένη παρὰ ταῦτα ἡ ἀποκάλυψις, μήτε ἐφαπτομένη μήτε γειτνιῶσα τούτων μηδενί, σχεδὸν ὡς εἰπεῖν μηδὲ συλλαβὴν πρὸς αὐτὰ κοινὴν ἔχουσα... ἔτι δὲ καὶ διὰ τῆς φράσεως τὴν διαφορὰν ἔστι τεκμήρασθαι τοῦ εὐαγγελίου καὶ τῆς ἐπιστολῆς πρὸς τὴν ἀποκάλυψιν. τὰ μὲν γὰρ οὐ μόνον ἀπταίστως κατὰ τὴν Ἑλλήνων φωνήν, ἀλλὰ καὶ λογιώτατα ταῖς λέξεσι, τοῖς συλλογισμοῖς, ταῖς συντάξεσι τῆς ἑρμηνείας γέγραπται. πολλοῦ γε δεῖ βάρβαρόν τινα φθόγγον, ἢ σολοικισμόν, ἢ ὅλως ἰδιωτισμὸν ἐν αὐτοῖς εὑρεθῆναι. ἑκάτερον γὰρ εἶχεν, ὡς ἔοικε, τὸν λόγον, ἀμφοτέρους αὐτῷ χαρισαμένου τοῦ Κυρίου, τόν τε τῆς γνώσεως, τόν τε τῆς φράσεως. τούτῳ δὲ ἀποκάλυψιν μὲν ἑωρακέναι, καὶ γνῶσιν εἰληφέναι καὶ προφετείαν οὐκ ἀντερῶ· διάλεκτον μέντοι καὶ γλῶσσαν οὐκ ἀκριβῶς ἑλληνίζουσαν αὐτοῦ βλέπω, ἀλλ' ἰδιώμασίν τε βαρβαρικοῖς χρώμενον, καί που καὶ σολοικίζοντα. ἅπερ οὐκ ἀναγκαῖον νῦν ἐκλέγειν· οὐδὲ γὰρ ἐπισκώπτων, μή τις νομίσῃ, ταῦτα εἶπον, ἀλλὰ μόνον τὴν ἀνομοιότητα διευθύνων τῶν γραφῶν.

'Some before us have set aside and rejected the book [the Apocalypse of John] altogether, criticizing it chapter by chapter, and pronouncing it without sense or argument, and maintaining that the title is fraudulent. For they say that it is not the work of John. . . . But I could not venture to reject the book, as many brethren hold it in high esteem. . . . And that this book is the work of one John, I will not deny. For I fully admit that it is the work of a holy and inspired man. But I should not readily admit that he was the Apostle, the son of Zebedee, the brother of James, by whom the Gospel of John and the Catholic Epistle were written. For I conclude from the character of both [writings], and the form of the language, and the general construction of the book [of the Revelation] that [the John there mentioned] is not the same. . . . And from the thoughts too, and from the words and their collocation, it may be reasonably conjectured that this one is different from that one [*i.e.* the writer of the Apocalypse is different from the writer of the Gospel and the Epistle]. For the Gospel and the Epistle agree with each other, and begin in like manner. The one says, "In the beginning was the Word"; the other, "That which was from the beginning." . . . He is consistent with himself, and does not depart from his purposes, but discusses everything under the same heads and names; some of which we will briefly recall. Any one who examines carefully will find the phrases, "the life,"

NOTE F

"the light," "turning from darkness," frequently occurring in both; also continually, "truth," "grace," "joy," "the flesh and blood of the Lord." . . . In fact, it is plainly to be seen that one and the same character marks the Gospel and the Epistle throughout. But the Apocalypse is different from these writings and foreign to them; not touching, nor in the least bordering upon them; almost, so to speak, without even a syllable in common with them. . . . Moreover, it can also be shown that the diction of the Gospel and of the Epistle differs from that of the Apocalypse. For they were written not only without error as regards the Greek language, but also most artistically in their expressions, in their reasonings, and in the arrangements of explanations. They are far indeed from betraying any barbarism or solecism, or any vulgarism whatever. For the writer had, as it seems, both the requisites of discourse,—that is, the gift of knowledge and the gift of expression—as the Lord had bestowed them both upon him. I do not deny that the other writer saw a revelation and received knowledge and prophecy. I perceive, however, that his dialect and language are not accurate Greek, but that he uses barbarous idioms, and, in some places, solecisms. It is unnecessary to point these out here, for I would not have any one think that I have said these things in a spirit of ridicule—let no man think it—but only with the purpose of showing clearly the difference between the writings.'

NOTE G.

THE OXYRHYNCHUS 'SAYINGS OF JESUS.'

The 'Sayings of Jesus.' IN 1897, when Dr. Grenfell and Dr. Hunt began excavating at Oxyrhynchus, they discovered in a mound amongst a number of other Greek Papyri, the leaf of a papyrus codex, containing what purported to be eight Sayings of Jesus. The idea of new Sayings of Jesus was not in itself strange. It is suggested by various statements in the Gospels, such as Luke i. 1-4, John xx. 30 f., as well as by the existence in early Christian literature and tradition of a member of so-called *Agrapha*.[1] But here there was tangible evidence of a Collection of these Sayings, which, as the leaf could not be dated later than the beginning of the third century, probably ran back to the middle of the second century, and possibly even to the first century.

All manner of questions were at once raised as to the source and consequent authority of the Sayings, and interest in them was still further quickened by a fresh discovery of a similar character at Oxyrhynchus in 1903. Unlike the earlier collection, however, which, as we have seen, formed the leaf of a papyrus book, the five new Sayings were written on the back of a survey list of various pieces of land, and were prefaced by an Introduction or Heading to this effect: 'These are the (wonder-

---

[1] For a convenient collection of these, see C. G. Griffinhoofe, *The Unwritten Sayings of Christ*, Cambridge and London, 1903.

NOTE G

ful?) words which Jesus the living (lord) spake to J . . . and Thomas . . .'

It is impossible to enter here into any discussion on the true character of these two sets of Sayings, which may well have formed originally parts of one collection, but there seems to be no good reason to doubt that, while they show traces of the sub-Apostolic environment out of which they sprang, they contain a distinct residuum of the Lord's teaching, rescued from the floating tradition of the time.

The deep interest, in any case, of the Sayings will appear from the Editors' reconstruction and translation of the two first of the new Sayings (see Plate IV.).

> 'Jesus saith, Let not him who seeks . . . cease until he finds, and when he finds he shall be astonished; astonished he shall reach the kingdom, and having reached the kingdom he shall rest.
>
> 'Jesus saith, (Ye ask? who are those) that draw us (to the kingdom, if) the kingdom is in Heaven? . . . the fowls of the air, and all beasts that are under the earth or upon the earth, and the fishes of the sea, (these are they which draw) you, and the Kingdom of Heaven is within you; and whosoever shall know himself shall find it. (Strive therefore?) to know yourselves, and ye shall be aware that ye are the sons of the (almighty?) Father; (and?) ye shall know that ye are in (the city of God?), and ye are (the city?).'

The two collections of Sayings have been edited by the discoverers as separate publications for the Graeco-Roman Branch of the Egyptian Exploration Fund under the titles ΛΟΓΙΑ ΙΗΣΟΥ (*Sayings of our Lord*), 2s. nett or 6d. nett, and *New Sayings of Jesus and Fragment of a Lost Gospel from Oxyrhynchus*, 1s. nett, both at the Oxford University Press. They also appeared in *Oxyrhynchus Papyri*, i. p. 1 ff. and iv. p. 1 ff.

<small>Literature.</small>

APPENDIX

'Of the literature to which they have given rise in this country it is sufficient to notice, *Two Lectures on the Sayings of Jesus*,' by Professors W. Lock and W. Sanday (Oxford, 1897, 1s. 6d. nett) with a useful Bibliography, an important article on the interpretation of the New Sayings by Professor H. B. Swete in *The Expository Times*, xv. p. 488 ff., and two publications by Dr. Charles Taylor, *The Oxyrhynchus Logia and the Apocryphal Gospels* (Oxford, 1899, 1s. 6d. nett) and *The Oxyrhynchus Sayings of Jesus* (Oxford, 1905, 2s. nett).

A pamphlet by Professor Harnack, *Über die jüngst entdeckten Sprüche Jesu* (Freiburg, i. B., 1897), was translated in *The Expositor*, V. vi. pp. 321 ff., 401 ff.

Those who desire to see the use to which the Sayings may be turned for homiletic purposes may consult such books as *Jesus Saith*, by J. Warschauer (London, no date), and *The Newly-found Words of Jesus*, by W. Garrett Horder (London, 1904).

NOTE H.

PAPIAS AND IRENAEUS ON THE ORIGIN OF THE GOSPELS.

THE testimony of Papias as to the origin of the Gospels of St. Mark and St. Matthew is very familiar, but in view of its great importance and the references made to it in the Lectures, it may be well to give the passage in full, as it has been preserved for us in Eusebius' *Ecclesiastical History*.

Καὶ ἄλλας δὲ τῇ ἰδίᾳ γραφῇ παραδίδωσιν Ἀριστίωνος τοῦ πρόσθεν δεδηλωμένου τῶν τοῦ κυρίου λόγων διηγήσεις καὶ τοῦ πρεσβυτέρου Ἰωάννου παραδόσεις· ἐφ' ἃς τοὺς φιλομαθεῖς ἀναπέμψαντες, ἀναγκαίως νῦν προσθήσομεν ταῖς προεκτεθείσαις αὐτοῦ φωναῖς παράδοσιν ἣν περὶ Μάρκου τοῦ τὸ εὐαγγέλιον γεγραφότος ἐκτέθειται διὰ τούτων

Καὶ τοῦθ' ὁ πρεσβύτερος ἔλεγε. Μάρκος μὲν ἑρμηνευτὴς Πέτρου γενόμενος, ὅσα ἐμνημόνευσεν, ἀκριβῶς ἔγραψεν, οὐ μέντοι τάξει, τὰ ὑπὸ τοῦ κυρίου ἢ λεχθέντα ἢ πραχθέντα. οὔτε γὰρ ἤκουσεν τοῦ κυρίου οὔτε παρηκολούθησεν αὐτῷ, ὕστερον δέ, ὡς ἔφην, Πέτρῳ· ὃς πρὸς τὰς χρείας ἐποιεῖτο τὰς διδασκαλίας, ἀλλ' οὐχ ὥσπερ σύνταξιν τῶν κυριακῶν ποιούμενος λογίων,[1] ὥστε οὐδὲν ἥμαρτεν Μάρκος οὕτως ἔνια γράψας ὡς ἀπεμνημόνευσεν. ἑνὸς γὰρ ἐποιήσατο πρόνοιαν, τοῦ μηδὲν ὧν ἤκουσε παραλιπεῖν ἢ ψεύσασθαί τι ἐν αὐτοῖς.

Papias *c.* A.D. 130.

Euseb. *Hist. Eccles.* iii. 39. 14-16, ed. Schwartz.

---
[1] *v.l.* λόγων.

ταῦτα μὲν οὖν ἱστόρηται τῷ Παπίᾳ περὶ τοῦ Μάρκου· περὶ δὲ τοῦ Ματθαίου ταῦτ' εἴρηται

Ματθαῖος μὲν οὖν Ἑβραΐδι διαλέκτῳ τὰ λόγια συνετάψατο, ἡρμήνευσεν δ' αὐτὰ ὡς ἦν δυνατὸς ἕκαστος.

'Papias also gives in his own work other accounts of the words of the Lord on the authority of Aristion who has been mentioned above, and traditions of the Presbyter John. To these we refer those who are fond of learning, but for our present purpose we must add to the words of his, which have already been quoted, a tradition which he sets forth regarding Mark who wrote the Gospel. It is in the following terms—

And the Presbyter said this also: Mark having once acted as interpreter (or catechist) of Peter[1] wrote down accurately, though not indeed in order,[2] all that he remembered of what was either spoken or done by the Lord. For he neither heard the Lord, nor followed Him, but afterwards, as I said, [attached himself to] Peter, who used to adapt his instructions to the needs [of his hearers], but with no intention of giving a connected account of the Lord's oracles.[3] Mark then fell into no error, while he thus wrote down some things just as he recalled them to mind: for he made it his one care, not to omit any of the things which he had heard, or to state anything falsely in [his narrative of] them.

---

[1] That γενόμενος refers to an office or relationship that was past is rendered very probable by the regular usage of the term in the papyri, *e.g. Oxy. Pap.* i. p. 82, No. 38 ¹¹ˡ· (A.D. 49-50) (=*Selections*, p. 53), ἐπὶ τοῦ γενομένου τοῦ νομοῦ στρατηγοῦ Πασίωνος, 'before Pasion, who was ex-strategus of the nome.'

[2] For an interesting attempt to find in τάξει the thought not so much of chronological, as of 'rhetorical order, that ordering which will produce a satisfactory and readable work,' see F. H. Colson in the *Journal of Theological Studies*, xiv. p. 62 ff.

[3] Or, discourses (λόγων).

NOTE H

These then are the things narrated by Papias regarding Mark. And regarding Matthew these things are said—

'So then Matthew composed the oracles in the Hebrew tongue, and each one interpreted them as he was able.'

The question as to the exact identity of the Presbyter John, to whom Papias refers as his authority for the foregoing statements regarding Mark and Matthew, is a very intricate one. But there is not a little to be said for the view that there was only one John at Ephesus who was both Apostle and Presbyter.[1] {Identity of the Presbyter.}

Whether, however, this be so or not, it will be at once recognized how much added interest is given to the statements, if we can refer them in the last instance to the author of the Fourth Gospel. On this point Dr. Sanday writes as follows in the article 'Bible' in Hastings' *Encyclopaedia of Religion and Ethics*, ii. (Edinburgh, 1909), p. 576:

'The present writer fully believes that the two important extracts from the work of Papias preserved by Eusebius relate, the one to our extant Gospel of St. Mark, and the other to the second document disclosed by criticism which in the extract is referred to the Apostle St. Matthew. He believes that the authority quoted for these statements is none other than the writer of the Fourth Gospel, the John who played such a leading part at Ephesus towards the end of the first century A.D. He would observe that the statements made bear a great stamp of verisimilitude, just because they are so little obvious and not at all such as could be inferred from a superficial study of the Gospels. The statement about St. Mark in particular points to criticisms upon that Gospel (especially as to its want of completeness and chronological order) that we can understand being made at an early stage in the history

[1] Cf. most recently Dom Chapman, *John the Presbyter and the Fourth Gospel*, Oxford, 1911.

of the Gospel, and by no means so well later. It is interesting to note the calm matter-of-fact way in which the Fourth Evangelist (if it were really he) speaks of his predecessors' work; and we believe that it throws a welcome light upon the composition of his own Gospel.'

Irenaeus c. A.D. 180-190.

The evidence of Irenaeus, so far as it refers to St. Mark and St. Matthew, is obviously based on Papias; but it raises new points of interest with reference to the other two Gospels, as well as to the early recognition of the four Gospels as a whole.

The following extracts are taken from Harvey's edition of Irenaeus' great work *Adversus Haereses*; but one or two emendations in the Greek text suggested by Hort have been introduced. For these last see Souter, *Text and Canon of the New Testament*, p. 170 ff.

Adv. Haer. iii. 11. 11.

Ἐπειδὴ γὰρ τέσσαρα κλίματα τοῦ κόσμου ἐν ᾧ ἐσμεν, καὶ τέσσαρα καθολικὰ πνεύματα, κατέσπαρται δὲ ἡ ἐκκλησία ἐπὶ πάσης τῆς γῆς, στῦλος τε καὶ στήριγμα ἐκκλησίας τὸ εὐαγγέλιον καὶ πνεῦμα ζωῆς· εἰκὸς τέσσαρας ἔχειν αὐτὴν στύλους, πανταχόθεν πνέοντας τὴς ἀφθαρσίαν, καὶ ἀναζωπυροῦντας τοὺς ἀνθρώπους. ἐξ ὧν φανερὸν ὅτι ὁ τῶν ἁπάντων τεχνίτης Λόγος, ὁ καθήμενος ἐπὶ τῶν χερουβὶμ καὶ συνέχων τὰ πάντα, φανερωθεὶς τοῖς ἀνθρώποις, ἔδωκεν ἡμῖν τετράμορφον τὸ εὐαγγέλιον, ἑνὶ δὲ πνεύματι συνεχόμενον.

'For since there are four quarters of the world in which we live, and four universal winds, and the Church is scattered over all the earth, and the Gospel is the pillar and ground of the Church and the breath of life, it is likely that it should have four pillars, breathing immortality from all sides, and kindling afresh the life of men. Whence it is evident that the Word, the artificer of all things, Who sitteth upon the Cherubim and holdeth all things together, having been made manifest to men, gave us the Gospel under a four-fold form, but held together by one Spirit.'

ὁ μὲν δὴ Ματθαῖος ἐν τοῖς Ἑβραίοις τῇ ἰδίᾳ διαλέκτῳ αὐτῶν καὶ γραφὴν ἐξήνεγκεν εὐαγγελίου, τοῦ Πέτρου καὶ τοῦ Παύλου ἐν Ῥώμῃ εὐαγγελιζομένων καὶ θεμελιούντων τὴν ἐκκλησίαν. μετὰ δὲ τὴν τούτων ἔξοδον Μᾶρκος ὁ μαθητὴς καὶ ἑρμηνευτὴς Πέτρου καὶ αὐτὸς τὰ ὑπὸ Πέτρου κηρυσσόμενα ἐγγράφως ἡμῖν παραδέδωκεν. καὶ Λουκᾶς δὲ ὁ ἀκόλουθος Παύλου τὸ ὑπ' ἐκείνου κηρυσσόμενον εὐαγγέλιον ἐν βιβλίῳ κατέθετο. ἔπειτα Ἰωάννης ὁ μαθητὴς τοῦ κυρίου, ὁ καὶ ἐπὶ τὸ στῆθος αὐτοῦ ἀναπεσὼν καὶ αὐτὸς ἐξέδωκεν τὸ εὐαγγέλιον ἐν Ἐφέσῳ τῆς Ἀσίας διατρίβων.

Adv. Haer. iii. 1. 2.

'Matthew then put forth a written Gospel among the Hebrews in their own tongue, while Peter and Paul were preaching the Gospel in Rome and laying the foundation of the Church. And after their decease Mark, the disciple and interpreter of Peter, also transmitted to us in writing the subjects of Peter's preaching. And Luke, the companion of Paul, put down in a book the Gospel preached by him. Afterwards John, the disciple of the Lord, who also leaned back on His breast, likewise published his Gospel, while staying at Ephesus in Asia.'

NOTE I.

ALTERNATIVE ENDINGS OF ST. MARK'S GOSPEL.

The ordinary ending of St. Mark's Gospel.

THE textual difficulties with regard to the ending of St. Mark's Gospel have become familiar to English readers through the Revised Version. It will be noted that after c. xvi. 8 a considerable space has been left blank, and that vv. 9-20 are introduced by a note in the margin to the effect that they are omitted in the two oldest Greek manuscripts and some other authorities, while still other authorities have a different ending to the Gospel.

External evidence.

The two Greek manuscripts referred to are of course the Vatican and Sinaitic codices, and the manner in which they end the Gospel is significant. In the former the scribe follows the closing words of c. xvi. 8, ἐφοβοῦντο γάρ, with the subscription κατὰ Μᾶρκον, but leaves a whole column blank before beginning St. Luke's Gospel, as if he were conscious that more should have followed in St. Mark, though at the time he was not in a position to supply it. In the latter, the Codex Sinaiticus, as will be seen from the Facsimile at p. 195, the closing words of v. 8 are enclosed in a kind of arabesque ornament, followed by the subscription εὐαγγέλιον κατὰ Μᾶρκον, and the remainder of the column is left blank.[1]

---

[1] Little stress can be laid on this latter feature, as similar blank spaces are found at the ends of the Gospels both of St. Matthew and of St. Luke. In the case of the Vatican Codex, half a column is left blank at the end of St. Matthew's Gospel. No conclusion can be

NOTE I

The witness of another authority, discovered since the publication of the Revised Version, is still more emphatic for the omission of the verses. In the Codex of the Old Syriac Gospels, as transcribed from photographs taken by Mrs. Lewis and Mrs. Gibson at the monastery of St. Catherine on Mount Sinai in 1892 and 1893, a space is found between Mark xvi. 8 and the beginning of St. Luke's Gospel, filled up by the words in red ink, 'Here endeth the Gospel of St. Mark,' then a line of ornamental dots, and then, 'The Gospel of Luke,' also in red. There can be no doubt therefore that in this very important Codex the closing verses of St. Mark, as we have them in our ordinary Bibles, never existed.[1]

Nor is this all, but the doubts which are thus cast upon them by external evidence are confirmed by the internal character of the passage as a whole. Both in language and style it differs markedly from the rest of the Gospel, while its general object is clearly didactic rather than historical. *Internal evidence.*

In all these circumstances, it is now very generally admitted by critics that the present ending of St. Mark formed no part of the original Gospel,[2] but was an independent narrative, dealing with the Appearances of the Risen Christ, which was added at a later date to round off the mutilated Marcan narrative (see p. 182). And it is at least possible, on the evidence of a note in a copy of the Gospels in Armenian written in A.D. 986, that the real author of this Appendix was Ariston, or rather Aristion, whom Papias mentions as one of the disciples *Its probable author.*

drawn as to the scribe's practice from St. Luke's Gospel, as it finishes at the foot of a column.

[1] See the frontispiece to Mrs. Lewis's *Translation of the Four Gospels from the Syriac of the Sinaitic Palimpsest*, London, 1894.

[2] See, however, Burgon's vigorous defence of the passage in *The Last Twelve Verses of the Gospel according to St. Mark*, Oxford and London, 1871.

276 APPENDIX

of the Lord.¹ It is certain, at any rate, that the ending, whatever its exact source, was generally accepted at an early date, as it is found in practically all Greek manuscripts and versions, with the exception of those already noted above.

The shorter ending. That, however, its position was not wholly unchallenged is proved by the fact that we have also evidence of another and shorter ending. The principal witness for this is Codex Regius (L), an eighth century manuscript of the Gospels now in Paris, which, as a matter of fact, with certain other manuscripts, contains both endings; though as in this case the shorter comes first, it would appear to have been preferred by the scribe.²

It runs as follows :

Πάντα δὲ τὰ παρηγγελμένα τοῖς περὶ τὸν Πέτρον συντόμως ἐξήγγειλαν. Μετὰ δὲ ταῦτα καὶ αὐτὸς ὁ Ἰησοῦς ἀπὸ ἀνατολῆς καὶ ἄχρι δύσεως ἐξαπέστειλεν δι' αὐτῶν τὸ ἱερὸν καὶ ἄφθαρτον κήρυγμα τῆς αἰωνίου σωτηρίας.

' But all that had been enjoined they reported briefly to Peter and his companions. And after-

---

[1] This suggestion was first made by Mr. F. C. Conybeare, who discovered the Armenian manuscript in the Patriarchal Library of Edschmiatzin in Nov. 1891: see the *Expositor*, IV. viii. p. 241 ff., and cf. Swete, *The Gospel according to St. Mark*, p. ciii ff., with the instructive Facsimile of the ending of St. Mark in the Edschmiatzin manuscript. The Facsimile is also reproduced in Nestle's *Textual Criticism of the Greek N.T.* Plate ix.

[2] The full textual evidence will be found in Souter's edition of the *Novum Testamentum Graece* (Oxford, at the Clarendon Press). To the authorities containing both endings he now (*Text and Canon of the N.T.* p. 30, n²) adds a Graeco-Sahidic manuscript published by Heer in *Oriens Christianus*, 1912, p. 1 ff. They are also found on the *verso* of the interesting Gospel manuscript (? seventh century) published by Dr. Rendel Harris in *Biblical Fragments from Mount Sinai* (London, 1890), No. 12, Fol. 3, as I learn from the editor's own corrected copy to which he has kindly given me access.

NOTE I

wards Jesus Himself sent out by them from east even to west the sacred and imperishable proclamation of eternal salvation.'

The origin of this shorter ending is obviously much the same as that of the longer, though instead of being an independent composition to begin with, it would seem to have been specially composed to complete the broken-off ending of St. Mark. Its origin and character.

Dr. Hort finds in it certain resemblances in style to St. Luke's Prologue,[1] and Dr. Swete notes one or two verbal similarities with the Epistle of Clement.[2] But in any case there is again general agreement that it formed no part of the original St. Mark, nor from the absence of references to it in early Christian writings does it seem ever to have become widely known.

Apart from these two endings, an interpolated form of the first ending of the Gospel has recently been brought to light. It cannot indeed be said to be wholly new, for part of it is given in a well-known passage in St. Jerome's 'Dialogue against the Pelagians.' But as no Greek manuscript support for this passage has hitherto been available, little weight has been attached to it. The new ending.

That support is now, however, forthcoming in a new uncial codex of the Gospels, which has been named the Washington manuscript (W) in view of its future home, though it is popularly known as the Freer manuscript, because it is the possession of Mr. C. L. Freer of Detroit, Michigan, U.S.A. The manuscript, or rather manuscripts, for they are four in number, are said to have been formerly in the White Monastery near Sohag, opposite Akhmîm; but Professor Sanders, to whom their publication has been entrusted, prefers to think rather of the monastery of the The Washington or Freer manuscript.

---

[1] *Introduction to the New Testament in the Original Greek*[2], p. 298 f.

[2] *Gospel according to St. Mark*, p. ci.

APPENDIX

Vinedresser, which was located near the third pyramid.[1] In some such ruined monastery at any rate they were found about the year 1906, and apart from the richness of their contents,[2] their importance is shown by the fact that their date cannot be later than the sixth century, and may go back perhaps even to the fourth.

The complete publication of the manuscripts in facsimile is eagerly awaited, but meanwhile an account of the new ending of St. Mark in the Gospel manuscript has been given by Professor Gregory of Leipzig in a short study entitled *Das Freer-Logion* (Leipzig, 1908) with illustrations, from which Plate VI. at p. 182 has been reproduced. And the interesting point for our present purpose is, that in this Freer manuscript we find, as has already been indicated, what is apparently the original from which St. Jerome quotes, along with an additional passage giving our Lord's answer to the Eleven.

For the purposes of comparison it may be well to give St. Jerome's version first.

> 'In quibusdam exemplaribus et maxime in Graecis codicibus iuxta Marcum in fine eius evangelii scribitur: Postea, quum accubuissent undecim, apparuit eis Iesus et exprobravit incredulitatem et duritiam cordis eorum, quia his, qui viderant eum resurgentem, non crediderunt. et illi satisfaciebant dicentes: Saeculum istud iniquitatis et incredulitatis sub Satana est, quod non sinit per immundos spiritus veram dei apprehendi virtutem: idcirco iam nunc revela iustitiam tuam' (*Dialogus contra Pelagianos*, ii. 15).

The new passage in the Freer codex comes immediately after St. Mark xvi. 14 in our usually received text. In

---

[1] *The Old Testament Manuscripts in the Freer Collection*, Part I. (New York, 1910), p. 2 ff.

[2] They contain the books of Deuteronomy and Joshua, the Psalms, the Gospels, and fragments of the Pauline Epistles.

NOTE I

the following transcript the lines of the original manuscript (see Plate VI.) have been preserved, but breathings, accents, and punctuation have been added.

κἀκεῖνοι ἀπελογοῦντε[-το] λέγοντες· ὅτι ὁ
αἰὼν οὗτος τῆς ἀνομίας καὶ τῆς ἀπιστίας
ὑπὸ τὸν σατανᾶν ἐστιν, ὁ μὴ ἐῶν τὰ ὑπὸ
τῶν πνευμάτων ἀκάθαρτα τὴν ἀλήθειαν
τοῦ θεοῦ καταλαβέσθαι δύναμιν. διὰ
τοῦτο ἀποκάλυψον σοῦ τὴν δικαιοσύ-
νην ἤδη. ἐκεῖνοι ἔλεγον τῷ Χριστῷ. καὶ ὁ
Χριστὸς ἐκείνοις προσέλεγεν· ὅτι πεπλήρω-
ται ὁ ὅρος τῶν ἐτῶν τῆς ἐξουσίας τοῦ
σατανᾶ, ἀλλὰ ἐγγίζει ἄλλα δινά [sc. δεινά], καὶ ὑ-
περ ὧν ἐγὼ ἁμαρτησάντων παρεδόθην
εἰς θάνατον, ἵνα ὑποστρέψωσιν εἰς τὴν
ἀλήθειαν καὶ μηκέτι ἁμαρτήσωσιν·
ἵνα τὴν ἐν τῷ οὐρανῷ πνευματικὴν καὶ ἄ-
φθαρτον τῆς δικαιοσύνης δόξαν
κληρονομήσωσιν. ἀλλὰ πορευθέν-
τες κτλ.

'And they defended themselves, saying: "This world of lawlessness and of unbelief is under Satan, which does not suffer those unclean things that are under the dominion of spirits to comprehend the true power of God. On this account reveal Thy righteousness now." They said (these things) to Christ. And Christ replied to them: "There has been fulfilled the term of years of the authority of Satan, but other dreadful things are drawing nigh, even (to those) for the sake of whom as sinners I was delivered up to death, in order that they might return to the truth and sin no more; in order that they might inherit the spiritual and incorruptible glory of righteousness which is in heaven" [Mark xvi. 15]. But go...'

280   APPENDIX

General character of the new ending.
Into the different questions which this ending raises, we are unable to enter at present. It must be enough to say that there is no better reason for regarding it as authentic, in the sense of its having formed part of the original Marcan Gospel, than was the case with the longer and shorter endings previously noted. Rather from the natural way in which the new words fit in between vv. 14 and 15, they would seem to have formed part of a still longer recension, and for some unknown reason to have been excised from the ending in general use.

Bibliography.
Till the completion of the facsimile edition, those who desire further information regarding the manuscripts as a whole may be referred to the articles by Sanders in the *Biblical World* (Chicago), Feb. 1908 and May, 1909, both with plates, and in the *American Journal of Archaeology*, xii. (1908) p. 49 ff. and xiii. (1909) p. 130 ff., both again with plates; to the articles by E. J. Goodspeed in the *Biblical World*, March, 1908, and in the *American Journal of Theology*, xiii. (1909) p. 597 ff.; to the notices by Harnack and Schmidt in the *Theologische Literaturzeitung*, 1908, p. 168 ff. and p. 359 ff.; and to the accounts by Jacquier, *Histoire des Livres du Nouveau Testament*, iii. (Paris, 1908) p. 338 ff., and by Oesterley, *Our Bible Text*, London, 1909, p. 32 ff.

The text of the new Marcan ending can be very conveniently studied in *Two New Gospel Fragments*, ed. H. B. Swete (Cambridge: Deighton, Bell and Co., 1908, price 6d.), p. 9 ff., being the English edition of Lietzmann's *Kleine Texte für Theologische Vorlesungen und Übungen*, No. 31.

NOTE J.

THE GOSPEL ACCORDING TO PETER.

THOUGH the Akhmîm fragment was discovered in the winter of 1886-87, it was not till November, 1892, that the text was first published by M. Bouriant in the *Mémoires publiés par les membres de la Mission Archéologique Française au Caire*, IX. i. (Paris: E. Leroux). Almost immediately afterwards, a tentatively corrected text was issued in this country by Professor Swete, which, after revision, was reprinted along with a valuable Introduction and Notes in *The Akhmîm Fragment of the Apocryphal Gospel of St. Peter* (London, 1893). From this edition, with Dr. Swete's kind consent, I have taken the following transcription and translation of the passage shown in the facsimile, Plates IX., X.

<small>Gospel of Peter.</small>

IX. Τῇ δὲ νυκτὶ ᾗ ἐπέφωσκεν ἡ κυριακή, φυλασσόντων τῶν στρατιωτῶν ἀνὰ δύο δύο κατὰ φρουράν, μεγάλη φωνὴ ἐγένετο ἐν τῷ οὐρανῷ καὶ εἶδον ἀνοιχθέντας τοὺς οὐρανοὺς καὶ δύο ἄνδρας] κατελθόντας ἐκεῖθεν, πολὺ φέγγος ἔχοντας, καὶ ἐγγίσαντας τῷ τάφῳ. ὁ δὲ λίθος ἐκεῖνος ὁ βεβλημένος ἐπὶ τῇ θύρᾳ ἀφ' ἑαυτοῦ κυλισθεὶς ἐπεχώρησε παρὰ μέρος, καὶ ὁ τάφος ἠνοίγη καὶ ἀμφότεροι οἱ νεανίσκοι εἰσῆλθον. ἰδόντες οὖν οἱ στρατιῶται ἐκεῖνοι ἐξύπνισαν τὸν κεντυρίωνα καὶ τοὺς πρεσβυτέρους, παρῆσαν γὰρ καὶ αὐτοὶ φυλάσσοντες· καὶ ἐξηγουμένων αὐτῶν ἃ εἶδον, πάλιν ὁρῶσιν ἐξελθόντας ἀπὸ τοῦ τάφου τρεῖς ἄνδρας,[1] καὶ τοὺς δύο τὸν

---
[1] Cf. Dan. iii. 24 f.

ἕνα ὑπορθοῦντας, καὶ σταυρὸν ἀκολουθοῦντα αὐτοῖς· καὶ τῶν μὲν δύο τὴν κεφαλὴν χωροῦσαν μέχρι τοῦ οὐρανοῦ, τοῦ δὲ χειραγωγουμένου ὑπ' αὐτῶν ὑπερβαίνουσαν τοὺς οὐρανούς. καὶ φωνῆς ἤκουον ἐκ τῶν οὐρανῶν λεγούσης Ἐκήρυξας τοῖς κοιμωμένοις·[1] καὶ ὑπακοὴ ἠκούετο ἀπὸ τοῦ σταυροῦ [ὅ]τι Ναί.[2]

X. Συνεσκέπτοντο οὖν ἀλλήλοις ἐκεῖνοι ἀπελθεῖν καὶ ἐνφανίσαι ταῦτα τῷ Πειλάτῳ. καὶ ἔτι διανοουμένων αὐτῶν φαίνονται πάλιν ἀνοιχθέντες οἱ οὐρανοὶ καὶ ἄνθρωπός τις κατελθὼν καὶ εἰσελθὼν εἰς τὸ μνῆμα. ταῦτα ἰδόντες οἱ περὶ τὸν κεντυρίωνα νυκτὸς ἔσπευσαν πρὸς Πειλᾶτον, ἀφέντες τὸν τάφον ὃν ἐφύλασσον, καὶ ἐξηγήσαντο πάντα ἅπερ εἶδον, ἀγωνιῶντες μεγάλως καὶ λέγοντες Ἀληθῶς υἱὸς ἦν θεοῦ. ἀποκριθεὶς ὁ Πειλᾶτος ἔφη Ἐγὼ καθαρεύω τοῦ αἵματος τοῦ υἱοῦ τοῦ θεοῦ, ὑμῖν δὲ τοῦτο ἔδοξεν. εἶτα προσελθόντες πάντες ἐδέοντο αὐτοῦ καὶ παρεκάλουν κελεῦσαι τῷ κεντυρίωνι καὶ τοῖς στρατιώταις μηδὲν εἰπεῖν ἃ εἶδον· συμφέρει γάρ, φασίν, ἡμῖν ὀφλῆσαι μεγίστην ἁμαρτίαν ἔμπροσθεν τοῦ θεοῦ, καὶ μὴ ἐμπεσεῖν εἰς χεῖρας τοῦ λαοῦ τῶν Ἰουδαίων καὶ λιθασθῆναι. ἐκέλευσεν οὖν ὁ Πειλᾶτος τῷ κεντυρίωνι καὶ τοῖς στρατιώταις μηδὲν εἰπεῖν.

XI. Ὄρθρου δὲ τῆς κυριακῆς[3] Μαριὰμ ἡ Μαγδαληνή, μαθήτρια[4] τοῦ κυρίου (φοβουμένη διὰ τοὺς Ἰουδαίους, ἐπειδὴ ἐφλέγοντο [ὑπὸ τῆς ὀργῆς, οὐκ ἐποίησεν ἐπὶ τῷ μνήματι τοῦ κυρίου ἃ εἰώθεσαν ποιεῖν αἱ γυναῖκες ἐπὶ τοῖς ἀποθνήσκουσι καὶ τοῖς ἀγαπωμένοις αὐταῖς), λαβοῦσα μεθ' ἑαυτῆς τὰς φίλας ἦλθε ἐπὶ τὸ μνημεῖον ὅπου ἦν τεθείς.

IX. Now on the night when the Lord's Day was drawing on, as the soldiers kept guard by two and two in a watch, there was a great voice in heaven,

---

[1] Cf. 1 Pet. iii. 18.
[2] Cf. 2 Cor. i. 20.
[3] Cf. Rev. i. 10.
[4] Cf. Acts ix. 36.

and they saw the heavens opened, and two men] descend from thence with much light and draw nigh unto the tomb. And the stone which had been cast at the door rolled away of itself and made way in part, and the tomb was opened, and both the young men entered in. The soldiers, therefore, when they saw it, awakened the centurion and the elders (for they were also there keeping watch); and as they told the things that they had seen, again they see three men coming forth from the tomb, two of them supporting the other, and a cross following them; and the head of the two reached to heaven, but that of Him who was led by them overpassed the heavens. And they heard a voice from the heavens, saying, Thou didst preach to them that sleep; and a response was heard from the cross, Yea.

X. They took counsel therefore with one another to go and shew these things unto Pilate. And while they yet thought on this, the heavens again appeared to open, and a man descended and entered into the sepulchre. When they saw this, they of the centurion's company hastened by night to Pilate, leaving the tomb which they were guarding, and told all that they had seen, greatly distressed and saying, Truly He was the Son of God. Pilate answered and said, I am clean from the blood of the Son of God, but this was your pleasure. Then they all came near and besought him, and entreated him to command the centurion and the soldiers to say nothing as to the things which they had seen; for it is expedient for us (they said) to be guilty of a very great sin before God, and not to fall into the hands of the Jews and be stoned. Pilate therefore commanded the centurion and the soldiers to say nothing.

XI. Now at dawn on the Lord's Day Mary Magdalene, a female disciple of the Lord—afraid by reason of the Jews, forasmuch as they were inflamed [with wrath, she had not done at the sepulchre of the Lord what women are wont to do for those who die and who are dear to them—took with her her female friends, and came to the sepulchre where He was laid.

It is impossible here to discuss the many questions which the Gospel according to Peter suggests. But as illustrating its peculiarities, attention may be drawn in c. ix. to the mention of the three men of supernatural height who issued from the tomb, the most majestic being supported by the other two; to the personification of the cross; and to the preaching in Hades: in c. x. to the writer's marked desire to free Pilate from blame, in order to emphasize the guilt of the Jews: and, in c. xi., to the ascribing to fear the delay in the women's visit to the tomb.

Elsewhere the docetic character of the Gospel, to which Serapion refers in its criticism of it (Eus. *H.E.* vi. 12) comes out very clearly, notably in the loud cry attributed to the Lord upon the cross, Ἡ δύναμίς μου, ἡ δύναμίς μου, κατέλειψάς με, 'My power, my power, thou hast forsaken me' (c. v.). The Divine Christ, that is, was 'taken up,' while the Human Christ remained upon the cross.

The exact date of the Gospel is uncertain, but it may be placed about A.D. 150.

Literature.

For further information regarding the Gospel, the English student may be referred to *The Gospel according to Peter, and the Revelation of Peter*, by J. Armitage Robinson[1] and Montague Rhodes James (London, 1892),

---

[1] A revised edition of Dean Armitage Robinson's translation of the Gospel fragment has since appeared in the Additional Volume of the *Ante-Nicene Christian Library* (Edinburgh, 1897), p. 7 f.

and to *A popular account of the newly-recovered Gospel of S. Peter*, by J. Rendel Harris (London, 1893), as well as to articles by J. O. F. Murray in *The Expositor*, VII. iv. p. 50 ff., and by V. H. Stanton in *The Journal of Theological Studies*, ii. (1901), p. 1 ff.

Amongst the most important studies of the Gospel by foreign scholars are *Evangelii secundum Petrum et Petri Apocalypseos quae supersunt* . . . , by A. Lods, Paris, 1892; *Bruchstücke des Evangeliums und der Apokalypse des Petrus* (being *Texte u. Untersuchungen*, ix. 2) by A. Harnack, Leipzig, 1893; *Das Evangelium des Petrus*, by Theodor Zahn, Erlangen u. Leipzig, 1893; and *L'Évangile de Pierre et les Évangiles Canoniques*, by A. Sabatier, Paris, 1893.

NOTE K.

THE MURATORIAN FRAGMENT ON THE CANON.

Muratorian Canon.

THIS fragment of a Roman second century canon was first published by its discoverer Muratori in his *Antiquitates Italicae Medii Aevi* (Milan, 1740), iii. p. 851 ff., and has since been frequently revised and reprinted. Full information regarding it will be found in S. P. Tregelles, *Canon Muratorianus*, Oxford, 1867; in Westcott, *On the Canon*[5], Appendix C; and in Zahn, *Geschichte des Neutest. Kanons*, ii. p. 1 ff., and *Grundriss*[2], p. 76 ff. The results of a new examination of the Codex made by the Rev. E. S. Buchanan in 1906 will be found in the *Journal of Theological Studies*, viii. (1907), p. 537 ff. I am indebted to Professor Zahn for the Latin text of the Canon printed below, and to Professor Gwatkin for the accompanying translation from his *Selections from Early Writers* (London, 1905), p. 83 ff.

```
  quibus tamen interfuit et ita posuit
  tertio euangelii librum secundo lucan
  lucas iste medicus post ascensum [XPi]
  cum eo paulus quasi ut iuris studiosum
5 secundum adsumsisset numeni suo
  ex opinione conscribset dnm tamen nec ipse
  uidit in carne et idē prout asequi potuit
  ita et ad nativitate iohannis incipet dicere
  quarti euangeliorum iohannis ex decipolis
```

10 cohortantibus condescipulis et eps suis
dixit conieiunate mihi odie triduo et quid
cuique fuerit reuelatum alterutrum.
nobis ennarremus eadem nocte reue
latum andreae ex apostolis ut recognis
15 centibus cuntis iohannis suo nomine
cuncta discriberet et ideo licit uaria sin
culis euangeliorum libris principia
doceantur nihil tamen differt creden
tium fidei cum uno ac principali spu de
20 clarata sint in omnibus omnia de natiui
tate de passione de ressurrectione
de conuersatione cum decipulis suis
ac de gemino eius aduentu
primo in humilitate dispectus quod fo
25 it secundum potestate regali ... pre
clarum quod foturum est quid ergo
mirum si iohannes tam constanter
sincula etiā in epistulis suis proferam
dicens in semeipsu quae uidimus oculis
30 nostris et auribus audiuimus et manus
nostrae palpauerunt haec scripsimus uobis
sic enim non solum uisurem sed et auditorem.
sed et scriptorē omnium mirabiliū dñi per ordi
nem profetetur acta autē omniū apostolorum
35 sub uno libro scribta sunt lucas obtime theofi
le conprindit quia sub praesentia eius singula
gerebantur sicuti et semote passionē petri
euidenter declarat sed et profectionē pauli ab ur
be ad spaniā proficiscentis epistulae autem
40 pauli quae a quo loco uel qua ex causa directe
sint volentibus intellegere ipse declarant
primū omnium corintheis scysmae heresis in
terdicens deinceps b callactis circumcisione
romanis autē ordine scripturarum sed et
45 principium earum ... esse XPm intimans

prolexius scripsit de quibus sincolis neces
se est ad nobis desputari cum ipse beatus
apostolus paulus sequens prodecessoris sui
iohannis ordine non nisi nomenati sempte
50 ecclesiis scribat ordine tali a corenthios
prima. ad efesius seconda ad philippinses ter
tia ad colosensis quarta ad calatas quin
ta ad tensaolenecinsis sexta ad romanos
septima uerum corintheis et thesaolecen
55 sibus licet pro correbtione iteretur una
tamen per omnem orbem terrae ecclesia
deffusa esse denoscitur et iohannis enī in a
pocalebsy licet septe eccleseis scribat
tamen omnibus dicit verū ad filemonem una
60 et at titū una et ad tymotheū duas pro affec
to et dilectione in honore tamen eclesiae ca
tholice in ordinatione eclesiastice
discepline scificate sunt. fertur etiam ad
laudecenses alia ad alexandrinos pauli no
65 mine fincte ad heresem marcionis et alia plu
ra quae in catholicam eclesiam recepi non
potest fel enim cum melle misceri non con
cruit epistola sane iude et superscrictio
iohannis duas in catholica habentur et sapi
70 entia ab amicis salomonis in honore ipsius
scripta apocalapse etiam iohanis et pe
tri tantum recipimus quam quidam ex nos
tris legi in eclesia nolunt pastorem uero
nuperrim e temporibus nostris in urbe
75 roma herma conscripsit sedente cathe
tra urbis romae aeclesiae pio spē fratre
eius et ideo legi eum quidē oportet se pu
plicare vero in eclesia populo neqe inter
profetas completum numero neqe inter
80 apostolos in finē temporum potest
arsinoi autem seu ualentini uel mitiadis

nihil in totum recipemus qui etiam nouū
psalmorum librum marcioni conscripse
runt una cum basilide assianom catafry
85 cum constitutorem.

Fragment of Muratori on the Canon.

'... but at some he was present, and so he set them down.

The third book of the Gospel, that according to Luke, was compiled in his own name in order by Luke the physician, when after Christ's ascension Paul had taken 5 him to be with him like a student of law. Yet neither did *he* see the Lord in the flesh; and he too, as he was able to ascertain [events, so set them down]. So he began his story from the birth of John.

The fourth of the Gospels [was written by] John, one 10 of the disciples. When exhorted by his fellow-disciples and bishops, he said, 'Fast with me this day for three days; and what may be revealed to any of us, let us relate it to one another.' The same night it was revealed to Andrew, one of the apostles, that John was to write all things in his own name, and they were all to certify. 15

And therefore, though various elements are taught in the several books of the Gospels, yet it makes no difference to the faith of believers, since by one guiding Spirit all things are declared in all of them concerning the Nativity, 20 the Passion, the Resurrection, the conversation with his disciples and his two comings, the first in lowliness and contempt, which has come to pass, the second glorious with royal power, which is to come. 25

What marvel therefore if John so firmly sets forth each statement in his Epistle too, saying of himself, 'What we have seen with our eyes and heard with our ears and our 30 hands have handled, these things we have written to you'? For so he declares himself not an eyewitness and

T

a hearer only, but a writer of all the marvels of the Lord in order.

The Acts however of all the Apostles are written in one book. Luke puts it shortly to the most excellent Theophilus, that the several things were done in his own presence, as he also plainly shows by leaving out the passion of Peter, and also the departure of Paul from town on his journey to Spain.

The Epistles however of Paul themselves make plain to those who wish to understand it, what Epistles were sent by him, and from what place, and for what cause. He wrote at some length first of all to the Corinthians, forbidding schisms and heresies; next to the Galatians, forbidding circumcision; then to the Romans, impressing on them the plan of the Scriptures, and also that Christ is the first principle of them, concerning which severally it is [not] necessary for us to discuss, since the blessed Apostle Paul himself, following the order of his predecessor John, writes only by name to seven churches in the following order—to the Corinthians a first, to the Ephesians a second, to the Philippians a third, to the Colossians a fourth, to the Galatians a fifth, to the Thessalonians a sixth, to the Romans a seventh; whereas, although for the sake of admonition there is a second to the Corinthians and to the Thessalonians, yet *one* Church is recognized as being spread over the entire world. For John too in the Apocalypse, though he writes to seven churches, yet speaks to all. Howbeit to Philemon one, to Titus one, and to Timothy two were put in writing from personal inclination and attachment, to be in honour however with the Catholic Church for the ordering of the ecclesiastical mode of life. There is current also one to the Laodicenes, another to the Alexandrians, [both] forged in Paul's name to suit the heresy of Marcion, and several others, which cannot be received into the Catholic Church; for it is not fitting that gall be mixed with honey.

NOTE K

The Epistle of Jude no doubt, and the couple bearing the name of John, are accepted in the Catholic [Church]; and the Wisdom written by the friends of Solomon in his honour. The Apocalypse also of John, and of Peter [one Epistle, which] only we receive; [there is also a second] which some of our friends will not have read in the Church. But the Shepherd was written quite lately in our times by Hermas, while his brother Pius, the bishop, was sitting in the chair of the church of the city of Rome; and therefore it ought indeed to be read, but it cannot to the end of time be publicly read in the Church to the people, either among the prophets, who are complete in number, or among the Apostles.

But of Valentinus the Arsinoite and his friends we receive nothing at all; who have also composed a long new book of Psalms; together with Basilides and the Asiatic founder of the Montanists.'

NOTE L.

THE ORDER OF THE NEW TESTAMENT WRITINGS.

Earliest N.T. collections. WE have seen that during the greater part of the period of which we have been treating the different New Testament writings were circulated either singly or in small groups (cf. p. 204). Of these last the most important were ΕΥΑΓΓΕΛΙΟΝ, 'the Gospel,' and ΑΠΟΣΤΟΛΟΣ, 'the Apostle,' the separate books in these collections being provided not only with their own titles, but also frequently with individual prefaces or prologues.[1]

Gradually, however, the practice began of combining the scattered groups into one or more volumes. And in such a process it was inevitable that the order in which these groups and their constituent members were arranged should vary greatly. No good purpose would be served by reproducing here the elaborate tables or lists of these varying orders which have been drawn up. The curious reader will find full particulars in the literature mentioned below. But it may be of interest to indicate very generally a few of the principal facts, especially in so far as they bear upon the order of books to which we are accustomed in our English New Testament.

---

[1] The very interesting Latin Marcionite Prologues to St. Paul's Epistles can now be conveniently studied in Souter, *Text and Canon of the New Testament*, p. 205 ff.: cf. also the later editions of Burkitt's *Gospel History and its Transmission*.

NOTE L

1. We begin with the main groups or sections into which our New Testament writings as a whole fall. And here the Gospels are almost invariably placed first, owing to the nature of their contents and the honour paid to their authors. Any change in this position, as when Chrysostom places them after the Pauline Epistles, was doubtless due to liturgical reasons.

1. Order of main groups of N.T. writings. Gospels.

The desire to keep the historical books together ensured that as a rule the book of the Acts of the Apostles followed the Gospels, though in one of our oldest and most important codices, the Codex Sinaiticus, it is placed after the Pauline Epistles and the Epistle to the Hebrews.[1]

Acts.

Contrary to the order to which we are accustomed in our English version, the Catholic Epistles are found immediately after the Book of Acts and before the Pauline Epistles in almost all our Greek manuscripts, partly, doubtless, as the writings of the principal Apostles, and partly because of their encyclical or general character.[2] And this place, as is well known, continues to be assigned to them in many recent critical editions of the Greek New Testament, such as those of Tischendorf or of Westcott and Hort.

Catholic Epistles.

Then come the Pauline Epistles, and finally the Apocalypse, whose place would be determined by the difficulty

Pauline Epistles. Apocalypse.

---

[1] It may be noted that Acts occupies the same place in the earliest *printed* Greek Testament, A.D. 1514. This Testament formed part of the great Complutensian Polyglott of Cardinal Ximenes, and was not actually published till the completion of that work in 1520, four years after the issue of Erasmus's edition of the Greek New Testament (Basle, 1516).

[2] 3 John is the only one of the seven which does not fall under this last category, and it is quite possible that had it not been for the habit of inscribing it along with its companion 2 John on one roll with the rest of the group, these two short Epistles might have been lost to us altogether.

APPENDIX

it had found in winning acceptance in certain quarters, as well as by its own inherent character.¹

2. Order of individual writings in groups.

2. When we pass to the individual constituents of these different groups, the orders in which they are found are almost bewildering in their variety, nor in many cases is it possible any longer to discover the principles on which the scribes acted.

Gospels.

But here again the order of the Gospels to which we are accustomed—Matthew, Mark, Luke, John—is the prevailing one in nearly all the Greek and Syriac manuscripts, and rests apparently on various early traditions regarding their origin and authorship.²

Of other arrangements, perhaps the most interesting is that of Codex Bezae and certain Old Latin manuscripts, where Matthew and John come before Luke and Mark, apparently on the ground that the Gospels of Apostles should precede the Gospels of followers of Apostles.³ The precedence assigned to Luke's Gospel over Mark's may be due simply to its greater length. On the other hand, in a Canon of unknown date, bound up in the sixth century Codex Claromontanus of St. Paul's Epistles, Mark comes before Luke.

---

[1] Cf. p. 223 f. In the so-called *Decretum Gelasianum*, the Apocalypse comes after the Pauline and before the Catholic Epistles, but this Decree, instead of belonging to the end of the fourth century as was formerly believed, is now assigned to the sixth century: see E. von Dobschütz, *Das Decretum Gelasianum de Libris Recipiendis et Non Recipiendis* (Leipzig, 1912), cited by Souter, *Text and Canon*, pp. 218, 229 f.

[2] Cf. *e.g.* Irenaeus, *adv. Haer.* iii. 1. 2 (as in Additional Note H), and the views of Origen, as stated in Eusebius, *Hist. Eccles.* vi. 25. 3-6, who says that he has learned by tradition (ἐν παραδόσει) that Matthew wrote first, then Mark as Peter instructed him (ὡς Πέτρος ὑφηγήσατο αὐτῷ), thirdly Luke (τὸ ὑπὸ Παύλου ἐπαινούμενον εὐαγγέλιον), and last of all John (ἐπὶ πᾶσιν τὸ κατὰ Ἰωάννην).

[3] This 'Western' order is also found in the recently discovered Freer manuscript (cf. Additional Note I, p. 277 f.).

NOTE L

Chrysostom places John first, and arranges the other Gospels in the order—Matthew, Luke, Mark, an order which seems to have been known to Tertullian,[1] and corresponds, as Gregory has pointed out,[2] with the order found in the lectionaries or books of Gospel lessons, in which John was read at Easter, Matthew at Whitsuntide, Luke at Michaelmas, and Mark in Lent.

Catholic Epistles.

The Catholic Epistles were later than the Pauline in being collected into a single book, but from the fourth century onwards they generally appear in the order—James, Peter, John, Jude. When any change is made, Peter is placed first owing to the ecclesiastical position of the writer, and the others follow in all possible variations.

Pauline Epistles.

In the case of the Pauline Epistles, the earliest order with which we are acquainted is found in Marcion's Canon (cf. p. 217), in which Galatians is placed first, perhaps on dogmatic grounds, though it is worth noting that this place is assigned to it chronologically by many modern critics.[3]

In the Muratorian Canon (cf. Additional Note K), on the other hand, the Epistles to the Corinthians come first, and the Epistle to the Romans at the end, immediately before Philemon and the Pastorals, a position which may help to explain some of the textual difficulties connected with its closing chapters (see p. 182 ff).

Another variation that frequently occurs is the placing of Colossians after 2 Thessalonians.

On the whole, however, the order of the individual Epistles to which we are accustomed has been the prevailing order from the fourth century onwards. And the fact that there is no earlier evidence for it suggests that

---

[1] *adv. Marc.* iv. 2: 'nobis fidem ex apostolis Johannes et Matthaeus insinuant, ex apostolicis Lucas et Marcus instaurant, iisdem regulis exorsi.'

[2] *Textkritik*, ii. p. 856, cf. i. p. 339.

[3] See the note in my commentary on *Thessalonians*, p. xxxvii f.

it may have formed 'part of the textual and critical revision which the New Testament underwent, chiefly, but not exclusively, at the hand of Alexandrian scholars, in the fourth century.'[1] In the main it would seem to have been determined on the two grounds that the Epistles addressed to Churches should precede those addressed to persons, and that the longer Epistles should come before the shorter.

Epistle to the Hebrews.

The position assigned to the Epistle to the Hebrews is of importance, especially in connexion with the question of authorship. In the earlier Greek manuscripts it is placed between the Epistles of St. Paul to the Churches and the Pastoral Epistles;[2] but in the majority of late Greek manuscripts it comes at the end of all the Epistles usually attributed to St. Paul, and may therefore be regarded as a kind of appendix to them.

Literature.

Those who desire further particulars may consult Moffatt's carefully prepared lists in his *Historical New Testament*, p. 108 ff., and more recently in his *Introduction to the Literature of the New Testament*, p. 13 ff., and the discussions in Zahn, *Geschichte des Neutestamentlichen Kanons*, ii. p. 343 ff., Gregory, *Textkritik des Neuen Testamentes*, ii. p. 848 ff., and (in a condensed form) Jacquier, *Le Nouveau Testament dans l'Église Chrétienne*, ii. p. 59 ff. The Latin evidence is given by S. Berger, *Histoire de la Vulgate* (Paris, 1893), pp. 301 ff., 339 ff. Many of the most interesting 'Catalogues' are printed in the Appendices to Westcott's and to Souter's works on the Canon. Some interesting remarks on the whole subject will also be found in a paper by the Rev. A. Wright, *Some New Testament Problems* (London, 1898), p. 195 ff.

---

[1] Lake, *The Earlier Epistles of St. Paul*, p. 358, n[2].
[2] See also the Festal Letter of Athanasius, Additional Note M.

NOTE M.

EXTRACTS FROM FESTAL LETTER XXXIX. OF ATHANASIUS, A.D. 367.

THE earliest list of the books of the New Testament, which includes all the books of our own Canon and no others, is given by Athanasius in one of his Festal Letters. The following extracts are taken from Zahn's Greek text in his *Geschichte des Neutestamentlichen Kanons*, ii. p. 210 ff., and reprinted in his *Grundriss der Geschichte des Neutestamentlichen Kanons*², p. 87 f.

Athanasius.
† A.D. 373.

Μέλλων δὲ τούτων μνημονεύειν χρήσομαι πρὸς σύστασιν τῆς ἐμαυτοῦ τόλμης τῷ τύπῳ τοῦ εὐαγγελιστοῦ Λουκᾶ,[1] λέγων καὶ αὐτός· ἐπειδήπερ τινὲς ἐπεχείρησαν ἀνατάξασθαι ἑαυτοῖς τὰ λεγόμενα ἀπόκρυφα καὶ ἐπιμίξαι ταῦτα τῇ θεοπνεύστῳ γραφῇ, περὶ ἧς ἐπληροφορήθημεν καθὼς παρέδοσαν τοῖς πατράσιν οἱ ἀπ' ἀρχῆς αὐτόπται καὶ ὑπηρέται γενόμενοι τοῦ λόγου, ἔδοξε κἀμοὶ προτραπέντι παρὰ γνησίων ἀδελφῶν καὶ μαθόντι ἄνωθεν, ἑξῆς ἐκθέσθαι τὰ κανονιζόμενα καὶ παραδοθέντα πιστευθέντα τε θεῖα εἶναι βιβλία, ἵνα ἕκαστος, εἰ μὲν ἠπατήθη, καταγνῷ τῶν πλανησάντων, ὁ δὲ καθαρὸς διαμείνας χαίρῃ πάλιν ὑπομιμνησκόμενος.

Ἔστι τοίνυν τῆς μὲν παλαιᾶς διαθήκης βιβλία τῷ ἀριθμῷ τὰ πάντα εἰκοσιδύο. . . . . .

[1] Cf. Luke i. 1-4.

Τὰ δὲ τῆς καινῆς πάλιν οὐκ ὀκνητέον εἰπεῖν. ἔστι δὲ ταῦτα· Εὐαγγέλια τέσσαρα κατὰ Ματθαῖον, κατὰ Μᾶρκον, κατὰ Λουκᾶν, κατὰ Ἰωάννην. Εἶτα μετὰ ταῦτα Πράξεις ἀποστόλων καὶ Ἐπιστολαὶ καθολικαὶ καλούμεναι τῶν ἀποστόλων ἑπτὰ οὕτως· Ἰακώβου μὲν μία, Πέτρου δὲ δύο, εἶτα Ἰωάννου τρεῖς καὶ μετὰ ταύτας Ἰούδα μία. Πρὸς τούτοις Παύλου ἀποστόλου εἰσὶν ἐπιστολαὶ δεκατέσσαρες, τῇ τάξει γραφόμεναι οὕτως· πρώτη πρὸς Ῥωμαίους, εἶτα πρὸς Κορινθίους δύο, καὶ μετὰ ταῦτα πρὸς Γαλάτας μία, πρὸς Ἐφεσίους μία, πρὸς Φιλιππησίους μία, πρὸς Κολοσσαεῖς μία, καὶ μετὰ ταύτας πρὸς Θεσσαλονικέας δύο καὶ ἡ πρὸς Ἑβραίους· καὶ εὐθὺς πρὸς μὲν Τιμόθεον δύο, πρὸς δὲ Τίτον μία καὶ τελευταία ἡ πρὸς Φιλήμονα μία· καὶ πάλιν Ἰωάννου ἀποκάλυψις.

Ταῦτα πηγαὶ σωτηρίου, ὥστε τὸν διψῶντα ἐμφορεῖσθαι τῶν ἐν τούτοις λογίων· ἐν τούτοις μόνοις τὸ τῆς εὐσεβείας διδασκαλεῖον εὐαγγελίζεται· μηδεὶς τούτοις ἐπιβαλλέτω μηδὲ τούτων ἀφαιρείσθω τι.

'Seeing that I am about to make mention of these matters, I will use to support my boldness the example of the Evangelist Luke, and I will also say: Since certain men have taken in hand to draw up for themselves (a list of) the books called apocryphal, and to mix these up with the God-inspired Scripture, concerning which we have been fully informed, in accordance with what those who were from the beginning eye-witnesses and servants of the word have handed down to the fathers, it has seemed good to me also, seeing that I have been urged on by the true brethren, and have learned (the course of all things accurately) from the first, to set forth in order the books that are in the canonical list and have been handed down and believed to be Divine, in order that each person, if he has been deceived, may pass judgment on those who led him astray, and he who has continued blameless may rejoice, when he is again reminded (of the truth).

These then are the books of the Old Testament, in number altogether twenty-two. . . . . . .

Nor must I shrink from mentioning the books of the New Testament in their turn. They are these: Four Gospels, according to Matthew, according to Mark, according to Luke, according to John. Then after these Acts of Apostles and Epistles of the Apostles, which are called Catholic and are seven in number as follows: of James one, of Peter two, then of John three, and after these of Jude one. In addition to these there are fourteen Epistles of Paul the Apostle, which are written in order thus: the first to the Romans, then two to the Corinthians, and thereafter to the Galatians one, to the Ephesians one, to the Philippians one, to the Colossians one, and after these to the Thessalonians two and the Epistle to the Hebrews; and forthwith to Timothy two, and to Titus one, and last of all the Epistle to Philemon one; and of John again the Revelation.

These are springs of salvation, so that he who is athirst may be filled with the oracles in them. In them alone is the teaching of piety proclaimed as good news. Let no one add to them, or take away aught from them.'[1]

---

[1] In the curious Syriac work *The Doctrine of Addai*, which in its present form may be dated in the second half of the fourth century, though it evidently embodies a much earlier tradition, the writer lays a somewhat similar charge upon his presbyters in his closing speech : 'The Law and the Prophets and the Gospel, wherein ye read every day before the people ; and the Epistles of Paul which Simon Kephas sent us from the city of Rome ; and the Acts of the Twelve Apostles,

Athanasius then proceeds to certain other writings such as the so-called Teaching of the Apostles and the Shepherd, which, though not included in the canonical list, are nevertheless useful for those who come to be instructed in the true religion (κατηχεῖσθαι τὸν τῆς εὐσεβείας λόγον). And finally he adds another warning with regard to the apocryphal books which are often palmed off as ancient by the heretics, in order that they may have an excuse for deceiving in this way the simple (ἵνα ὡς παλαιὰ προφέροντες πρόφασιν ἔχωσιν ἀπατᾶν ἐκ τούτου τοὺς ἀκεραίους).

Councils of Laodicea and Carthage.

It may be added that at the Council of Laodicea, held four years earlier (A.D. 363), when for the first time a definite pronouncement was made regarding the canonical books of the Old and New Testament, the list agrees exactly with the foregoing, except that the Apocalypse is omitted. At the Council of Carthage A.D. 397 (cf. p. 227), the Apocalypse was added, and the Epistles of St. Paul and the Epistle to the Hebrews ('Epistolae Pauli apostoli tredecim, eiusdem ad Hebraeos una') are placed after Acts and before the Catholic Epistles.

The text of both these lists, along with many other documents relating to the history of the Canon, are given by E. Preuschen, *Analecta*[2], ii. *Zur Kanonsgeschichte*, Tübingen, 1910.

which John the son of Zebedee sent us from Ephesus: these writings (or Scriptures) shall ye read in the Churches of Christ, and beside them nothing else shall be read' (ed. Phillips, p. 46).

NOTE N.

RECENT LITERATURE ON THE CANON OF THE NEW TESTAMENT.

THE great storehouse for all that is concerned with the history of the New Testament Canon is Zahn's *Geschichte des Neutestamentlichen Kanons*, Erlangen und Leipzig, 1888-1892, together with his *Forschungen zur Geschichte des neutestamentlichen Kanons und der altkirchlichen Literatur*, of which eight parts have appeared, Erlangen and Leipzig, 1881-1907. For the ordinary student, the same writer's *Grundriss der Geschichte des Neutestamentlichen Kanons*², Leipzig, 1904, originally intended as a supplement to his *Einleitung in das Neue Testament*, will be found a most useful compendium. {Literature on the Canon.}

In 1889 Professor Harnack published a critique of the first part of Zahn's *Geschichte* in a short but significant brochure entitled, *Das Neue Testament um das Jahr* 200 (Freiburg i. B.). And to this Zahn replied in *Einige Bemerkungen zu Adolf Harnacks Prüfung der Geschichte des neutestamentlichen Kanons*, Erlangen und Leipzig, 1889.

More recent is the *Geschichte des neutestamentlichen Kanons* by the Egyptologist, Dr. J. Leipoldt, Leipzig, 1907-08, which may be regarded as in the nature of an eirenicon between his two great predecessors. In any case, he acknowledges his indebtedness to both, and sums up his view of the position as follows:

'Harnack understands by the New Testament Canon a

collection of books to which authority was assigned, because they were regarded as Holy Scripture. Accordingly he places the rise of the New Testament at the end of the second century. Zahn, on the other hand, equally finds the New Testament in a collection of books, possessed of authority, but he does not insist that this authority should be based on that dictum : " The New Testament is Holy Scripture." It is enough for him that the Gospels are an authority, because of the authority of the Lord's sayings which they contain. Zahn can therefore speak of a New Testament Canon a hundred years earlier than Harnack can. The actual facts, which are involved, are hardly touched by the controversy' (i. p. 4). Leipoldt's own attitude is further shown by his insistence throughout on Luther's maxim, ' Heilige Schrift ist, was Christum treibt' (i. p. v, cf. p. 268 ff.).

Short German studies on the subject which may be mentioned are G. Krüger, *Die Entstehung des Neuen Testamentes*, Freiburg i. B. und Leipzig, 1896 ; P. Ewald, *Der Kanon des Neuen Testaments* (in *Biblische Zeit- und Streitfragen*), Gr. Lichterfelde—Berlin, 1906 ; H. Lietzmann, *Wie würden die Bücher des Neuen Testaments heilige Schrift?* (in *Lebensfragen*), Tübingen, 1908 ; and H. Holtzmann, *Die Entstehung des Neuen Testaments*[2] (in the series of *Religionsgeschichtliche Volksbücher*), Tübingen, 1911.

Many of the leading documents in connexion with the history of the Canon will be found in H. Lietzmann's useful collection of *Kleine Texte für Theologische Vorlesungen und Übungen*, Bonn, 1902, of which an English edition, under the title *Materials for Theological Lecturers and Students*, has been brought out by Deighton, Bell & Co., Cambridge.

Amongst the sections devoted to the subject of the Canon in the various Introductions to the New Testament, special mention may be made of the stimulating chapters in A. Jülicher's *Einleitung in das Neue Testament* [5 and 6], Leipzig, 1906. An English translation of the second edition of this book by Miss Janet P. Ward appeared in 1904. For the more traditional views, Salmon's *Historical Introduction to the Study of the Books of the New Testament* [7] (London, 1894) should still be consulted.

The most comprehensive work in English, however, is Bishop Westcott's *General Survey of the History of the Canon of the New Testament*, first published London, 1855. The seventh edition appeared in 1896. The substance of this book in simpler form, for the use of general readers, was issued under the title, *The Bible in the Church: a popular account of the Collection and Reception of the Holy Scriptures in the Christian Churches*, in 1864, and has since been revised and reprinted at various dates.

Much material of the highest importance for the study of the Canon will also be found in Bishop Lightfoot's *Essays on the Work entitled Supernatural Religion* (London, 1889), and in Dr. Sanday's Bampton Lectures on *Inspiration*, first published in 1893. With these last may be compared the same writer's art. 'Bible (B) New Testament I. *Canon*,' contributed to the eleventh edition of the *Encyclopaedia Britannica*, Cambridge, 1910.

In his *Canonicity*, Edinburgh, 1880, based on Kirchhofer's *Quellensammlung*, Professor Charteris has brought together a very complete collection of early testimonies to the canonical books of the New Testament. For a more general statement, reference may be made to his Croall Lecture, *The New Testament Scriptures: their Claims, History, and Authority*, London, 1882. The case as regards the Gospels is fully stated by Professor Nicol of Aberdeen in the Baird Lecture for 1907, *The Four Gospels in the Earliest Church History*, Edinburgh and London, 1908.

The Canon forms the first part of Professor C. R. Gregory's volume in the 'International Theological Library,' *Canon and Text of the New Testament* (Edinburgh, 1907), a volume which has appeared in a revised form in German, *Einleitung in das Neue Testament*, Leipzig, 1909. In Professor Souter's *The Text and Canon of the New Testament*, which has just appeared in Duckworth's series of 'Studies in Theology,' London, 1913, the order of treatment is reversed. And though the size of the book does not admit of lengthened discussions, all the leading questions are fully noted, while room is found for a number of useful ' Selected Documents,' edited with great exactness and skill.

With these two books may be mentioned the attractively written volumes by the Abbé Jacquier on *Le Nouveau Testament dans l'Église Chrétienne*, the first of which has for its subject, ' Préparation, formation et définition du Canon du Nouveau Testament' (Paris, 1911).

The New Testament in the Christian Church (New York, 1904) is the title given to eight lectures by Professor E. C. Moore of Harvard University, in which the Canon of the New Testament is related to the Organization of the Church for Government, and the Rule of Faith.

Of a more popular character are two other books also hailing from America: *The Formation of the New Testament*, by G. H. Ferris, and *Our New Testament, How did we get it?* by H. C. Vedder, both published at Philadelphia without date.

As introductory to the main points at issue, *The Rise of the New Testament*, by D. S. Muzzey, New York, 1904, and *Faith and the New Testament* (lectures to a Church Reading Society), by A. W. F. Blunt, Edinburgh, 1912, may also be mentioned.

The article on the New Testament Canon in the *Encyclopaedia Biblica* is by Dean Armitage Robinson, and in Hastings' *Dictionary of the Bible*, by Professor V. H. Stanton. A paper on the subject by Dr. Sanday will be found in *Oxford House Papers*, Third Series, London, 1897, p. 105 ff., and a lecture by Bishop Chase in the St.

Margaret's Lectures on *Criticism of the New Testament*, London, 1902, p. 96 ff. Much of importance relating to the Canon will also be found in Dr. C. H. Turner's valuable series of papers entitled 'Historical Introduction to the Textual Criticism of the New Testament' in the *Journal of Theological Studies* for 1909-10.

INDEXES.

I. SUBJECTS.

Accidence, 62 f.
Acts of the Apostles, 161 ff.
Addresses of N.T. writings, 17 ff.
Agrapha, 266.
Apocalypse of St. John, 117 ff., 223 f., 257 f., 262 ff.
Apocryphal books, 213.
Aramaic, 36 f.
Autographic conclusions, 24 f.
Autographs, New Testament, 6 f.

'Biblical' words, 70 ff.

Canon, New Testament: formation of, 206 ff.; recent literature on, 301 ff.
Catholic Epistles, 107 ff.
Christian vocabulary, 58 f.
Circulation of the N.T. writings, 173 ff.
Codex form, 188 ff.
Collection of the N.T. writings, 203 ff.
Colossians, Epistle to the, 100 f., 177.
Commendatory letters, 88 f., 255 f.
Contractions in MSS., 25, 247.
Corinthians, Epistles to the, 97 f.
2 Corinthians, integrity of, 184 ff.
Corpus Evangelicum, 217 ff.; *Paulinum*, 215 ff.

Dates of N.T. documents, 172 f.
Delivery of N.T. writings, 30 ff.
Diatessaron, 218 f.
Dictation, 21 ff., 27 ff., 99, 241 f.
Didache, 217 f.

Ephesians, Epistle to the, 85, 98 ff., 174.
Epistolary form, 85 ff., 107; phraseology, 93, 260; plural, 259.
Evangelion Da-Mepharreshê, 219.

Freedom of literary reproduction, 178 ff.

Galatians, Epistle to the, 96.
Gospel name and form, 130 f.
Greek: use of Greek in Palestine, 37 ff.; character of N.T. Greek, 43 ff.; uniformity of the Κοινή, 48 f.; influences affecting N.T. Greek, 49 ff.

Handwriting of N.T. texts, 25 f., 190, 195.
Hebraisms, 50 ff.
Hebrews, Epistle to the, 108 ff., 181, 225, 252, 296.
Heretics, use of N.T. by, 214 f.

James, Epistle of, 38 f., 111 f.
John, Epistles of, 115 ff.
John, Gospel of, 153 ff., 186 f.

Laodiceans, Epistle to the, 85.
Letters, early use of, 86 f.
Literary tendencies in N.T., 55 ff.
Logia of Papias, 137 f., 269 ff.
Logia, The Oxyrhynchus, 131, 266 ff.
Lucan source, special, 138 f.
Luke, Gospel of, 149 ff.

Marginalia, 14, 187 f.
Mark, Gospel of, 38, 134 f., 143 ff., 177; endings of, 182, 274 ff.
Morphology, 63 ff.
Muratorian Canon, 222, 286 ff.

New Testament Documents: rise of, 4 ff.; outward form of, 7 ff.; writing of, 21 ff.; delivery of, 30 f.; language of, 35 ff.; literary character of, 83 ff.; circulation of, 171 ff.; collection of, 203 ff.; permanent value of, 32, 80, 228 f.
Notae Tironianae, 246.

Old Testament, early supremacy of, 205 f.; Canon of, 206 f.
Oral teaching, 3 f., 129.
Order of N.T. Writings, 292 ff.
Orthography, 62 f.

Papyri, study of Greek, 233 ff.
Papyrus: manufacture of, 9 ff.; ordinary letters on, 255 ff.; N.T. texts on, 248 ff.
Paragraphs, 25.
Parchment: manufacture of, 191 f.; Christian documents on, 192 f.; codices on, 194 ff.
Pastoral Epistles, 85, 101 ff.

Pauline Epistles: authenticity of, 84 f.; form of, 87 ff.; plan of, 93; literary character of, 94, 104; speech, character of, 103; relation of, to Jewish literature, 104 ff.; originality of, 106 f.
Peter, Gospel according to, 213, 281 ff.
Peter, Epistles of, 112 ff.
Pocket Bibles, 196.
'Poor Men's Bibles,' 191.
Prepositions, lax use of, 65 ff.
Preservation of rolls, 20.
Pseudepigrapha, 114.
Public Worship, use of N.T. in, 210 ff.
Punctuation, 25 f.

Q (as Gospel source), 136 f., 152.
Quotations in Pauline Epistles, 27 ff.

Realien, 77 ff.
Recto and *Verso*, 13.
Romans, Epistle to the, 97; ending of, 182 ff.

'Sayings of Jesus,' 190, 266 ff.
Scilitan martyrs, 211 f.
Sealing, 17 ff.
Semitisms, see Hebraisms.
Septuagint, 53 f., 106, 206 f.
Shorthand, 26, 242 ff.
Signature, authenticating, 23.
Subscriptions of the N.T. writings, 237 ff.
Synoptic Gospels: name of, 132; sources of, 133 ff.; evolution of, 139 ff.; conditions of writing, 141 f.; aim of, 142 f.; unity of, 152 f.
Syntax, 65 ff.

Testimonia, 207 f.

I. SUBJECTS

Text of the N.T., 60 f., 176 ff., 197 ff.
Thessalonians, Epistles to the, 84, 96.
Titles of the N.T. writings, 237 ff.
Travel-diary, 163 f.
Two-Document Hypothesis, 133 ff.

Ur-Marcus, 135.

Vocabulary, N.T., 69 ff.

Writing, early use of, 4 f.
Writing materials, 8 ff.

II. AUTHORS.

Abbott, E. A., 72, 134.
Abbott, T. K., 42.
Allen, W. C., 38, 136, 236.
Allon, T. W., 247.

Bachmann, 186.
Bacon, 135, 153.
Barth, 181.
Bartlet, 139, 217.
Baur, 84.
Bell, H. I., 79, 234.
Benson, 121.
Berger, 296.
Biesenthal, 38.
Bigg, 114.
Birt, 10, 15, 16, 20, 60, 175, 192.
Blass, 62, 65, 104, 109, 163, 167, 252.
Blau, 8, 19.
Bleek, 111.
Blunt, A. W. F., 304.
Böhlig, 104.
Bonhöffer, 57.
Bouriant, 281.
Bousset, 122.
Brooke, A. E., 115, 158, 236.
Buchanan, E. S., 286.
Buckley, 145.
Bultmann, 57.
Burgon, 275.
Burkitt, F. C., 135, 152, 153, 160, 177, 208, 219, 292.

Chapman, 271.
Charles, R. H., 106.
Charteris, 303.
Chase, F. H., 67, 113, 168, 304.
Clement, 179.
Colson, F. H., 270.
Conybeare, F. C., 276.

Dalman, 37.
Deissmann, 7, 18, 24, 47, 48, 51, 57, 62, 70, 71, 76, 78, 79, 86, 88, 95, 104, 105, 106, 111, 119, 154, 155, 164, 234 f., 251, 257, 260.
Dittenberger, 16, 75, 154.
Dobschütz, von, 84, 294.
D'Orville, 243.
Dziatzko, 10, 14, 20, 179.

Erasmus, 293.
Erman, 234.
Ewald, P., 302.

Farrar, 47, 132.
Ferris, G. H., 304.
Feltoe, 262.
Foat, 245.
Frame, J. E., 84, 236.
Friedländer, 31.

Gaertringen, H. von, 51.
Gardner, P., 56, 166.
Gardthausen, 10, 12, 192, 245.

II. AUTHORS

Gerhard, 260.
Goodspeed, E. J., 18, 280.
Gray, G. B., 111.
Green, A. V., 153.
Gregory, C. R., 191, 241 f., 248, 250, 278, 295, 296, 303.
Grenfell, B. P., 31. *See also* Grenfell-Hunt.
Grenfell-Hunt, 17, 18, 19, 21, 22, 25, 26, 50, 51, 66, 72, 73, 74, 79, 109, 117, 162, 189, 190, 194, 196, 233, 244, 248, 249, 250, 251, 252, 255, 256, 266 f., 270.
Griesbach, 132.
Griffenhoofe, 266.
Grimm-Thayer, 70, 72, 74.
Grotius, 13.
Gunkel, 122.
Gwatkin, 286.

Harnack, 84, 85, 111, 112, 121, 149, 163, 164, 165, 168, 172, 174, 175, 226, 268, 280, 285, 301.
Harris, Rendel, 28, 117, 208, 252, 276, 285.
Hatch, E., 208.
Hatch, W. H. P., 59.
Hausrath, 184.
Hawkins, 136, 148, 152, 164.
Heinrici, 104.
Heitmüller, 67.
Helbing, 62, 236
Hemphill, 218.
Herwerden, van, 235.
Hicks, 17.
Hill, Hamlyn, 218.
Hobart, 56, 150.
Hogarth, 51.
Holtzmann, 100, 302.
Horder, 268.
Hort, 46, 65, 76, 85, 125, 177, 184, 196, 272, 277. *See also* Westcott and Hort.

Hunt, A. S., 20, 23, 190, 196, 233, 252, 253, 254. *See also* Grenfell-Hunt.

Jackson, H. L., 153.
Jacquier, 280, 296, 304.
James, M. R., 284.
Jannaris, 235.
Jowett, 5.

Keim, 144.
Kenyon, F. G., 8, 11, 13, 14, 25, 79, 94, 191, 198, 234, 236, 244, 248.
Knowling, 56, 84, 167.
Krebs, 234.
Krüger, G., 302.

Lagarde, 9.
Lake, Kirsopp, 137, 167, 184, 186, 296.
Laudien, 234.
Laurent, 14.
Law, 109, 115 f.
Leemans, 65, 244.
Leipoldt, 224, 301 f.
Lewis, F. W., 186 f.
Lewis, Mrs., 275.
Lietzmann, 186, 234, 280, 302.
Lightfoot, J. B., 22, 46, 79, 97, 115, 166, 167, 184, 209, 216, 303.
Lock, 28, 268.
Lods, A., 285.
Loisy, 135.
Luther, 96, 302.

Mahaffy, 143, 233.
Marquardt, 245.
Mayor, J. B., 39, 114.
M'Giffert, 262.
Menzies, A., 135, 186.
Mill, 197.
Milligan, W., 123, 125.
Mitteis, 10, 234.

Moellendorf, 107.
Moffatt, 84, 101, 136, 145, 146, 158, 163, 175, 296.
Moore, E. C., 304.
Moulton, J. H., 44, 48, 55, 59, 62, 64, 65, 112, 113, 121, 149, 152, 162, 235, 257.
Murray, J. O. F., 285.
Muzzey, D. S., 304.

Nägeli, 57, 98, 102.
Nestle, 7, 9, 13, 191, 197, 276.
Nicol, 220, 303.
Nicole, J., 12.
Niese, 41.
Norden, 107, 131, 149.

Oesterley, 280.
Overbeck, 181.

Paley, 101.
Peake, 164.
Peter, H., 261.
Petrie, Flinders, 131.
Peyron, 45.
Phillimore, 164, 243.
Pick, Bernard, 162.
Pistelli, 249.
Plummer, 151, 236.
Preisigke, 73.
Preuschen, E., 300.
Psichari, 54.
Putnam, H., 178, 179.

Radermacher, 235.
Ramsay, W. M., 5, 58, 102, 119, 125, 137, 162, 165, 166, 175.
Reitzenstein, 131.
Renan, 87, 149.
Richards, G. C., 55.
Roberts, A., 236.
Robinson, J. Armitage, 67, 85, 103, 159, 212, 217, 236, 258, 260, 284, 304.
Ropes, J. H., 149.

Rouffiac, 183.
Ryle, H. E., 206.

Sabatier, A., 285.
Salmon, 142, 303.
Sanday, 15, 99, 101, 134, 135, 139, 141, 145, 146, 181, 268, 271 f., 303, 304.
Sanders, 277 f., 280.
Scheil, F. V., 249.
Schmidt, 250, 280.
Schmiedel, 42, 62.
Schubart, 12, 13, 259.
Schürer, 42.
Simcox, 103.
Simonides, C., 7.
Skeel, 175.
Smith, G. A., 40 f.
Smith, W. Robertson, 180.
Smyly, 72, 79.
Soden, von, 237 ff., 248 ff.
Souter, A., 56, 101, 194, 199, 272, 276, 292, 294, 296, 304.
Spitta, 111, 114, **186**.
Stanton, V. H., 285, 304.
Strauss, 158.
Streeter, 136, 139 ff., 145, 146, 156.
Swete, 16, 54, 86, 93, 118, 119, 123, 124, 125, 147, 268, 276, 277, 280, 281 ff.

Taylor, C., 177, 268.
Thackeray, H. St. John, 54, 62, 65, 86, 106, 235.
Thayer, *see* Grimm-Thayer.
Thompson, E. M., 236.
Thumb, A., 48, 235.
Tischendorf, 293.
Traube, 247.
Tregelles, S. P., 286.
Turner, C. H., 65, 305.

Usener, 86.

Vedder, H. C., 304.
Vigoroux, 166.

Vischer, 121.
Vitelli, 79, 254.
Vollmer, 106.

Wackernagel, 53.
Ward, J. P., 303.
Warschauer, 268.
Weiss, J., 57, 104.
Weizsäcker, 29.
Welldon, 198.
Wellhausen, 37, 38, 144.
Wendland, 86, 103, 107, 207, 260.
Wendling, 135.
Wessely, 234, 245, 248, 249.
Westcott, 32, 64, 66, 85, 194, 221, 262, 286, 293, 296, 303. *See also* Westcott and Hort.
Westcott and Hort, 19, 62, 63, 119, 199, 293.
Wilcken, 10, 11, 12, 13, 17, 234, 236, 244.
Wilson, J. M., 168.
Winer-Schmiedel, 43, 62.
Witkowski, S., 234.
Wordsworth and White, 160.
Wright, A., 296.

Ximenes, Cardinal, 293.

Zahn, 13, 15, 36, 113, 114, 187, 217, 219, 285, 286, 296, 297 f., 301.
Ziemann, 260.

III. REFERENCES.

1. BIBLICAL.

DEUTERONOMY.	PAGE
iv. 10	223

2 SAMUEL.	
xi. 14 f.	87

2 KINGS.	
xix. 14	87

EZRA.	
iv. 8 ff.	36
vii. 12 ff.	36

PSALMS.	
xl. 7	11
xlv. 1	243

ISAIAH.	
liv. 1	205

JEREMIAH.	
xxix.	87

EZEKIEL.	
ii. 9	12
iii. 1 ff.	12

DANIEL.	
ii. 4 ff.	36

ST. MATTHEW.	PAGE
i.	139
i. 1-9, 12, 14-20	249
ii.	139
v.-vii.	147
vi. 1-18	148
vi. 16	78
vi. 27	74
vii. 28	148
viii.-ix.	148
ix. 13	205
x. 13	63
x. 32-xi. 5	254
xi.	147
xi. 1	148
xii. 32	64
xiii.	147
xiii. 22	75
xiii. 52	147
xiii. 53	148
xv. 37	63
xvi. 10	63
xix. 1	148
xxiii.	148
xxv. 12-15, 20-23	254
xxvi. 1	148
xxvi. 29	63
xxviii. 19	4, 66

ST. MARK.	
i. 1	156
iii. 8	63

III. REFERENCES

	PAGE		PAGE
iv. 28	65	vii. 53-viii. 11	188
v. 41	37	viii. 30	69
vii. 34	37	viii. 56	259
viii. 8, 20	63	ix. 11	154
xii. 37	35	x. 25	157
xii. 38	50	xi. 45	250
xiii.	145 f.	xiv. 26	208
xiv. 9	64	xvii. 3	67
xiv. 25	63	xix. 20	36
xv. 15	79	xx. 11-17, 19-25	250
xv. 34	37	xx. 30 f.	266
xvi. 9 ff.	182, 274 ff.	xx. 31	156
xvi. 20	78	xxi. 7	161
		xxi. 24	157

St. Luke.

	PAGE
i.	139
i. 1-4	129, 130, 266, 297
i. 3	151
i. 74-80	249
ii.	139
ii. 52	74
iv. 1 f.	250
iv. 16 ff.	151, 210
v. 3-8	249
v. 30-vi. 4	249
vii. 18 ff.	249
vii. 36-45	249
x. 38-42	249
xii. 18	63
xv. 13	79
xix. 3	74
xxii. 18	63
xxiv. 25, 44 f.	204

St. John.

	PAGE
i. 14	64
i. 15, 32	157
i. 18	66
iii. 11	157
iii. 14-17, 17 f., 31 f.	254
v. 36	157
vi. 63	35
vii. 15	21

Acts.

	PAGE
ii. 5	41
iii. 15	75
iv. 13	21
iv. 31-37	250
iv. 36	111
v. 2-9	250
v. 31	75
vi. 1-6, 8-15	250
vi. 5	65
vi. 9	41
viii. 35	204
ix. 25	63
ix. 36	282
xiii. 15	173, 210
xvi. 10-17	163
xvi. 12	76
xvii. 6	74
xviii. 18	183
xviii. 26	111
xviii. 28	204
xx. 5, 15	163
xx. 35	208
xxi. 1-18	163
xxi. 8	139
xxi. 40 ff.	36, 42
xxvi. 24	21
xxvii. 1 ff.	163
xxviii. 31	168

ROMANS.

	page
i. 1-7	251
ii. 14-15	14
ix. 5	26
xv. xvi.	182 ff.
xvi. 5	216
xvi. 7	64
xvi. 19	14
xvi. 22	23

1 CORINTHIANS.

i. 17-20	251
i. 25-27	252
ii. 6-8	252
iii. 8-10, 20	252
iv. 21	50
v. 9	5, 185
vi. 13-18	251
vii. 3, 4, 10-14	251
vii. 10	208
vii. 18-viii. 4	252
viii. 1-9	28
x. 21	51 f.
xi. 23	208
xiii.	97
xv. 31	259
xv. 32	216
xvi. 1 f.	72
xvi. 8, 19	216
xvi. 19	183
xvi. 21	23

2 CORINTHIANS.

i. 1	98, 174
i. 8 f.	216
i. 20	282
i. 22	73
i.-ix.	185
ii. 13	31
iii. 1	18, 88
iii. 2	4
iii. 6	35
iii. 7	203
iii. 14	173

	page
iv. 2	78
iv. 7	3, 8
v. 5	73
vii. 6, 13 f.	31
vii. 8	184
ix. 10	63
x. 1	29
x. 10	5, 83
x.-xiii.	185
xi. 28	5
xii. 16	29

GALATIANS.

i. 2	174
iii. 1	79
iii. 16	105
v. 12	74
vi. 11	24

EPHESIANS.

i. 1	85, 174
i. 3-14	98
i. 3, 20	99
i. 10	4
i. 14	73
i. 15-23	98
ii. 6	99
iii. 1-13	98
iii. 10	99
vi. 12	99
vi. 21 f.	31

PHILIPPIANS.

ii. 19	29
iii. 9-17 and iv. 2-8	252
iv. 2-8	252
iv. 10	29
iv. 18	78

COLOSSIANS.

ii. 14	16
iv. 14	150
iv. 16	5, 85, 211
iv. 18	23

III. REFERENCES

1 Thessalonians.

	page
i. 1	93
iii. 8	96
iv. 15	208
v. 27	211

2 Thessalonians.

ii. 2	211
iii. 1	171
iii. 17	5, 23, 211
iii. 18	23

1 Timothy.

i. 3	102
iv. 13	173
iv. 19	183

2 Timothy.

iv. 9-22	85
iv. 13	3, 9, 19 f.
iv. 19	183

Titus.

i. 11-15	253
ii. 3-8	253

Philemon.

Ver. 1 ff.	94
,, 18	73

Hebrews.

i. 1	181, 251
ii. 9	68
ii. 10	75
ii. 14-v. 5	252
v. 12	108
vi. 4	68
vi. 9	108
ix. 12-19	253
ix. 16, 17	75
x. 7	11
x. 8-xi. 13	252
x. 32	108
xi. 28-xii. 17	252
xii. 2	75

	page
xii. 4	108
xiii. 18	51
xiii. 22-25	108

James.

i. 1	112
i. 3	76
ii. 1	112
ii. 14-26	112
ii. 19-iii. 9	254

1 Peter.

i. 1	174
i. 7	76
ii. 2	77
iii. 18	282
v. 12	22
v. 13	117

2 Peter.

ii. 13	75
iii. 15 f.	83
iii. 16	205

1 John.

iv. 11-12, 14-17	250

2 John.

Ver. 1	116, 259
,, 4, 8	117
,, 12	9

3 John.

Ver. 9	117
,, 13	9, 16, 17
,, 15	258

Revelation.

i. 1	118
i. 3	83, 118, 223
i. 4	117, 120
i. 4-7	253
i. 10	282
iii. 5	16

REVELATION—Cont.	PAGE				PAGE
iii. 14 ff.	85	xii.			122
v. 1	13, 17	xiii.-xx.			122
vi. 14	16	xiv. 6			171
vii. 4-8	122	xxii. 7			118, 223
xi. 1-13	122	xxii. 10			118
xi. 15	126	xxii. 18			118
		xxii. 21			117

2. ANCIENT TEXTS AND WRITINGS.

	PAGE		PAGE
Apollonius of Tyana, i. 18 -	243	Dionysius of Alexandria	123, 262 ff.
Aristeas, § 176	8	Doctrine of Addai -	299 f.
Athanasius, *Festal Letter* xxxix.	297 ff.	Eunapius, p. 138 -	243
Aulus Gellius, *Noct. Att.* xvii. 9	246	Eusebius :	
		De vita Constantini, iv. 36	193
Catullus, xxxv. 2	9	*Hist. Eccles.* iii. 24. 3 -	2
Cicero, *ad Attic.* i. 9. 1	31	,, iii. 24. 4 -	6
,, ,, iv. 4. 1	19	,, iii. 25.	223
,, ,, viii. 1. 1	24	,, iii. 36.	176
,, ,, xiii. 24	193	,, iii. 37. 2 -	170
,, ,, xiii. 32. 3	246	,, iii. 39. 4 -	209
,, *ad Fam.* v. 8 -	186	,, iii. 39. 14 ff. 137, 145, 269 f.	
,, ,, xv. 21. 4	95	,, iv. 23. 11 -	213
,, *pro Archia*, 23	34	,, iv. 23. 12 -	179
1 Clement	216, 225	,, v. 20. 6 -	220
2 Clement	205	,, v. 25.	176
Clement, Alex., *Strom.* ii. 9. 45	220	,, vi. 12.	213, 284
Clement, Alex., *Strom.* vi. 18	168	,, vi. 14. 6 f. -	145
		,, vi. 14. 7 -	156
Clement, Alex., *Strom.* vii. 16. 94 ff.	220	,, vi. 25.	223, 294
		,, vi. 25. 7 -	6
		,, vi. 25. 11 ff.	109
Decretum Gelasianum	294	Freer MS. of the Gospels -	279
Diatessaron	218 f.	Galen -	150, 243
Didache	217 f.		
Diogenes Laertius, ii. 48	243	Hieronymus, *ad Hedibiam*, 120	30
Diognetus, Epistle to, xi. 2	128		
,, ,, xi. 6	202		

III. REFERENCES

	PAGE
Hieronymus, *Dial. c. Pelag.* ii. 15	278
Hieronymus, *Epist.* cxli.	193
Hippocrates	150
Horace, *Serm.* ii. 3. 1	193
Ignatius, *Ephes.* xii.	216
,, *Philad.* viii.	229
,, *Rom.* x.	22
Inscriptions :	
American School at Athens, Papers of the, ii. 57	59
Dittenberger, *Orientis Graeci Inscriptiones Selectae :*	
No. 218	16
Dittenberger, *Sylloge Inscriptionum Graecarum*[2] :	
No. 325	75
439	16
807	155
Ios, inscription from	155
Priene, Inschriften von, 115	51
Irenaeus, *adv. Haer.* iii. 1.	
2	273, 294
Irenaeus, *adv. Haer.* iii. 11. 8	220
Irenaeus, *adv. Haer.* iii. 11. 11	272
Isidore, *Orig.* i. 22	246
Josephus, *Antt. Jud.* xix. 329	41
Josephus, *Antt. Jud.* xx. 264	39
Josephus, *Bellum Jud., proem.*	36
Justin, *Apol.* i. 66. 67	212
,, *Dial.* 103	212
Juvenal, iv. 24	9
Lactantius, *Instit.* iv. 20	202
Lucian, *imag.* 8	16

	PAGE
Marcion	217, 292
Martial, iii. 2	9
,, iii. 100	31
,, xiii. 3	175
,, xiv. 208	246
Melito, *Eclogae*	207
Muratorian Fragment	222, 286 ff.
Origen	223
Papyri :	
Amherst Papyri, No. 3	251
Berliner Griechische Urkunden,	
No. 37	18, 24
597	64
601	12
615	91, 257
846	92, 259
1079	50, 73
British Museum Papyri,	
No. 121	13, 244
417	94
1213	79
Cairo Papyri, No. 8	18
Fayûm Papyri, No. 12	51
Flinders Petrie Papyri, Nos. 45, 144	164
Florentine Papyri, Nos. 61, 99	79
Geneva Papyri, No. 52	12
Giessen Papyri, No. 17	91, 258
Greek and Latin Papyri, Nos. 1, 3	254

INDEXES

Papyri:
Grenfell Papyri,   PAGE
  No. 30 - - - 31
      67 - - - 73
     111 - - - 194

Leyden Papyri,
  C - - - - 65
  N - - - - 244

Oxyrhynchus Papyri,
  No. 2 - - 189, 248
      38 - - - 270
      45 - 25, 89 f., 256
     106 - - - 17
     119 - - - 74
     208 - - 189, 249 f.
     209 - - - 251
     275 - - - 21
     292 - - - 18
     293 - - - 244
     294 - - - 66
     301, 381 - - 19
     402 - - - 250
     497 - - - 22
     523 - - - 51
     654 - - - 267
     657 - - 109, 252
     724 - - 26, 244
     744 - - 18, 116
     746 - - 88 f., 255 f.
     840 - - - 196
     849, 850 - - 162
    1008, 1009 - - 252 f.
    1067 - - - 23
    1078 - - 109, 253
    1079 - - - 253 f.
    1080 - - - 196
    1153 - - - 20
    1170, 1171 - - 254

Papyri:
Rylands Papyri,   PAGE
  No. 4 - - - 253
      5 - - 190, 253

Strassburg Papyri,
  No. 32 - - - 73

Tebtunis Papyri,
  Nos. 16, 41 - - 50
      58 - - - 72
     100 - - - 79
     316 - - - 22

Passio Sanct. Scilitanorum   212
Peter, Gospel according to
                213, 281 ff.
Pliny maj., Nat. Hist. xiii.
  11 ff. - - 10, 192
Pliny min., Epist. iii. 5. 14   245
    ,,   ,, vii. 12 - 31
    ,,   ,, ix. 36. 2   245
Plutarch, Cato min. xxiii. - 245 f.
Polycarp, ad Philipp. xiii. - 176
Proclus, de forma epist. - 82

Quintilian, Inst. Orat. x. 3.
  31 - - - - 193
Quintilian, Inst. Orat. xi. 2.
  25 - - - - 247

Seneca - - - - 246
Strabo, xiii. 1. 54 - - 178
Suetonius, Tit. 3 - - 247

Tertullian, adv. Marc. iv. 2   295
    ,,   ,, iv. 5   221
Tertullian, de praescr. hae-
  ret. 22 - - - 128
Tertullian, de praescr. hae-
  ret. 36 - - - 6
Theodore of Mopsuestia - 93

IV. GREEK WORDS.

ἀγάπη, 58.
ἀγράμματος, 21.
ἀδελφός, 59.
ἄδολος, 77.
αἰώνιος, 59.
ἀκριβέστερον, 111.
ἀκωλύτως, 168.
ἀνάγνωσις, 173.
ἀναστατόω, 73.
ἀναστρέφομαι, 51.
ἀπάτη, 75.
ἀπέχω, 78.
ἀποθνήσκω, 259.
ἀπομνημονεύματα, 131, 212.
ἀπόστολος, 59, 292.
ἀρραβών, 73.
ἀρχηγός, 75.
ἀσπάζομαι, 23, 31.
ἀσωτεύομαι, 79.
αὐτάρκεια, 57.
ἀφθονία, 190.

βιβλίον, 10, 14, 20, 194.
βίβλος, 10.
βλέπω ἀπό, 50.
βραδέως, 22.
βύβλος, 10.

γέγοναν, 63.
γέγραπται, 205.
γένημα, 63.
γενόμενος, 270.

γεύομαι, 68.
γραφή, 205.

διά, 22.
διαθήκη, 75.
διήγησις, 130.
διφθέρα, 8.
δοκίμιος, 76.

ἐάν (for ἄν), 64.
Ἑβραϊστί, 36.
ἐγώ, 155.
εἰς and ἐν, 66.
ἐλλογάω, 73.
ἐμβατεύω, 177.
Ἐμμανουήλ, 256.
ἐν (instrumental), 50.
ἐξαλείφω, 16.
ἐπακολουθέω, 78.
ἐπίσκοπος, 59.
ἐπιστολαὶ συστατικαί, 88, 254 f.
ἐπουράνιος, 99.
ἔρρωσο, 24, 256.
ἐρωτάω, 51.
ἐσχατοκόλλιον, 11.
ἑτεροδιδασκαλεῖν, 102.
εὐαγγέλιον, 130, 292.

ἡλικιά, 74.

θεοδίδακτος, 71.
θρησκεία, 59.

ἵνα, 67, 259.

καί, 154.
κάλαμος, 9, 17.
κάνων, 194.
κενεμβατεύω, 177.
κέρας, 11.
κεφαλιόω, 177.
κεφαλίς, 11.
κίστα, 20.
Κοινή, 44, 48.
κολαφίζω, 177.
κόλλημα, 10.
κολοβοδάκτυλος, 144.
κύριος (as title of address), 116, 259.

λογεία, 72.
λόγια, τά, 131, 137.

μαστιγόω, 79.
μέλας, 16.
μεμβράνα, 20.
μερίς, 76.
μόλιβδος, 194.

ὀμφαλός, 11.
ὄνομα, κατ', 258.
ὀξυγράφος, 243.

πάπυρος, 9.
παράγραφος, 25.
παρουσία, 59.
περγαμηνή, 192.
πιστεύω, 69.

πλήρης, 64.
πρεσβύτερος, 59.
προγράφομαι, 79.
προκόπτω, 74.
πρωτόκολλον, 11.
πρῶτος, 162.

σελίς, 14.
σημειογράφος, 26, 244, 246.
σημεῖον, 244, 246.
σημειόω, 25, 256.
σίλλυβος, 19.
σπέρμα, 105.
σπορά, 105.
συμφυλέτης, 71.
συνείδησις, 57.
συστατικός, 18.
σφραγίς, 17.
σφυρίς, 63.
σχίδες, 10.
σωτήρ, 59.

τάξις, 270.
ταχέως γράφειν, 243.
τετράδιον, 194.
τόμος, 15.

ὑποσημειόω, 243.

φελόνης, 20.

χαίρειν, 93.
χαρίζομαι, 79.
χάρτης, 9, 10, 12.

www.ingramcontent.com/pod-product-compliance
Lightning Source LLC
Chambersburg PA
CBHW061423300426
44114CB00014B/1515